W9-DDD-089

MOTHERHOOD IN THE
TWENTY-FIRST CENTURY

Psychoanalysis & Women Series

The Embodied Female
Edited by Alcira Mariam Alizade (2002)
Studies on Femininity
Edited by Alcira Mariam Alizade (2003)
Masculine Scenarios
Edited by Alcira Mariam Alizade (2003)
On Incest
Edited by Giovanna Ambrosio (2005)

MOTHERHOOD IN THE TWENTY-FIRST CENTURY

edited by

Alcira Mariam Alizade

A Volume in the Psychoanalysis & Women Series
for the Committee on Women and Psychoanalysis
of the International Psychoanalytical Association

KARNAC

LONDON   NEW YORK

ST CHARLES COMMUNITY COLLEGE
LIBRARY
WITHDRAWN

First published in 2006 by
H. Karnac (Books) Ltd.
6 Pembroke Buildings, London NW10 6RE

Copyright © 2006 The International Psychoanalytical Association
Copyright © 2006 Arrangement and Preface by Alcira Mariam Alizade,
and individual chapters by the contributors.

The rights of the editor and contributors to be identified as the authors
of this work have been asserted in accordance with §§ 77 and 78 of the
Copyright Design and Patents Act 1988.

All rights reserved. No part of this publication may be reproduced,
stored in a retrieval system, or transmitted, in any form or by any means,
electronic, mechanical, photocopying, recording, or otherwise, without
the prior written permission of the publisher.

British Library Cataloguing in Publication Data

A C.I.P. for this book is available from the British Library

ISBN 1 85575 369 3

Edited, designed and produced by The Studio Publishing Services Ltd,
www.publishingservicesuk.co.uk
E-mail: studio@publishingservicesuk.co.uk

Printed in Great Britain

10 9 8 7 6 5 4 3 2 1

www.karnacbooks.com

CONTENTS

FOREWORD   ix

CONTRIBUTORS   xiii

CHAPTER ONE
Motherhood is unending   1
  Ruth F. Lax

CHAPTER TWO
The twenty-first century: what changes?   11
  Giovanna Ambrosio

CHAPTER THREE
Motherhood in a fertile new world   23
  Diane Ehrensaft

CHAPTER FOUR
Artificial pregnancy   35
  Jacqueline Amati Mehler

CHAPTER FIVE
The non-maternal psychic space   45
  Alcira Mariam Alizade

CHAPTER SIX
Why do you want to have a child?   59
  Estela V. Welldon

CHAPTER SEVEN
The place of motherhood in primary femininity   73
  Emilce Dio Bleichmar

CHAPTER EIGHT
Reconstructing Oedipus? Considerations of the   85
psychosexual development of boys of lesbian parents
  Toni Vaughn Heineman

CHAPTER NINE
Maternity and femininity: sharing and splitting in the   97
mother–daughter relationship
  Florence Guignard

CHAPTER TEN
The parents, the baby, and the high-tech stork   113
  Fanny Blanck-Cereijido

CHAPTER ELEVEN
Motherhood and work   123
  Herta E. Harsch

CHAPTER TWELVE
The bodies of present-day maternity   135
  Leticia Glocer Fiorini

CHAPTER THIRTEEN
New reproductive realities: paradoxes, parameters,   145
and maternal orientations
  Joan Raphael-Leff

CHAPTER FOURTEEN
Parenthood and HIV/AIDS. An investigation of the   161
INPer based on psychoanalytic and gender theory
  Teresa Lartigue

CHAPTER FIFTEEN
New methods of conception and the practice   177
of psychoanalysis
  Sylvie Faure-Pragier

CHAPTER SIXTEEN
The impossible being of the mother   191
  Alicia Leisse de Lustgarten

REFERENCES   199

INDEX   215

FOREWORD

In the twenty-first century, with its frenzy and heterogeneity, where the mixture of modernity and postmodernity is not without danger, motherhood cannot escape the impact of social and cultural transformations.

This book takes a fresh look at women in their maternal role—in the fullest sense of the term, from gestation to bringing up children—in order to highlight the hitherto unknown aspects to which social and cultural change have given rise. Not all twenty-first century mothers treat motherhood in accordance with the established model. Psycho-history, the accumulation and variety of psychoanalytic theories of femininity and motherhood, the contribution of gender studies, cross-disciplinary research, and listening to what our patients have to say—all this has yielded, in the past few decades, much controversial data that challenges orthodox classical thinking with respect to the role and function of women as mothers.

In its praise of motherhood, psychoanalysis has on occasion gone too far: even in the earliest texts on the subject, mothers have taken centre stage with regard to the mental life of human beings, and their accomplishments or shortcomings have been considered decisive for subsequent mental health or illness—not only for the child but also in adolescence or adulthood. Excessive idealization—the fantasy of the phallic mother—or accusation—the kind of mothering that leads to mental disorder—are typical of the two opposite poles.

The absolute and unmitigated demand that mothers be perfect and know no flaws—an impossible requirement—ignores the fact that the capacities of all women are finite; embodied in the maternal figure, she can never be (to paraphrase Winnicott) quite-good-enough as a mother—and perhaps may even turn out to be decidedly pathogenic or sadistic.

Mothers in the twenty-first century confront us, both in clinical practice and in theory, with fascinating challenges that to some extent subvert the traditional maternal ideal: the motherhood of single women, motherhood in which the mother–child relationship seems minimal (in the case of very busy working mothers), teenage motherhood, in which there is no true awareness of the maternal function, motherhood in couples of homosexual women, men who take upon themselves the maternal function (men-mothers), complex motherhood by virtue of the multiple variants that have nowadays become possible thanks to new reproductive techniques, shared motherhood, surrogate motherhood, sublimated motherhood, perverse motherhood . . .

The different psycho-social and situational contexts in which a woman has or does not have a child, wants or does not want to have a child—consciously or unconsciously—not only create a hiatus between reproduction and sexuality, but also stand as a source of new fantasy and symbolic scenarios, which take the psychoanalyst in his or her daily clinical practice by surprise.

Many theoretical structures call for re-thinking and even questioning, given the framework of freedom of thought typical of the quasi-revolution of recent times in the habits and customs of contemporary society. The solidly-based idea of a primary maternal stage, thought to lie at the very heart of every female human being, is countered by fresh hypotheses that highlight the frequent pathology inherent in the wish for a child and emphasize the importance of considering women as having a psychic organization independent of the maternal function. This latter proposition dissociates femininity from motherhood; women take their rightful place in the arena of life that concerns wishes and desires, without having to put their capacity for procreation into action.

The innovative work in this book concerning reproduction technology and its psychic consequences is a confirmation of the plurality of voices that henceforth express the phenomenon of motherhood.

This book, above all, opens on to fresh perspectives; it will be a thought-provoking instrument for all psychoanalysts who are eager to explore a territory of the mind that invites us to constant reflection.

Alcira Mariam Alizade
COWAP chairperson (2001–2005)

Alcira Mariam Alizade, MD, is a psychiatrist and training analyst of the Argentine Psychoanalytic Association. She is the current overall chair of the IPA Committe on Women and Psychoanalysis (2001–2005), and former COWAP Latin-American co-chair (1998–2001). She is the author of: *Feminine Sensuality* (Karnac, 1992); *Near Death: Clinical Psychoanalytical Studies* (Amorrortu, 1995); *Time for Women* (Letra Viva, 1996); *The Lone Woman* (Lumen, 1999); *Positivity in Psychoanalysis* (Lumen, 2002), and Editor of IPA-COWAP Karnac Series (*The Embodied Female; Studies on Femininity; Masculine Scenarios*) and of the collected papers of COWAP Latin-American Intergenerational Dialogues (Lumen).

Giovanna Ambrosio is a full member of the Italian Psychoanalytical Association (AIPsi) and the International Psychoanalytical Association. She is Secretary of AIPsi, Chief Editor of the journal *Psicoanalisi*, and European co-chair of the Committee on Women and Psychoanalysis. Her main scientific interests include the field of the intrapsychic interaction relationship between "truth and the false", the meanings of "lies" and issues related to the well known problem of the"'confusion of tongues".

Fanny Blanck-Cereijido, MD, is a Member of the Mexican and Buenos Aires Psychoanalytic Association, and Training Analyst of the Mexican Psychoanalytic Association. Among other books and articles, she has published "A study on feminine sexuality" (*International Journal of Psychoanalysis*, 64: 93–104, 1983); "Panel report: infertility, surrogacy and the new reproductive technique" (*International Journal of Psychoanalysis*, 77: 129–133, 1997); "Psicoanálisis y nuevas técnicas reproductivas" in: *El laberinto de las estructuras* (Siglo XXI, 1998).

Emilce Dio Bleichmar, MD, is a Member of the Argentinian Psychoanalytical Association and of Regiomontana Psychoanalytical Association. Mexico, Head and Professor of Graduate Studies in Psychotherapy and Psychoanalytical Clinical Practice of Child and Family at the Universidad Pontificia Comillas, Madrid, and Head of the Women's Studies Department at ELIPSIS. She is the author of the following books: *La Sexualidad Femenina. De la niña a la mujer* (Paidós, 1998); *Género, Psicoanálisis, Subjetividad* (compiler with M. Burin) (Paidós, 1996); *La Depresión en la Mujer* (Temas de Hoy, 1991); *El Feminismo Espontáneo de la Histeria. Trastornos narcisistas de la feminidad.* (Siglo XXI, 1991); *Temores y Fobias. Condiciones de Génesis en la Infancia* (Gedisa, 1981). Emilce Dio Bleichmar is also the author of articles in collective and specialized works, mostly on the subjects of femininity, female sexuality, and motherhood.

Sylvie Faure-Pragier is a psychiatrist and psychoanalyst, Full Member of the Paris Psychoanalytical Society (SPP) and of the International Psychoanalytical Association (IPA). She is Head of the Paris Institute of Psicoanálisis, Former Registrar in the Faculty of Medicine, Paris University, and a Board Member of the Gynaecology and Psychosomatic Obstetrics Society.

Leticia Glocer Fiorini is a training psychoanalyst of the Argentine Psychoanalytic Association, a former member of the Editorial Board of the *Revista de Psicoanálisis* (1998–2002), and current chair of the Publications Committee of the Argentine Psychoanalytic Association. She won the Association's Celes Cárcamo Prize (1993) for her paper: "The feminine position. A heterogeneous construction". She is the author of *The Feminine and the Complex Thought* (Lugar

Editorial, 2001). She also published: "Assisted fertilization. new problems" in *Prevention in Mental Health* (Lugar Editorial, 2002), "The sexed body and the real, its meaning in transsexualism" in *Masculine Scenarios* (Karnac, 2003) and "Psychoanalysis and gender. Convergence and divergence" in *Psychoanalysis and Gender Relations* (2004). Her papers on maternity and female sexuality were selected for presentation in the IPA Congresses in Santiago, Chile (1999) and Nice (2001).

Florence Guignard. Born in Geneva, Florence Guignard settled in Paris in 1970, where she still practises as a child, adolescent, and adult psychoanalyst. In 1982 she was elected a Full Member of the Paris Psychoanalytical Society (SPP) and has served two terms as Vice-President of that Society. She is a member of the Committee on Child and Adolescent Psychoanalysis (COCAP) of the International Psychoanalytical Association (IPA). Together with Annie Anzieu, she founded, in 1984, the Association for Child Psychoanalysis, and in 1994, the European Society for Child and Adolescent Psycho-analysis (SEPEA). She has been the Editor-in-Chief of the *Année Psychanalytique Internationale* since its creation in 2002. This is an annual review, published in French under the aegis of the *International Journal of Psychoanalysis*. She has written over 200 articles, collaborated in several joint publications and is the author of two books: *Au Vif de l'Infantile* (Delachaux et Niestlé, 1996); and *Épître à l'Objet* (Presses Universitaires de France, 1997).

Herta E. Harsch, is a psychology graduate, psychoanalyst practis-ing in Karlsruhe, Gemany, and is married with two children. She is IPA-training analyst and supervisor for the German Psychoanalytic Association, and 1996–1998 president of the Heidelberg-Karlsruhe Psychoanalytic Institute. She is the author of various publications about "mothers, children, and surrogate caregivers" from psycho-analytic, historical, and cultural perspectives.

Teresa Lartigue has a PhD in Psychology (Iberoamericana Univer-sity) and is a training analyst with the Institute of Psychoanalysis, Mexican Psychoanalytic Association. She is a full member of the International Psychoanalytic Association, a child and adolescent psychoanalyst (Mexican Psychoanalytic Association), and Director of the Institute of Psychoanalysis (Mexican Psychoanalytic Association). She is also Chair of the Epidemiology Reproductive Department, National Institute of Perinatology (Mexico).

Ruth F. Lax is a Member, faculty, and training analyst, IPTAR, New York Freudian Society and International Psychoanalytic Association. She is also a Fellow, American Psychological Association and American Board of Professional Psychology, and a Member of the American Psychoanalytic Association. Dr Lax has published many articles on masochism, character neurosis, and issues in female psychosexual development, her main areas of interest. *Becoming and Being a Woman* is her most recent book, published in 1997 by Jason Aronson, New York. In addition to an active private practice in psychoanalysis, psychotherapy, and couples counselling, Dr Lax initiated and formerly co-chaired IPA NGO at the UN, and has been a representative at the UN of the International Council of Psychologists. She now chairs, at the American Psychoanalytic Association, a study group dealing with the psychoanalytic causes of socially sanctioned violence against women.

Alicia Leisse de Lustgarten is a Full Member Training Psychoanalyst , Psychoanalytical Society of Caracas, Official Supervisor of Candidates of the Psychoanalytical Training Programme, and a Full Member Teacher in the Psychoanalytical Training Programme. She is also a Teaching Collaborator in Postgraduate Studies of Psychiatry and Clinical Psychology, Hospital of the Central University of Caracas, and Teaching Collaborator in Postgraduate Studies of Clinical and Community Psychology, Catholic University Andres Bello. She has given various talks and presentations in hospitals, centres of social services, and varied scientific circuits of the country, and is the author of regular publications in the journal *Trópicos* of the Psychoanalytical Society of Caracas. At present she is President of the Psychoanalytical Society of Caracas, and has been Treasurer and Director of Scientific Activities, and Director of the Institute of Psychoanalysis.

Jacqueline Amati Mehler is a full-time practising training and supervising analyst, currently the Director of the Institute at the Italian Psychoanalytic Association (AIPsi). Former Secretary and

Vice president of the IPA, she is the author of numerous clinical and theoretical papers published in several international journals including "Hope and hopelessness" (1990); "Love and male impotence" (1992); "The exiled language" (1995); and chapters in several books. She has also co-authored a book on multi-lingualism, *The Babel of the Unconscious* (1993, International Universities Press). Her main interest is in early mental processes, memory and symbolic function development, as well as in the theory and technique of the psychoanalytic treatment of psychoses. In 1998 she was a recipient of the Mary S. Sigourney Honorary Award.

Joan Raphael-Leff is a Fellow of the British Psychoanalytical Society. As Professor in the Department of Psychology at University College London, she heads the MSc programme in Psychoanalytic Developmental Psychology based at the Anna Freud Centre, London. Until 2003 she was Professor of Psychoanalysis at the Centre for Psychoanalytic Studies at the University of Essex, UK and remains Visiting Professor there. Since qualification as a psychoanalyst in 1976 she has specialized in treating patients with reproductive, perinatal, and parenting issues, with over eighty single author publications in this field, and nine books, including: *Psychological Processes of Childbearing*, 4th edition 2005; *Parent–Infant Psychodynamics: Wild Things, Mirrors and Ghosts*, (Ed.) (Whurr /Wiley 2003); *Pregnancy: the Inside Story* (Karnac , 2001); *Spilt Milk: Perinatal Loss and Breakdown* (Ed.), (Routledge, 2000); *Between Sessions and Beyond the Couch* (Ed.), (University of Essex, 2002); *Female Experience: Three Generations of British Women Psycho-Analysts on Work with Women* (co-edited with Rosine Josef Perelberg), (Routledge, 1997). She was inaugural Overall Chair of COWAP from 1998 and remains ongoing Consultant. Currently she is a member of the IPA Committee for Social Exclusion.

Toni Vaughn Heineman has been in practice as a child and adult psychologist for over twenty years. In addition to providing psychotherapy and parent consultation, she has done extensive work with separating and divorcing parents, including lesbian couples. Dr Heineman is the author of numerous articles and presentations, and *The Abused Child: Psychodynamic Understanding and Treatment* (1998, Guilford Press). She is the founder and Executive Director of

"A Home Within", a non-profit organization devoted to meeting the mental health needs of foster children and youth and their families.

Estela V. Welldon, MD, DSc (Hon), FRC PSYCH, is Honorary Consultant Psychiatrist in Psychotherapy at Tavistock Portman NHS Clinics, founder and ex-Director of the Diploma Course in Forensic Psychotherapeutic Studies at the University College London, founder and Honorary Elected President for Life of the International Association for Forensic Psychotherapy, Member of the British Association for Psychotherapy, the Institute of Group Analysis and of the International Association of Group Psychotherapy. She is the author of *Mother, Madonna, Whore: the Idealization and Denigration of Motherhood* (Free Association Books, 1988); *Sadomasochism. Ideas in Psychoanalysis* (2002, Icon Books UK and Totem Books USA); and main editor of *A Practical Guide to Forensic Psychotherapy* (Jessica Kingsley, 1997).

CHAPTER ONE

Motherhood is unending[*]

Ruth F. Lax

ll societies have created and evolvingly continue to create stereotypic arch-types of The Mother and Motherhood. These became the ideals of a given society whose form and content depend on the ethos of the era, and on the vicissitudes of the individual. In each generation the prevailing idealized stereotypes become incorporated and influence both the female and the male psyche. The girl child, however, becomes primed for motherhood almost from birth.

In most societies, Feminine and Mother are combined to form a single representation of WOMAN—and for most women in the world this still is their only self-representation. Motherhood is a state of being. Although the specifics are expressed idiosyncratically, primary preoccupation with the child, availability to the child, self-sacrifice for the child, are values upheld as inherent in good

---

* A wider development of this subject has been published in another paper: "Motherhood is an ebb and flow—it lasts a lifetime: the vicissitudes of mother's interaction with her 'fantasy child' ", published in *The Inner World of the Mother*, Dale Mendell and Patsy Turrini (eds.), Psychosocial Press, 2003.

motherhood. Transmitted from generation to generation, this stereotype expresses unconscious childhood wishes, expectancies, and hopes of what a mother should be like, and how she should behave towards her child.

It is still culturally inconceivable and unacceptable that a "good mother" may have conflicts regarding her culturally assigned, and frequently consciously and unconsciously self-imposed, role. Further, it is inadmissible that these conflicts may evoke feelings of anger or, even worse, hate for the child in the mother and a wish to vent it aggressively, to act out her frustration. To account for such feelings, regarded as "unnatural" in a "good mother", images of witches, child-eaters, wicked stepmothers, and evil mothers-in-law have been created. These stereotypes of maternal monsters have been endowed with feelings of jealously, unjustified angers, infused with cruelty and sadism, murderous wishes, and treachery, emotions that, according to the stereotypic ideal, no good mother could conceivably ever experience.

The inescapable conflicts evoked by aspirations to embody and enact the mother-ideal, and the contradictory emotions caused by a mother's wishes and needs for a space and time "of her own" for the fulfilment of ego goals self-directed and propelled, are probably characteristic of all mothers. The diversity of feelings prevalent towards the child at different times can already be observed in a girl's play and attitude towards her first doll, her baby doll, the chosen doll, the discarded doll, and the doll family. Little girls are by no means always loving towards their dolls. They frequently hit their dolls mercilessly and when asked about it may say: "She is always a bad girl, she never listens. I'll pound some sense into her yet." Most telling is a girl's frequent response when told to go and play with her dollies: "I want to do something else." Dollies, babies, could never be everything a woman wants . . . yet we know of the sacrifices mothers do make. The image of Mater Dolorosa is a part of western culture.

The craving to have a child, which has been considered mistakenly to originate from an innate "maternal instinct", actually stems from an unconscious response to pressures that still predominantly define a woman's role and being in terms of motherhood. These pressures are both open and disguised, they are of religious, societal, and family origin. However, a uniquely significant contributory factor is a girl's conscious and unconscious interaction with her mother. This pivotal relationship of love and idealization, anger, hate, envy, and competition, which undergoes many vicissitudes, eventually forms the basis for a girl's ideal of motherhood. When the woman's childhood experiences were good, identification with her own mother is the basis for this ideal. When childhood memories are filled with anger and pain, ambivalence prevails and the ideal may be determined by reaction formations. However, the ideal of motherhood also unconsciously contributes to the wish for a child, a fantasied opportunity to play out the role of mother and child in an unambivalent idealized form desired in the woman's childhood. In this fantasy the woman wants to be the mother she wanted to have.

The fantasies of motherhood undergo typical vicissitudes during the negative and positive oedipal conflagrations; they become latent and may become reactivated in various versions during subsequent developmental phases.

During a wanted pregnancy, positive conscious and unconscious fantasies and wishes originating in childhood become activated. Alternations in the woman's object–libidinal and narcissistic equilibrium occur. A marked shift toward libidinal concentration on the self takes place. This specific type of narcissism cathects the expanding dual self-representation consisting of mother and internal baby. It enables the pregnant woman to feel that the growing body within her constitutes an integral part of herself. The physical symbiosis of pregnancy is augmented by the woman's preoccupation and daydreams about her future child, which she moulds in fantasy in accordance with her wishes and ego ideal. In this sense the infant-to-be becomes uniquely mother's own, physically and mentally existing only within her.

The pregnant woman's feeling of changes within her body, and the inner spontaneous movements of the foetus, bring about psychic states of "inwardness" during which the "fantasy child" and her interrelationship with it is formed. When the child is wanted, the bond of possession and love is formed. The feeling, fuelled with narcissistic cathexis, evokes a powerful sense of "it's mine, totally so".

However, the maternal experience of total union is disrupted eventually by the motility of the foetus, which follows a rhythm of its own. The awareness of apartness from the being within, a process culminating in birth, establishes the physical separateness.

Birth usually does not disrupt the unique mother–child bond, but tending to the baby now has to be done volitionally. This constant preoccupation with the baby can only be sustained because the infant continues to be cathected with both narcissistic and object libido. Analytic work with women reveals that the intensity and kind of libidinal investment a mother makes in her infant will depend, in large measure, on the extent to which the infant is unconsciously regarded as an extension of the self, on its unconscious symbolic meaning and on the degree to which it embodies, for the mother, her fantasy child.

The manifold unconscious aspects the infant and growing child has for the mother will have a significant importance in determining mother's shifts in the fusion of narcissistic–libidinal and object–libidinal cathexis, the amount of aggression felt towards the child, and the balance that will prevail.

Maternal inwardness, the creation and enjoyment of the "fantasy child", and the fantasy of the interactional relationship with this child, is the most significant preparatory state for motherhood. However, these feelings do not comprise the entirety of a pregnant woman's psychic state. Physical discomfort and the extent to which it occurs may disrupt the enjoyment of pregnancy. It happens quite frequently that the pregnant woman, in moments of stress, would like to escape from her physical condition.

The sense of loss of control, the awareness that the pregnancy progresses in a pre-programmed way with the mother-to-be having no say about it, makes some women quite anxious and others quite depressed. They remember themselves as active and decisive, and now are suddenly, to quote a patient, "a helpless, passive bystander".

Every woman wishes to be a good mother. However, the confines of a harmonious complementary relationship with the infant and growing child may have an extremely taxing impact on the family constellations. With the arrival of the first-born, husbands frequently feel pushed into second place and may find it difficult to be helpful. Unconscious jealousy follows, and may detrimentally affect the man's relationship to both mother and child. For the mother, the presence of one or more older children in the family makes the arrival of the newborn especially difficult. In such cases the mother, as a patient said, "feels torn" between her love and loyalty to the older children and her wish to be able to devote herself exclusively to the newborn.

The significance of the infant and the growing child's correspondence to mother's "fantasy child" created during pregnancy is an important factor. It facilitates and may even assure mother's "falling in love" with her baby. Sometimes an aspect of the baby's behaviour the mother had wished for, consciously or unconsciously, is the decisive factor. The vicissitudes of Mrs A's interaction with her first-born depicts the various aspects of the mother–child relationship. After birth, when she returned to analysis, Mrs A said: "You know, I wanted a girl, but he is the most wonderful baby you can imagine. He immediately knew how to nurse and I enjoy it." The patient recalled being told many times by her mother that she had been a "poor and lazy" suckling. This always made the patient feel her mother had been angry and dissatisfied with her. Thus, her child fulfilled a wish she had had about herself. She continued, "You know, nursing is quite erotic, exciting in a way I never imagined or experienced such feelings before. I look forward to it."

The patient had feared throughout the pregnancy that she would find it difficult to enjoy staying home and caring for the baby during her three-month leave. She thought she'd be in conflict because she would miss the excitement of the office and her flirtatious play with her boss. She reported after a month, "Jamie [her son] and I get along almost perfectly. We fit. He nurses often and that gives me pleasure, and I also get pleasure from his pleasure. Then he falls asleep and I do too. It's almost like a love affair." For Mrs A, the unexpected erotic gratification became a significant factor in establishing the bond and preoccupation with her infant.

The strength and significance of this early idyll became apparent when, at seven months, Jamie began giving clear indications that he no longer was interested in nursing and started turning away from the breast. Mrs A at first thought it was just accidental. However, when she had to face the reality, she felt rejected and also very angry, and said, "He pushes me away."

Analysis made Mrs A aware of the extent to which she had used the child for her own gratification and as a pretext for being less available to her husband. She also realized that she displaced her anger at Jamie on to her husband. A period of partial withdrawal from her son followed, which she rationalized by saying that Jamie did not need her "as much as before". She no longer experienced Jamie as the wonderful "perfect" child, and began to find fault with him. Analysis helped her to discover and face (although with difficulty) that the child had been fulfilling an erotic need for her that she had wanted to continue. She felt ashamed and guilty, but primarily angry with her husband for not being a better lover. Ambivalence and impatience were now quite predominant in the relationship with both her husband and her son. For Mrs A the "fit" between the "fantasy child" and the real baby diminished. This affected her emotional and behavioural attitude towards Jamie.

Variations in maternal attitudes towards her child (Coleman, Kris, & Provence, 1953) occur throughout mother's lifelong interaction with it. These may be caused by aspects of the child's maturation that do not correspond to mother's expectations, the child's unique proclivities and character, friends the child selects, the pursuit of specific interests, the wish for independence, the need to cling, etc. Mother's attitudes and her intrapsychic reaction to the child may change depending on the degree to which there is a corresponding complementarity and attunement between them. This may relate to their personality style, temperament, needs, and wishes. Thus, periods of greater and lesser harmonious interaction are inevitable. Significant during periods of dissonance is the maintenance of Mother's feeling: "In spite of it all, this is *my* child I love." Such an attitude in large measure depends on mother's recognition of elements belonging to the "fantasy child" in the persona of her child.

Mrs A's awareness of her own needs increased after Jamie's self-weaning, which she experienced as a painful rejection. She said, "I'm with him all day long, and I must admit, I am getting bored. I think I want to spend more time in the office. I need adult stimulation. 'Mother-talk' and 'baby-talk' can get very stifling. I do love him very much, and he is a sweet boy, but he doesn't need me as much as he used to so I can do things for myself." Mrs A had great difficulty tolerating her feeling of anger and ambivalence towards Jamie. Rationalization was one of the main defences. Mrs A explained her planned separations from Jamie as motivated by her wish to "stimulate his growth of independence", unaware that she was trying to counteract her unconscious dependence on him. She accepted an offer from her firm to work three full days on a project that interested her greatly. After a short period of elation, a boost to her self-esteem, and enjoyment of the playful flirtation with her boss, Mrs A developed guilt feelings about Jamie. She felt that he was no longer as joyful as he used to be and she blamed herself. Turmoil and an inner conflict started. Mrs A asked, "Do I have a right to personal self fulfilment at the expense of my child? I feel torn." Her feelings oscillated between the need to be a "good mother who sacrifices herself for the child", and her wish for gratification from work and contact with colleagues.

Mrs A questioned herself (and me): "Does a woman have a right to have a child if she isn't totally devoted to it?" She recalled that her own mother, with whom she had a very bad relationship, stayed at home. Thus, Mrs A realized, "Just staying at home with the child" was not the answer. She began with difficulty to analyse the qualities that really "make for a good mother". Eventually, Mrs A concluded that her wish to be a different mother than her mother was led to the development of an idealized mother image based on what she, as a child, wished her mother to be. She understood that this did not necessarily correspond to what would constitute a good mother for Jamie. Mrs A began to demand that I tell her "what the principles of good motherhood are". She was furious when I did not comply. We analysed, via the transference, the underlying reasons for her fury with me. This was a stormy period during which Mrs A accused me of not caring for Jamie's well-being, not being helpful to her, being smug and unresponsive, not "giving a damn".

The following vignette presents a case of mother's disappointment with her newborn.

Mrs C did not want to know the sex of her baby before birth. I saw her a month following the birth of her daughter. She was sullen and silent for quite a while, then began speaking in a whisper which ended in a crescendo. "I did not want a girl. In my family girls are not wanted—and she has red hair which means she'll have freckles. That is horrible. My great-aunt had red hair and freckles and nobody liked her. Why do I have to have such a daughter? I tried nursing her but she did not nurse well so I changed to a bottle.

She cries a lot, it makes everything so difficult. I am looking for a good nanny. I don't like the one we have."

During the first three months, Mrs C could not find any redeeming feature in her baby. She was amazed and annoyed that her husband played with the child. She could not understand why the baby gurgled and cooed when with him, also with the nanny, but not with her. As the baby grew, Mrs C became aware of feeling jealous. She complained: "Why doesn't she smile at me? I think she likes her father better than me. Everybody says girls like their fathers more than their mothers so that's just fate." I asked whom she had liked better. Mrs C was silent, and then said, "I don't remember. I am going to fire the nanny. She does not keep Fran clean enough."

During the first year of Fran's life Mrs C fired three nannies. Finally a pattern emerged. The dismissals occurred when Mrs C became aware of her daughter's attachment to her nanny. When I made this observation Mrs C at first angrily denied it. Eventually, however, it led to our exploration of her possessive feelings toward Fran. She said, "It's *my* daughter. I was pregnant with her. I gave birth to her. I went through all the pain and stress and look at her, now she loves a stranger better than me." She burst into angry crying and repeated, through sobs, "She's an ungrateful child. I hate her. I hate her." When she calmed down Mrs C said, "Do I really hate *her* if I get so upset that she loves her nanny better than me?" I said "I think you'd like Fran to love you best."

After we analysed her negative self-feelings, Mrs C became aware of the manifold conscious and unconscious reasons Fran failed as the wished for "fantasy child". These related to her own sense of inferiority because she was female. Mrs C recalled her childhood wish to be a boy. She had wished for a son during pregnancy. Having a boy, identifying with his achievements and glorying in them, would have been almost as good as having been a boy.

Pathological dissonance between mother and the child in reality may occur when a mother rigidly holds on to specific expectations based on the "fantasy child" imago. Mrs C enacted such a scenario in her relationship to Fran.

At times, a mother's wish for self-fulfilment through gratifying her ego needs and goals, her wish for "self-being" and "owning oneself", deviates greatly from what she believes to be her child's needs, the latter perhaps reflecting her own unconscious childhood wishes. Irrespective of age, however, since a child on the deepest conscious–unconscious psychic level always remains part of the mother's self, the propensity, mostly unconscious, towards self-deprivation in favour of "*my* child" persists. None the less, mother's capacity to tolerate self-deprivation in favour of the child depends in a large measure on the psychic fit prevailing between them. The greater the corresponding interactive attributes that are the basis of the psychic fit, the greater is mother's intrinsic gratification stemming from the child. When such a mother–child relationship prevails, the child is experienced as meeting mother's conscious–unconscious wish, and in this sense also provides a self-fulfilment for the mother. In such cases the feelings of self-deprivation are mitigated, since what is done for the child, an unconscious narcissistic libidinal self-object, is also gratifying to the self. Thus, to the extent to which the child, in the unconscious, never stops being part of the mother, the love directed towards it as a libidinal object also has narcissistic aspects that enhance the mother.

Often aspects of a mother's self, which the vicissitudes of life prevented her from attaining, are fulfilled when actualized by her "fantasy child". The scornful joke about the mother who proudly says, "*My* son, the doctor", epitomizes centuries of women's anger, frustration, and helplessness resulting from not being able to attain their self-goals because they were women. During those epochs a woman could achieve only through the achievements of her son, who therefore became "*her* pride". However, nowadays, the mother who boasts about her daughter's achievements may be to an even greater extent unconsciously gratifying her unfilled aspirations.

When children reach adulthood the relationship frequently changes. A patient who was painfully experiencing her "fantasy child's" subtle, yet persistent emotional distancing from her, tearfully said, "What hurts is that we lost the language we shared. I now know only superficialities. I long for the real deep loving that gives joy to being together. I no longer feel that during our visits."

Mothers remain mothers irrespective of the child's age. The "fantasy child" and their interactions with it continue within them as a psychic creation. However, as years pass by, a mother, unless she has been able to create her own emotional and ego gratifying life, becomes emotionally dependent on her child, especially if she is widowed or divorced. In such cases, the mother may experience her wonderful "fantasy child," now grown into a wonderful adult person involved in her/his own life, as emotionally distant, sometimes almost a stranger. When this happens, bitterness grows and anger frequently changes into depression. The spontaneity of the mother–child relationship and its warmth disappear. Mothers may begin to speculate about the way they should behave. They search for what they may have done wrong, try to understand the change in the relationship, and try to revive the closeness of the past. If these attempts fail, mothers frequently withdraw to avoid experiencing the pain, or else use anger as an unconscious defence. Patients' reports indicated that they sometimes soothe themselves by means of a fantasy, typical in childhood, which now may reoccur under conditions of hurt and anger. These patients, sometimes in tears, recalling a painful incident, say: "Oh, he/she will be sorry and miss me when I die, but by then it will be too late." Sometimes they fantasize their funeral; the eulogies, and even the imagined guilt of the child, are elaborated with details. Such consolation, however, is short-lived. When the mother's experience of having been abandoned prevails, fantasies about suicide may occur. Though the intention may appear as a wish for revenge, it seems predominantly to be an expression of unconsoled hurt and aloneness.

As understood in terms of our criteria, motherhood means a loving reliability, keeping the child's trust and faith, anticipating needs with sensitivity, being available to the child, and yes, if need be, with disregard for the self. This mandate of motherhood can only be fulfilled if the mother is aware of her ambivalent feelings and has the capacity to tolerate and contain them. She can then combine her ego ideal of good mothering with the fulfilment of her other ego needs and goals.

Can the mandate of good motherhood ever be totally fulfilled? Even knowing the *impossibility* of the task, mothers feel guilty when they can't meet the demand . . .

Motherhood is an ebb and a flow . . . lasting a lifetime . . .

CHAPTER TWO

The twenty-first century: what changes?

Giovanna Ambrosio

"God could not be everywhere and therefore he made mothers."

Jewish proverb

Parthogenetic mothers: narcissism and omnipotence

For the purpose of suggesting and, above all, sharing some thoughts and queries about the prospects of maternity in the twenty-first century, I should like to consider the matter from the viewpoint of historic and social change, paying particular attention to the psychic aspects.

First, I should like to say that my position on problems related to one's own body is that of respect for the principle of self-determination on the part of the subject, even more so since I live in a country where there is a troublesome tendency to legislate on many aspects of what is "private" and, even worse, in increasingly restrictive terms.

More specifically, I propose a brief reflection on the theme of maternity with reference to those particular clinical psychopathological situations of pathologies of the self and of narcissistic personality disorders. In fact, sometimes in these cases the fantasy of becoming a mother "at all costs" would seem to be mainly nourished by a system of needs belonging to the primary narcissism register and are completely remote from the possibility of acceding to recognition of the other and to the oedipal drive register.

Narcissistic events

We all know that the concept of narcissism represents a milestone in the Freudian meta-psychological edifice, and that his "Introduction to narcissism" (1914c), contains the basic arguments that led to the elaboration of the second topic (even though Freud wrote to Abraham in March 1914 that writing it had been "a difficult labour" and that the text bore "all the marks of a corresponding deformation") (1914c, p. 70).

Because of the importance that pathological narcissism has had in the past and continues to have in clinical work, this concept has been at the centre of post-Freudian theoretical revisions and relative controversies beginning with the fundamental contribution of Melanie Klein. Moreover, the history of the concept of narcissism in Freud's work follows pathways that are decidedly non-linear and are even sometimes contradictory. Before he elaborated the second topic, Freud placed narcissism between the stage of very early auto-erotism and that of object love. Subsequently, he indicated through the concept of primary narcissism a first state of life preceding the constitution of the ego, and he distinguished it from secondary narcissism.

While the concept of primary narcissism indicated an infantile state in which the child assumes himself as the love object, secondary narcissism indicated a more or less permanent structure of the subject and not necessarily an extreme regressive state. His formulations, however, always remained within the drive register.

This is not the place for a review of the extensive psychoanalytic literature on the concept; I refer readers to the excellent publication *Introduction to Narcissism* (1991), in which eminent psychoanalysts such as Grinberg, Baranger, Segal, and Grunberger, to mention but a few, have provided us with a re-reading of the concept.

Certainly, and, as Baranger (1991) emphasizes, "paradoxically", the elaboration of the concept of narcissism has given a fundamental impulse to the study of object relations, to the extent that "Freud's oscillations and contradictions have led to the need to redefine narcissism no longer as a phase of libido or Thanatos, but in relation to object relations" (my translation).

In clinical work, when we are faced with the complexity of the psychic structure, with the different stratified levels and with the different areas of the mind, it is not always easy to draw a clear line between primary and secondary narcissism; that is, between the quotas of narcissism that are necessary as drive components of the sense of self, and those that imprison primary narcissism. Probably one sometimes has to deal with areas of secondary narcissism that coagulate segments of primary narcissism.

It was precisely this entrapment within the meshes of primary narcissism inhabited by omnipotence that seemed to be common to certain of my patients who presented clinical pictures of pathology of the self and of narcissistic disorders, and who came into analysis because of problems regarding maternity or, in some cases, the difficulty of becoming mothers.

What always struck me in these cases was the emergence of an autopoietic, parthenogenetic representation of the self, far removed from the possibility of thinking of the self "in relation with". It was a scenario characterized by a painful image of mutilated maternity, even though it was sometimes presented with careless superficiality or with the "normality" of a claim to emancipation. In some cases—that were very difficult to handle in the transference–countertransference—it was necessary to help restore to the patient a representation of the self that was in its turn "generated", "belonging to".

Sometimes, for example, I have found myself working with women who have decided to resort to assisted reproduction techniques. Although the women were very different from each other, both from the point of view of intrapsychic economy and dynamics and in the organization of defences, I thought I could define in them a common modality by which the impulsive and coercive quality of seeing artificial insemination as being the only possibility of reproducing themselves—or, rather, of prolonging themselves—gradually decreased as, within the transference, and once a symbolic womb had been re-constructed, a progressive objectuality was reached. This generally came about when the fantasy of adopting a baby occurred. This was the moment that marked the passage from the representation of maternity as a mere duplication of the self, to the possibility of representing the self in a maternal function. They began to be able to think about the *other*.

One patient, who was already the mother of a psychotic adolescent, in her attempt to have another child through artificial insemination, told me that all her life she had thought of her son as her "exceptionally gifted little man", and that now she needed to console herself with "a good apple after the bad one".

Another patient, in confirmation of what Pines (1993) has so accurately described, said that for her the essential thing was to feel pregnant, while the idea of actually having a child seemed terrible: "What counts is the pregnancy; the idea of a child 'outside' terrifies me."

And yet another patient, who was entrapped in an incandescent fusional–incestuous area, cried out her right to have a child because "all my friends have had a family".

One patient came for a consultation and proudly told me how she had explained to her young grand-daughter that "The important thing is to have a baby by grabbing at any passing spermatozoa: try everything except risking the presence of a father."

What is prevented in these cases seems to be the passage to the "third" object by assuming this as the paradigm of being able to measure oneself in life with alterity and knowledge.

There have been many theoretical–clinical developments in psychoanalysis on this theme, beginning with the post-Freudian theoretic enrichments by Klein, Winnicott, Greenacre, Gaddini, Segal, Loch, Britton, and Green. Many analysts, especially during the past twenty years, have concentrated on the ubiquitous aspects of the primary scene, seen as a process (and not as an event), as that tortuous and complex event thanks to which one is able to "enter into relation with". There have been numerous contributions, also recently, on the importance of "third-ness" and of the "triangular space".

> The admission on the part of the child of the reciprocal relationship between the parents unites his psychic world, limiting it to a world shared with both parents in which different object relations can

exist. The closure of the oedipal triangle through the recognition of the link that unites the parents establishes a boundary that delimits the internal world. [Britton, 1990, my translation]

We can therefore assume that the passage to the third object is the true paradigm of the passage to survival.

Now let us return to our reflections upon the possible changes that may take place during the century that has just begun. Can we state, for example, that this theme of the recognition of the other as separate and different will, from our point of view, lose its paradigmatic value? Or that our psychoanalytic way of thinking will be able to do without referring to what is oedipal or pre-oedipal when (as already happens) we find ourselves faced with social change, female emancipation, new forms of procreation and of relations between the sexes, new family groups?

Again, will today's prevalence of narcissistic disorders and situations of self-pathology, compared with the classic neurosis of Freud's time, continue to consolidate, or will it give way to new and yet unknown pathological syndromes?

The theme of this book has led me to invent an imaginary game about time that I shall explain, because it describes a specific aspect of being a mother in relation to social and psychopathological changes. Assuming that the new century that has just begun is already well under way, what will we be able to say regarding our profession, our patients, our daily work of contact with psychic illness and mental pain? More explicitly, let us try to reply to certain questions as though we were already in the year 2030 or 2040; for example, will the economic, topical, dynamic, genetic, and adaptive functioning of psychism have changed significantly when compared with today? There can be any number of questions, and each reader can carry out the exercise by thinking of the present state of his or her major sphere of interest and then verifying it *back from the future*, to paraphrase the title of a popular American film of a few years ago.

Back from the future

In line with my non-medical training, my thinking in psycho-analytical terms is very much based on a historical rather than a sociological outlook. More precisely, I believe that a long-term approach when dealing with social change is still valid today, rather than a culture that is based on the so-called "immediate: or *événe-mentielle* history.

"The increasingly precise notion of the multiplicity of time and of the exceptional significance of a long period of time . . . should interest the other social sciences, our neighbours" (Braudel, 1969), my translation). Although these words were written several decades ago by one of the fathers of historic research of the twentieth century, I think that they are not only relevant today but are also necessary to our psychoanalytic thinking. More recently, Argentieri (2005) wrote: "The basic paradigms of psychism do not change with the changing of customs, and one or two generations are certainly not sufficient to transform the foundations of our theory" (p. 43).

I think that this assumption is fundamental in order to distinguish between one kind of time and another. As we know, there are two prevalent conceptions of time identifying different models of placement within reality. According to the first conception, which is that of the nearest and prevailing experience, time can be represented by a continuous horizontal line along which it is possible to identify, point by point, a "before" and an "after", and thus, beginning with the present, to determine a past and a future.

According to the second conception, to be found in certain religions, philosophies, or approaches to social history, the reference figure of the temporal dimension is not a straight line but a circle. Time has a circular dimension in which there is no before or after, but the same things can return according to an approach that owes much to the natural cycles of the stars or the seasons.

In one case, the predominant element is that of "progressing", of going forward towards a goal that, according to whether the approach is positive or negative, i.e. optimistic or pessimistic, takes the form either of a *progression* or of a loss. In the other case, there is no progress, but one remains stationary within a super-determined dimension that promptly and severely regulates the cycle of natural and human events.

It is obvious that these two conceptions represent views of the future that are radically opposed to each other; in the first, the future is seen as holding expectations and hopes, while in the second, the aspects of change are almost underestimated unless they are determinable from a historic point of view.

Let us try to reason according to the first approach. It is an approach that belongs to the last century, to the world of science fiction, to that literary delirium that imagined, and in many ways anticipated, tendencies that are now almost realities: voyages into outer space, the creation of robots and automatons, the prolonging of human life. Today science fiction is almost no longer needed; we only have to look at certain projects of public administrations or of important research groups: to have people living on Mars is planned for 2030, the mapping of human genomes is almost completed, as is the possibility of creating artificial beings from staminal cells, and so on. However, all this is not beyond the conception of a world marked, at least on the surface, by speed, change, and innovation.

On the other hand, according to a circular vision of time, human needs and components remain unvaried in the middle period: today as yesterday, sleep, hunger, and thirst, for example, are the prime necessities of the individual that must be satisfied first of all before the superior needs of well-being and psycho-physical integration can be taken care of. Seen from this viewpoint, many things have changed between our grandparents and ourselves, but on the surface and only apparently. Braudel (1969) wrote that history takes place beyond the bright lights, "beyond their flashing: we acknowledge, therefore, the existence of a deeper level . . . richer, from the scientific point of view, than the brilliant surface to which we are accustomed . . ." (my translation).

The generation gap has been constant but, at a certain level, always less than we might believe. Today, as in the time of our grandparents, certain problems of a biological nature and of psychodynamic character are still present, even though, through our therapeutic work, we are well aware of how our patients have changed compared with those described by Freud a century ago, and, above all, of how we analysts have changed.

The exercise that I want to propose now is well known in other disciplines. (In the world of economics it has given rise to "futurology"—of which I am very wary—that, starting from a linear temporality, attempts in some way to outline future scenarios in order to understand and hypothesize how the main variables of the production and distribution of products of work change.) The exercise starts from a so-called *symphonic*[1] vision of history within which different scales and rhythms of temporality combine, and in which not everything (I am obviously using a euphemism) can be manipulated, i.e., modified, on the basis of our expectations. In a circular vision of time, the future is not presented as an unexplored territory to reach and possess, but as a viewpoint from which to look backwards and verify the waves of change over a long period of time; in other words, *back from the future*.

Social change and structural mutations: very early levels and pathology of the self

Twenty years have gone by since Gaddini's fundamental work of 1984 in which he so clearly emphasizes how "the progressive expansion of psychopathology" also depends on the progress of psychoanalysis and the "experiential" tools of the analysts. Gaddini also tried to "period-ise" psychopathology: the hysteria of the post-First World War years, the subsequent displacement on to "character disorders", the borderline and narcissistic situation beginning with the end of the 1960s.

It seems to me that from the nosographical viewpoint, the state of affairs is basically unchanged, partly because the pathologies that emerge in particular socio-historic conditions are never new: they are psychopathological pictures that are already known, and that are becoming more and more visible as the result of certain external situations and of our own increased capacities to recognize them.

For example, in the 1950s Greenson, and ten years later Greenacre, were already describing psychopathological pictures that were "new" when compared with the experience of "the conservative analyst" (Greenacre, 1963).

Again, Gaddini noted that psychoanalysis had, as it were, inverted its direction: if at the beginning it had drawn away from psychosis, more recently it was turning towards psychosis again. "If, as it seems, all this is true, then we must conclude that it is as though, in spite of ourselves and with increasing speed, we were sailing towards the edge of a waterfall." Can we say that we have reached the edge of the waterfall, or that we have even fallen over it? I do not think that this has happened.

The main theme of development during these past twenty years that is still very much present—and is even increasing in intensification—has been the tendency towards undifferentiation, with a growing and painful loss of the sense of alterity. And so, what seems to have changed is not so much the clinical picture of reference, but the potential of energy with which it is being revealed today. It seems as though the Other, as such, is destined to be dangerously cancelled out or, rather, not seen.

I should mention that I do not wish to hastily liquidate the complex argumentation on globalization; I am simply interested in taking this as a paradigmatic sign of development of "mentalities" in this particular phase of history.

Once again using the game of *back from the future*, I think that from the psychopathological viewpoint we can suppose that clinical situations relative to narcissistic personalities and pathologies of the self will become consolidated and increasingly serious.

It seems likely that in the next few years psychoanalytic work will confirm and strengthen the register on which theory and clinical work have been moving over the last half century; that is, the register regarding very early phases of development, the difficult and complex vicissitudes linked to the processes of individuation and differentiation, and whether and how they combine with the oedipal levels, and the quality of these intersections.

In her paper on "Perversions", Amati Mehler (1999) reflects on the impact that the growing contemporary socio-cultural tendency towards sexual undifferentiation has on the destiny of identity and of gender identity. She notes that there is ". . . a confusion between the social, the ideological and the psychological levels, between mother and father figures, between male and female and maternal and paternal functions . . . ." She points out that ". . . undifferentiation is confused with equality and seems to have done away with the urge to discover, recognize and bear the different other, male or female; fused group ties seem to reign over a lost sense of individuality". She suggests that this merits reflection.

Recently, in a paper on incest, Argentieri (2005) wrote:

I think that in psychoanalysis the Oedipus complex, even though by most of us write it with a small "o", has preserved its main evolutionary, affective, and cognitive meaning under the shield of drives.

What might have changed, if anything, are the defences. . . . Today
our tolerance of atypical expressions of sexuality is greater: the
cross-dressing of adults and children, virtual sexuality, virtual
paedophilia, sex tourism, the category of transgender that now
unites transvestites and trans-sexuals in a single category. [p. 43]

Argentieri emphasizes that all this—as far as can be seen from our
clinical work—has already reverberated on the last two generations, who have been characterized by personality structures that
are "less rigid, more flexible, and with a superego that is less impos-
ing and an ego that is more fragile. . . . thus the oedipal knot is
loosened, if not avoided." (Argentieri, 2005, p. 44).

Returning to the idea of *back from the future*, what shall we be
able to say about maternity? Although it may be true that the oedipal register seems to be increasingly mortgaged by the growing
persistence of the pre-oedipal defences, shall we find ourselves
faced with fantasies of maternity that are always more exposed to
parthenogenetic and autopoietic risk? And especially, within this
context, what could "change" mean for us psychoanalysts, what
shall we have to change?

The change

Because our work as psychoanalysts has a transformative quality
(see Canestri, 2003), every day we face change, resistances to
change, defences ranged against it, and the oscillation between
anxiety of non-integration and anxiety of integration. It is not by
chance that our discipline is called "psychodynamic".

Our very special *time machine* is called *Nachträglichkeit*, that
formidable structure that allows us to resignify archaic elements in
forms relative to more evolved phases of development. Thanks to
this, we experience a temporality that seems to be "combined"—a
kind of continuous conjunction of circularity and linearity in continuity. It is also thanks to this instrument that we are able to promote
change and transformation.

We know, of course, that change does not necessarily in itself
bring about improvement; it can contain the seeds of impoverishment and lack of meaning. Through the history of ideas (for

instance, those of Marx, of Freud, of Nietzsche and his *Gaia Scienza*) we are in the habit of thinking not in terms of change and development, but in terms of the quality and "use" of development.

In his famous book *Il Gattopardo* (*The Leopard*), Giuseppe Tomasi di Lampedusa wrote: "cambiare tutto perché nulla cambi" (change everything so that nothing changes). I therefore believe that it is fundamental to think about change without diverting our attention from the *symphonic* quality of development, i.e., from the multiplicity of scales, rhythms, tones, and intensity of temporality. This means increasingly exploiting those tools that are useful for promoting a process of transformation in the minds of our patients. It means especially that we must not lose sight of the relationship between different forms of temporality—the time of social change and the time of psychic change—so as not to confuse, in the words of a well-known history book, merchants' time with Church time (the latter in the laital sense, of course).

If such confusion were to occur, I think that, in the gratifying illusion of feeling ourselves to be "politically correct" analysts, we should risk losing along the way the whole of our transformative equipment: setting, transference, countertransference, interpretation. Consequently, we should in this way lose the possibility of reorganizing the intrapsychic equilibrium and of promoting change and development.

"God could not be everywhere and therefore he made mothers." Continuing in the same ironic tone as this Jewish proverb, and if, instead of entrusting ourselves to God we are to entrust ourselves to mothers, then perhaps we must think about the fact that our future is partly entrusted to how these mothers are born, how they develop, and how they grow up into adults.

Notes

1. I have borrowed this word from the historian Michel Vovelle.

CHAPTER THREE

Motherhood in a fertile new world

Diane Ehrensaft

In the early twentieth century, classical psychoanalysis defined motherhood as the healthy developmental outcome for women. Females who repudiated motherhood for alternative endeavours were diagnosed as having a "masculinity" complex. Economic changes, historical shifts, and the advent of more effective birth control techniques led to an attack on this analytic stance. By the end of the twentieth century the "right to choose" replaced motherhood as the hallmark of healthy female development. The masculinity complex was now redefined as feminism and women were liberated to become mothers or not with no aspersion on their character. Maternal desire was superseded by the desire for self-actualization, which could include motherhood or not. With birth control pills on women's side, biology was no longer destiny.

As the dialectic of history typically plays its hand, entry into the twenty-first century has been accompanied by yet another radical turnabout in the phenomenon of motherhood. The introduction of rapidly evolving techniques of reproductive technology now offers infertile women, women partnered with infertile men, single heterosexual and lesbian women, and lesbian couples the opportunity to have children of their own. Typically driven by intense maternal desire, these are women who have transcended rather than accepted the destiny of their own biology by becoming biological mothers in ways Freud never contemplated when he wrote his first treatises on femininity.

As these women have entered the world of motherhood, our psychoanalytic understandings of sex, gender, and parenthood are once again torn asunder. A sexual union between a man and woman is no longer the prerequisite for procreation. An outside party has been introduced into the reproductive process—a man who donates his sperm, a woman who donates her egg, a woman who offers her womb as the gestational space for another woman or man's child. That person holds the status of the "birth other", an individual who will not become a parent but who will offer either gametes or womb so that his or her "partner(s)" in this process will be able to have a child.

This new maternity presents challenges to our psychoanalytic work with mothers and our working models of the psychology of gender, reproduction, and motherhood. We are encountering satisfied maternal desire divorced from sexuality, new maternal defences, a new phenomenon of part-object–whole object thinking, and a redefinition of the primal scene. I would like to address each one of these challenges in turn as I invite you to think with me about the complex psychological experience of becoming a mother with the aid of a birth other.

Love with an improper stranger

In discussion of erotic feelings that surface in psychotherapy, Jodie Davies stated: "Each of us is conceived out of the desire of two significant others" (Davies, 1998, p. 805). This sentence, as written, is no longer universally true. In the new paradigm of baby-making, the corrected quote would read, "Each of us is conceived out of the desire of one or two people, and possibly the help of one or more other people who participate in our conception not out of sexual desire but as a result of lending their bodies or their gametes so a baby could be made". Babies can now be born of libidinal *maternal* (or paternal) desire, divorced completely from sexual desire.

The logical conclusion is that the bifurcation of sex and reproduction and the removal of sexual desire from the equation will de-eroticize the experience of conception. Yet such logic is defied by the psychological experience of women who enter motherhood through the doors of the fertility clinic. The romance is understandably taken out of the experience of becoming a mother when it begins with hormone pills and shots, procreation in a cold sterile lab, or between a woman and a turkey baster, or in an exquisitely timed choreography between an egg donor and recipient, or after an ejaculation into a jar. Yet even with this new phenomenon of sexless conception, sexuality is not successfully expunged. Emotionally, it appears that our psyches, either because of genetic pre-programming and/or deeply rooted social constructs, do not allow for the total expulsion of sex from the garden of baby-making. On the other side of sterilized conception is induced sexualized procreation—in the form of dreams, fantasies, and anxieties.

A woman contemplating donor insemination reveals: "I've never told anyone this, but my husband is the only man I have ever had sex with. I'm afraid that having another man's sperm inside me would make me feel like I was sleeping with someone else" (Cooper & Glazer, 1994, p. 154). Alexis, a single woman in her early forties who wanted to become a mother, found a known sperm donor through her contacts in the gay community. During the period when the inseminations were taking place, Alexis reported romantic and sexual fantasies about the donor. Even though he was gay, she wished they could get together and do it the "old-fashioned way"; she enjoyed erotic fantasies about his body and their lovemaking together.

Concomitant erotic pleasure and sexual anxiety create psychological turmoil for the mother who thought she was simply having a baby with the help of the "nice woman" or the "nice man" who graciously donated a womb or a gamete to help her have a child. Surrounded by a culture that promotes monogamy and coupled love and emerging from a childhood filled with primal scenes and triangulated Oedipal dramas, the deeply imbedded scenario of man, woman, sex, and pregnancy remains stable, if not immutable. Fantasies of illicit sex, adultery, and a ménage a trois can take a mother by surprise. Experiences of parents using assisted reproductive technology inform us that you can take the reproduction out of sex, but it is presently far more difficult psychologically to take the sex out of reproduction.

Maureen and Craig very much wanted a baby, but Craig's sperm count was too low. While living abroad, they decided to try donor insemination. They found an anonymous donor from Southern France. They knew only that he was a blond heart surgeon. Years later they sat in my office talking about their decision to withhold from their daughter, Emily, the information that Craig was not her biological father. Maureen expressed extreme discomfort about telling their daughter her and Craig's personal history with sex, infertility, and reproduction. She also revealed her fantasy that if they decided to tell their daughter, Emily would quickly move the information into a sexual scenario, "You mean, Mummy, you did it with someone else?" Having met Emily, I thought Maureen's worry seemed more a projection of her own unconscious conflicts than an anticipated response to sexual pre-occupation on Emily's part. Maureen came across as a highly sexualized person, both in dress and demeanour. As she described with great pride the circumstances of Emily's conception using a blond French surgeon as the donor, she spoke as if she were describing the most erotic of intimate rendezvous rather than a medical procedure.

Cooper and Glazer advise that "Couples who ultimately choose this alternative means of family building [assisted reproductive technology] must be able to separate the act of lovemaking from the act of procreation" (1994, p. 154). Like many behavioural directives, deep psychological undercurrents block the successful execution of this task. The sperm donor, egg donor, or surrogate is not only a nice man or woman (if that), he or she is another person who enters the sexual arena of man and woman, woman or man alone, two women, or two men, a person who treads on the erotic terrain where babies are made.

The sexualized images that spring from the acts of assisted reproductive technology may be especially poignant for mothers who use donor insemination. In our culture sperm have been inextricably linked with sexuality, in a way that ova never are. Eggs symbolize birth, purity, even housing for the young. Sperm symbolize sexual passion, male virility, male dominance. This sensibility regarding sex and sperm is deeply embedded in our unconscious, despite our conscious awareness of sperm as merely the male seed that connects with the female egg. Diamond, Kezur, Meyers, Scharf,

& Wienshel (1999) describe a mother's feelings about sperm vs. egg donorship:

> Lou's father and brother both offered to donate sperm, but Felicia was repulsed by the "incestuous" aspect of using either man's sperm. However, Felicia said that if she had been infertile, she would not have had a problem using her sister's eggs because they bore none of the sexual connotations that sperm do. [p. 147]

A mother who uses an egg donor may be more liberated from the sexual disquiet that surfaces in response to gamete donorship. The woman who borrows someone else's eggs in order to conceive is placing something in her body that her own body would normally produce, rather than sexualized body substances from a man. It is a woman-to-woman phenomenon, and one that holds connotations of fecundity, pregnancy, and motherhood, rather than being associated with sexuality and lovemaking, as sperm are. However, as every egg needs a sperm to become a baby, if that egg is joined with her male partner's sperm, she is still not freed from the fantasy of the egg donor and her lover "doing it together".

The new primal scene and its sequelae

A birth other enters the arena of conception and birth and sexual scenarios swirl through the psyches of mothers, fathers, and birth others alike. Eroticism permeates the conception experience. In mothers who are coupled, the birth other symbolizes a potential sexual competitor.

> I felt like the odd woman out in the donor egg process, as my old friend from college was my donor, but this meant that her eggs would be fertilized by *my* husband's sperm. They are making the embryo/baby while I wait, then I'll carry *their* embryo that I didn't contribute to making. [Cooper & Glazer, 1994, p. 233]

This woman's experience as "the odd woman out", who watches her husband get together with another woman and even participates in their lovemaking by carrying *their* child, restimulates the original primal scene, the early and upsetting knowledge that her mother and father were engaging in a sexual act together, an act that excluded her.

Beginning with Freud (1924), psychoanalysts have argued that the primal scene is phylogenetic (Klein, 1932), while others say it is merely a social construction. However, most agree that within Western culture children are intrigued by what goes on behind the bedroom door, particularly their parents'. In this scenario children grow simultaneously excited and disquieted by the entry of a third person into the intimate scene of their parents' sexual union, whether it be themselves or another party. Residues of the drama carry into our intimate adult relationships, as evidenced in the rage and distress upon discovering a spouse or partner's love affair with another woman or man. Residues of the drama are now surfacing in the psyches of mothers who turn to a donor or surrogate to help them create a baby, stimulating fantasies of illicit extra-marital sex or ménages à trois.

The experienced inner chaos when a fantasized sexual competitor enters the scene can grow close to intolerable, at which point one calls on psychological defences to calm the storm. What I have witnessed in mothers (and fathers) who have conceived with the aid of a birth other is a form of denial I have labelled "immaculate deception" (Ehrensaft, 2000). A lesbian mother-to-be insisted that she and her partner were responsible for their baby's conception, no one else. The couple's child had been conceived by her partner and a known sperm donor. She accompanied her partner to the insemination, tucking the bag of fresh sperm into her armpit to keep it warm on the way to the doctor's office. She developed a new narrative to the birth story—she and her partner, rather than her partner and the donor, had conceived a child together, because she had hand-delivered the sperm that made the baby. Within this immaculate deception narrative, the mother, in annihilating the donor as a participant, simultaneously reinvented herself as the only partner in a seemingly sexualized scenario. Clear suggestions of erotic imagery emerge in the narrative of the warm sperm close to her body, as she remained close to her partner who was to be vaginally injected with the sperm that was kept alive only because of the heat of her own body. From that intimate, erotic closeness a baby was made.

Mothers who decide never to tell their children that they were conceived with the aid of someone else's sperm or egg or womb can also engage in a form of immaculate deception in which either the fact or the import of the insemination, donorship, or surrogacy is buried to such an extent that the mother herself grows to believe that there was no outside person in the process. The psychological mechanism for maintaining this level of denial is the reduction of whole objects to part objects. To assuage anxieties about the interloper, references are often made to the nice, generous men or women who dispassionately dispense their sperm or eggs or offer their wombs as selfless and sexless gifts to the childless. That construction, however, is not always a strong enough surge protector against the angst about the outsider's participation in the making of the baby. To better protect oneself against the anxiety stirred up by unconscious or conscious fantasies about sex, reproduction, and the intrusion of the "birth other," one can shrink the donor to a vial of sperm or a carton of eggs, or reduce the surrogate/gestational carrier to the status of an incubator.

In Klein's developmental theory of object relations (1958), the infant relies on body parts to represent the whole, especially breast = mother. As the infant grows, the baby discovers that mother is a whole being outside the baby's omnipotent control. As life progresses, times of stress may temporarily catapult one back to the earliest moments of life, when the whole is not more than the sum of its parts but is actually reduced to only a part in our inner fantasies. In the context of the anxieties stirred up by procreation with a birth other, I have witnessed such a reversion in the new equation: biological father = sperm, biological mother = ovum, gestational mother = womb. In ideation, such part-object reduction is a good strategy for keeping the birth other out of the bedroom. The downside, however, is that such fantasy denies the reality of the birth other as a whole person with thoughts and feelings.

Ironically, the exact opposite phenomenon may unfold—the inner creation of a whole person from a vial of sperm. Marlene, a single lesbian mother, inadvertently found out the identity of her daughter's sperm donor, who was supposed to remain anonymous. She lamented that her daughter did not have a father. She imagined presenting herself at his office to show him the pictures of "their" daughter and fill him in on the first ten years of the life he had been sorely missing. In her fantasies she completely overrode any question of desire or volition on his part, and was brought to a rude awakening when invited to entertain the possibility that this man's only involvement was to donate his sperm for a fee while a medical student. With no other parent in the picture, a single mother may grow anxious about leaving the father of her child in the status of a part-object—a vial of sperm. She longs to be able to fill in the missing piece of the family, to have some image of the man who has mixed his bodily fluids with hers, and has had genetic input in her child's being.

In the struggle to take the sex out of reproduction, we witness a paradox: a reversion to part-object relating and an illusional creation of whole objects where there is none. Within the present structures of family life, we have yet to come up with an alternative socially constructed concept of a "whole-object" donor, surrogate, or gestational carrier who is *not* a parent and not a sexual(ized) partner in the family. Mothers anxious about the interloper will be drawn towards part-object thinking, the reduction of the donor, surrogate, or carrier to a "thing" that presents no threat to her motherhood. Mothers who feel the absence of a parenting partner, or succumb to the erotic undertow of procreation with an outsider, will be more prone to conjure up a whole parent from a thread of genetic material, engaging in the fantasy of creating for themselves another parent, maybe even a lover.

Mother envy

Motherhood, of course, is not just about sexuality. It is about maternal desire, developing a bond with a child, and establishing a family. Any woman can enter this position, whether or not she is the biological mother of the child. A mother using assisted reproductive technology will attach to her child like any other mother, but she may be faced with an experience of "mother envy" for which she is ill prepared.

Agnes Rossi coined the term "feminisma," the female equivalent of machismo: "the essence of feminisma is the ability to create a living, breathing human being in the space between one's hipbones" (Rossi, 1998). Not every woman carries or breathes that essence, but when it does infiltrate a woman's being and she finds herself deprived of the opportunity to make and carry a child, a devastating sense of loss to her womanhood can ensue. Often there is no time to mourn this loss; time is of the essence and deep maternal desire drives one forward at a quick pace. Still in the process of mourning, an infertile woman who turns to an egg donor or surrogate to have a child must now embrace in her life another woman who faces no challenge to her feminisma. She must join with another woman who can produce viable eggs by the thousands or bring healthy foetuses to term between her hipbones, not only for herself but for others as well. Even if the mother never meets this woman, she exists in fantasies.

Mothers often express deep gratitude toward the egg donors or surrogates who have generously given of themselves so that the mothers can have babies. Yet, what often erupts unexpectedly is intense envy. I refer to this as mother envy, rather than maternal envy, to signify the relationship of the mother to the other woman with whom she will be "sharing" motherhood, either through the donation of her eggs or the use of her womb. "Mother envy" was first documented long ago in biblical times, when Hagar gave birth to Abraham's child so Sarah could become a mother:

> Sarah [of the bible] was the first, but by no means the last, woman to find that she had unanticipated reactions of jealousy and resentment to the pregnancy and childbirth experience of another woman, even one who was bearing a child for her. [Cooper & Glazer, 1994, p. 261]

Jealousy towards the "other woman," but more importantly, the deep desire to have what that other woman has, the ability to get pregnant, and the frustration of not having that ability, can become a constant and sometimes consuming source of pain for many women who have turned to egg donors or surrogates in order to have a child (Stuart-Smith, 2003).

Klein (1957) defined basic envy as an attack on what is perceived as good, most specifically, the mother. The frustration of not having what the mother has, or not getting what the mother has to offer, can sometimes lead the infant to want to get inside and attack the good mother. With time, the infant develops the capacity for gratitude for all that the mother gives, and that sense of gratitude calms the tides of envy so that the child can go on to live a productive and healthy life. But that earliest of feelings, intense envy towards some-one good, can resurface at any time in life, and does for many women who have had a child using an egg donor or surrogate. The experience of facing the failures in one's own body and turning to another female body in working order to fulfil one's maternal desire evokes the very earliest feelings of dependency on another female body that had everything the mother did not.

The envy can become overwhelming and manifest itself in many combinations and permutations. Maggie and Betty were a lesbian couple who wanted a child. They each longed for the experience of pregnancy, but Maggie, the older of the two, was to go first. She tried for several months to become pregnant using donor insemina-tion and the boost of fertility drugs. Nothing worked. Tensions mounted between her and Betty. They agreed that if Maggie did not get pregnant after twelve months of trying, Betty would start trying. Twelve months passed with no pregnancy. Per agreement, Betty started trying. Just at that time Maggie consulted another specialist who saw no reason why she could not conceive. So for a period of time both women tried to get pregnant, with the agreement that whoever got pregnant first, the other would stop trying. Maggie never got pregnant. Betty did, with little effort. That marked the beginning of the end of their relationship. Maggie could not tolerate the pain of Betty doing what she could not—bear a child. Maggie's envy was not towards a donor or surrogate, but towards her own lover who, in essence, had been transformed into the surrogate who would carry the child that Maggie could never make.

Mother envy is a woman-to-woman phenomenon, based not on sexual threat but maternal desire. Whether standing alone or hitched to concomitant sexual threat, such envy has the strength to transform maternal dreams into nightmares. In as much as insight breeds change, bringing these unanticipated inner conflicts to consciousness for analysis and understanding can restore the dream and strengthen the positive experience of motherhood with a birth other.

Conclusion

Sex has now been taken out of reproduction, so that women who heretofore were barred from biological motherhood can now become mothers, liberating infertile women, single heterosexual and lesbian women, and lesbian couples to satisfy their maternal desire for a child of their own. Yet, liberation never comes without complications. Eroticism is both constructed and deconstructed as women turn to birth others to help them become mothers, mother envy erupts, and new psychological defences are developed in which reversion to part-object thinking coexists with immaculate deception and fantasized partnerships with the birth other. Motherhood in the age of reproductive technology alerts us that maternal desire must be recognized in its own right as a force related to, but also existing independently of, sexual desire. The twenty-first century brings with it the opportunity to re-evaluate traditional theories of motherhood and examine collective anxieties about defying "mother nature" so the psychoanalytic community can offer proper support to women who grapple with the uncharted inner terrain of motherhood in partnership with a birth other.

CHAPTER FOUR

Artificial pregnancy

Jacqueline Amati Mehler

Introduction

One of the complex and still debated issues regarding motherhood in the twenty-first century is the variety of reasons that may account for a couple's sterility and the resources employed to solve it as well as the problems raised by those reasons. The latter inhabits the arena of debate throughout and beyond geographic, ethical, legal, and moral boundaries that I cannot discuss here. Suffice to say that different countries deal with assisted pregnancy in the most varied and contradictory manner, ranging from total flexibility, such as fertilization of singles or homosexual couples, to more repressive rules like exclusion of heterologue insemination or forced insemination of embryos even if genetically damaged. Cultural contexts may have a different impact on the way these issues are dealt with. As Malkah Notman[1] reminded me, in one of the international panels held on the subject of assisted pregnancy,[2] the clinical experience and concerns voiced by Europeans differed from those expressed by USA colleagues (personal communication).

I should state from the beginning that in regard to problems raised by assisted pregnancy I am unable to provide answers or to formulate elaborate psychoanalytical formulations; each individual, family, and social circumstance presents unique situations to psychoanalytic understanding. My aim is to raise and share some questions about situations that we, as psychoanalysts, are not yet sufficiently acquainted with. In considering this as a starting point, two issues come immediately to mind that I shall attempt to explore or at least to bring to our attention. One regards the motivations for the "choice" of artificial fecundation rather than that of adoption. The other regards something about which we are clinically more knowledgeable: the need to differentiate the wish to become pregnant from the desire for maternity (or paternity).

Assisted pregnancy

Several years ago, during a discussion on the opportunity of introducing "Artificial Pregnancy" as one of the themes in the Congresses of the IPA Psychoanalytic community, somebody remarked—and was indeed right—that there is no such thing as *artificial pregnancy*. One is or isn't pregnant, and what we are really talking about is *assisted pregnancy*. Although this is correct I still wanted to maintain the denomination of artificial pregnancy for my introduction at the first panel held on this subject (1993[1]), perhaps for the same reasons that I think it is correct to talk about artificial intelligence when referring to intelligent systems that are situated outside the human apparatus. Although these are certainly the product of the human brain, they nevertheless remain its surrogates. It is precisely this condition, of being a surrogate, that, for me, justifies, at least partly, the denomination of "artificial" for assisted pregnancy. Of course, this by no means implies a value judgement of any sort, nor does it imply that an assisted pregnancy is always and/or universally felt differently from a "non technically-assisted" pregnancy. It implies, however, that we are dealing with something different even when referring to those reproduction practices whose technological devices allow them to be circumscribed to the biological parents-to-be. We are confronted with the surrogate of something that for millennia has been contained within the boundaries of one single individual body when referring to pregnancy, and within two bodies only when referring to fertilization.

I mentioned "artificial intelligence" before, not only because it has occupied a lot of my own thinking and work, but because, when comparing human and artificial intelligence, the knowledge and realization of what cannot permeate from one to the other can highlight the organization of the mind; furthermore it has influenced the theories that attempt to explain its functioning. By the same token I think that the study of assisted pregnancy could contribute to further the psychoanalytical understanding of assumptions that are at the core of some of our own theories. I mean, for example, theories regarding issues of self-object differentiation processes and fantasies about internal (partial and total) objects and identification processes with primary figures, not to mention all the processes that we usually consider under the heading of the fusional aspects of the mother–child relationship and of the vicissitudes of the separation–individuation phases. To this we should add the influence of such concepts on the general understanding of the parent–child interaction, particularly in regard to the elements that may contribute to somehow mute the subjective sense of the child being the *real and true* child of the couple that will function as the social and psychological parents.

The differences in the psychological context between adoptive children and children born as a result of artificial reproduction are many. One is quite self-evident, especially from the mother's angle, and it regards the concrete creative engendering process of pregnancy, with all its physical and psychological implications, that is absent in the case of the adoptive mother. This does not mean, of course, that an adoptive parent will not develop a whole series of phantasies about the baby or child that is going to enter their lives. On the other hand, in the case of artificial fertilization, while a woman can say "This child is mine", regardless of whether it was conceived with her partner's or with a donor's sperm, a man might say "It is *as if* it were my child", perhaps in both circumstances but certainly so in the second case. I believe there may be many reasons, intrinsic to the specific bond and relationship of the couple, that play a role not only in the choice (when this is possible) between adoption and artificial reproduction, but also in the choice of the technological devices selected by the couple to engender a child. Since that first encounter in 1995, many colleagues have developed important considerations and clinical explorations to which I refer the reader (see Tubert, 1991).

Today, a baby may be conceived in a radically different way from the one that has ruled biology and interpersonal generative practices for thousands of years and that has, for some decades now, influenced our own ways of conceiving and interpreting fantasies about impregnation, female identity and maternity, parental imagos, and the vicissitudes of the "family romance".

Just to introduce some of our bewildering queries, let me quote an example, albeit quite extreme, that many may remember: a woman in Buffalo, aged fifty-three, gave birth to a baby that was the son of her daughter and her son-in-law. The baby was conceived in a laboratory with the sperm of the father and the ovule of his wife thereafter deposited in the grandmother's womb. Who is the biological mother here? Will it coincide with or be split from the internalization of the psychological mother? What will be the relation of the father with these two women, both somehow the mother of his child?

From a biological viewpoint the "true child" is the individual who derives from the bonding of the male and female germinal cells followed by its development in that same female's uterus until birth. A less "true child" lacks one of these characteristics in the sense that one of those who will then count as his/her social and psychological parent is substituted in one or more phases of this process by another person. The direct interpersonal interaction of two human bodies seems to be substituted in the generating act by parts or products of the genital organs (sperm, ova, uterus, and so on) that assume an almost autonomous existence, detached from the individual's body. Paradoxically, the truest possible child of assisted reproduction is the most artificial: the test-tube baby obtained from the parents' gametes and reintroduced in the mother's uterus. All the other forms of artificial reproduction require the intervention of at least one other person different from the aspiring parents. Thus, in some cases it is the genetic contribution of one or both parents that will be lacking; in other cases the pregnancy will inhabit a different uterus from that of the mother, whether the child was or was not engendered by the future father's sperm.

Most practices involve—when a third party is indicated—an anonymous donor. In the case of artificial insemination, when the baby is the child of the biological mother and an unknown donor, what will the phantasies about this unknown biological father be like? And in any case, how will the "imaginary baby" that inhabits the mind of all potential parents, long before the actual generating project takes off, be modified when donors and technological devices are brought into the picture? What has often been reported resembles a vague disturbing sense of the uncanny, (*unheimlich*). This can be a prevalent conscious or unconscious element in the configuration of the "imaginary child" in the mind of the pregnant mother and of the father-to-be.

Within the family dynamics, what will be the psychological implications of artificial insemination with donor? They could vary according to whether it is a recognized public action, or whether it will be kept as a secret. Sometimes it is concealed because the parents may be convinced that it is better for the child; other times because of a culturally determined need to protect the image of the father's manhood when the sperm is donated by another man. The variable philosophy of fatherhood should be kept in mind, and I think that it could be quite interesting to know more about the motivation of the donors themselves. They can be men who provide their semen to a bank for money; others do so because they have been vasectomized and wished to conserve seminal liquid in case they should change their mind about procreating. Other men yet donate their sperm because they are ill or subject to chemotherapy and wish to preserve their seminal fluid for the future, whether they stay alive or die. I think we are all acquainted with controversies about legal, ethical, and psychological problems ensuing from the use of deposited sperm after the donor's death. Furthermore, today scientific progress concerning the use or misuse of staminal cells and eventual genetic manipulations has rendered the destiny of procreative cells and embryos the centre of a debate that I shall not deal with here.

The criteria with which the donors could be chosen are also very important because this sort of programmed selection of paternal characteristics can inform us about the parental wishes or phantasies. (I am thinking here of the wishful phantasy to have a Nobel prize winner as donor, or one who has physical characteristics that resemble those of the man who will be socially recognized as the father.) And we know how deeply parental desires can influence development and personality organization in their offspring. Some parents appear to be very worried about the alien genetic aspects brought along by the donor (an anxiety that is also present in the case of adoption). Other parents trust in a suitable choice on the part of the doctor or institution involved, and others still rely much more on the relationship and the education provided to the child rather than on genetic factors. In cases of adoption we may hear such expressions as "It is as if it were my own child", or "It would be mine anyhow" when artificial fertilization through a donor has resulted in a pregnancy. A man who favoured adoption but was against artificial insemination told his wife "At least this way (through adoption) it is neither yours nor mine". Some men who view AID favourably seem able to overcome the sense of biological extraneousness through a close sharing intimacy of the pregnancy with their wives.

The case of a woman donor is again a very different story. In order to donate an ovum a small surgical intervention is necessary, and the ovum cannot be stored for delayed use as easily as the sperm. Or rather, its use can be more safely delayed if the ovum is already fecundated and thus in the state of an embryo. These embryos can then be deposited in the womb of the potential mother according to medical or institutionalized decision-making. Another possible variation is the artificial fecundation of a woman donor's ova, either through artificial insemination or *in vitro*, followed by the transfer to another female's womb, by virtue of a "women's agreement", as in the case of the woman in Buffalo mentioned above. And, of course, all these techniques could allow a woman who has never had intercourse or the experience of shared love or sex with a partner to become pregnant and bear a child (a practice that some lesbian couples have adopted). The wish to bear a child thus leads a sterile couple to undergo the methods of artificial fertilization, whether through a male or a female donor, leading to pregnancy and delivery—but not necessarily to the pregnancy of the woman who will be the future mother.

There is no doubt that scientific and technological developments have alleviated the sad situations of sterility, and while at a sociological level one must guard against ideological distortions when dealing with artificially assisted pregnancy, I think that our conceptual framework regarding maternity and its understanding may gain a lot from further psychoanalytic investigation of such cases. I am thinking particularly about those women who consider it their job to rent out their uterus for the sake of another woman's maternity. I don't believe in what has been for a long time called the innate maternal instinct, and precisely by virtue of this I can't help wondering—in the case of a rented uterus—about the fate of all those processes that contribute to the mental and physical construction of the mother–child relation during gestation, both in the woman who is pregnant and in the potential mother who is waiting for delivery to take place in order to take with her the creature that will be her baby from there on, by virtue of a previous agreement.

What I really think is at stake in the practices of artificial reproduction is the type and fate of the relationship with a significant Other recognized as such—whether it be the partner, an anonymous donor, or the offspring. In other words, we are confronted no more with a father and a mother but with a series of variable third parties involved in the procreation process. We know, of course, that also in nature (if I may use such an expression) all sorts of phantasies involving internalized primary objects of the parents are in any case involved in the process of making and having a child. But what variables are introduced when real concrete third parties are introduced between the future father and mother, that are furthermore liable to conscious intentional manipulations? This is relevant, for instance, in those cases in which the choice of donor—inspired by the illusion of procreating a genius with the sperm of a Nobel prize winner or someone who physically has a familiar "air"—has the flavour of a programmed selection. Again, I am here leaving aside all possible moral or ethical concerns. What I am trying to emphasize is the need to understand better if and which differences could exist between phantasies that are linked to one's internal objects and those promoted by external biological donor objects within the parental couple and the parent–child interactions. Paradoxically these objects have both a very real concrete quality and a concealed, prohibited, and sometimes forever unknowable quality to them.

The wish for maternity

The second issue about motherhood mentioned at the beginning of this chapter—also closely connected with phantasies and internal object and self-object representations mentioned above—is the need to differentiate the wish to become pregnant from the desire for maternity (or paternity). The phantasies that a woman has about herself as a mother-to-be or about the baby to come are not only crucial to the pregnancy's development but also to the future mother–infant relationship and the fate of the newcomer itself. In fact, the ways in which the feminine identity is organized and motherhood is experienced draws its source in childhood though the relationship with one's own mother or caretaker. Identification with mother as a developmental step towards feminine identity, contrary to what is generally thought, renders separation and individuation more difficult for the girl than for the boy. While psychological separation develops during growth, she will resemble mother in her femininity. Thus, two opposite processes are at stake; differentiation on the one hand and resemblance on the other. Pregnancy, especially the first one, may reshuffle the internal set-up since the psychological factors in play are so closely connected with early and bodily scenarios of identity formation and the achievement of alterity. Regression is often present during pregnancy, and biological fusion with the foetus might stir up phantasies related to the early fusional experiences of the mother-to-be. There is a further physiological regression following delivery that allows for the development of a particular sensibility and capacity to identify with the baby's needs, called "primary maternal preoccupation". It is in this area that the early relationship with one's own mother can play a role in the ways motherhood is experienced and in the balance between physiological regression to symbiotic experiences and the more mature recognition of the Other as such, whether it be the partner or the child that is engendered and then born. Aggression, envy, and guilt can play a role both during pregnancy and in the development of a harmonious mother–infant relationship.

There are, of course, many issues that interest us as psychoanalysts as to how pregnancy (and motherhood) is experienced, whether we are dealing with narcissistic needs or the mature desire to create a new life of a separate being. Are such issues linked with the choice of adoption or assisted pregnancy and, among the latter, the different possible methods to achieve pregnancy? What can we as analysts understand about women who, as mentioned above, may never have experienced a love relationship or had sex, but choose by means of assisted pregnancy to bear a child of their own? What are the differences (if any) between the mother–infant relationship in such cases, and in that of a woman who, having engendered a child with a partner, brings up the child alone without the father? I believe that possible differences lie in the internal psychic organization of the mother and above all in the *nature of the desire* to become a mother that in my opinion deserves great attention and careful psychoanalytic exploration. Under this generic label we can come across the mature desire to create a new life of a separate being as well as that of simply remaining pregnant in order to recreate a blissful fusional experience. The latter sometimes results in difficulty in carrying the pregnancy until the end and/or difficulties during the delivery. In my experience such patients are tormented by acute separation anxieties as the time for delivery approaches, and we are familiar, of course, with post-delivery depression. Another kind of wish relates to the need to conceive a new self, "flesh of one's flesh", that threatens the future autonomy of the child, who is destined to become a narcissistic extension of the mother at the service of her own lack.

To conclude, I wish to emphasize again that my queries about assisted pregnancy and the possible motivations to resort to its different techniques do not imply any value judgement about artificial reproduction, but are intended to single out situations that we need to learn more about because our practice will be increasingly confronted with them in our work with children, adult individuals, and families. The complicated integration of mental and biological phenomena is of the utmost importance to our theoretical and clinical practice and I think that the subject of assisted pregnancy can offer a vast clinical field of interest and psychoanalytic investigation.

Notes

1   I am very grateful to Malkah Notman for her critical comments.

2.   The panel was held during the congress in Amsterdam in 1993. Its title was: "Infertility,Surrogacy and the New Reproductive Techniques: Psychoanalytic Perspectives". Chair: Helen Meyers; introduction: Jacqueline Amati Mehler; presenters: Eva Lester, Dinora Pines; discussant: Marianne Springer-Kremer.

CHAPTER FIVE

The non-maternal psychic space

Alcira Mariam Alizade

Introduction

P sychoanalytic theories about mental development in women are closely linked to motherhood. A woman's maternal function is of some considerable importance on the psycho-analytic scene.

The ideas I would like to present here are geared towards thinking about and constructing a theory relating to the mental space in women that is independent from the psychic function or position of a mother. To this end, I shall explore the concept of a non-maternal psychic space and the processes that do not revolve around the equations and events directly related to motherhood.

This chapter is therefore an invitation to reconsider the subjectivity of women, their conscious and unconscious fantasies, and the psychodynamics of the relationship issues that involve these. To this end, it would be helpful to suspend preconceived ideas and generalities that can only introduce bias in the field of desire and human peculiarities.

Now that gestation may be controlled either to avoid pregnancy (contraception) or to achieve pregnancy by means of new reproductive techniques, in the following pages I endeavour to consider these issues impartially and without any *a priori* theoretical restrictions.

Psychoanalysis makes more flexible the thesis according to which the healthy development of every woman necessarily involves a desire to become pregnant, give birth, and raise children, so that the manner in which we listen to what women patients have to say is also modified. This new receptiveness will influence the direction of the treatment and the formulation of interpretations. It will make possible the detection both of pathological states in the desire for a child and of their opposite—normality or health—in the absence of any desire for a child. The concept of normality and pathology will be freed from the kind of inflexibility that bound them so tightly together.

Women may develop creatively *both within the context of their reproductive body and outside that context.*

Conflictual motherhood, the dark side of motherhood

Human beings possess the instinctive genetic reproduction endowment of the species—how would the species survive if the desire or instinct to mate did not exist? But as subjects of desire, permeated by language and by the weight of cultural tradition, the desire for pregnancy is a biological, psychological, and historical construction, involving both representations and affects, and not a universal instinct-based drive as such.

A certain aura of romanticism has turned motherhood into some supreme gift, a kind of exalted and idealized fulfilment and ultimate goal in life. In fantasy representation, the mother imago embodies the phallic mother, the all-powerful "hyper-mother". Even modern reproductive techniques, viewed as a set of procedures aimed at obtaining a certain product (a child)—with their multiple interventions that are more or less painful, disruptive, or unsettling—have on many occasions been wrongly equated with the means to deliver women from the great evil of not being a mother, thereby offering them the momentous gift of motherhood.

This way of thinking carries with it the weight and influence of cultural tradition, via the superego and the social imagery of affects and representations. Apparently natural from a simplistic syn-chronic perspective, a diachronic and interdisciplinary study high-lights the influence of gender mandates and the narcissistic ideals of each community. The study of motherhood necessarily becomes more complex and diversified.

This section, with the support of psychohistory, shows how many women feel rejection towards their children. Both history and the contributions of specialized research lead us to make a critical reappraisal of the existence of natural motherly love. An in-depth consideration of the hate or aversion that some mothers feel towards their children should function in clinical practice as a warning against indiscriminately advocating and encouraging motherhood in patients.

I have coined the term "the dark side of motherhood" to refer to the dark, Thanatos-related area in mothers where hate for the child reigns, together with deadly feelings of rejection and the conscious and unconscious persistent inflicting of damage. The dark side of motherhood, with its frequent and dramatic externalization, may also have been considered natural in previous centuries.

The dark side of motherhood attenuates the mythical aspects of motherly love that, with its dimension of unabated devotion, is far too excessive. Throughout history, the deadly aspect has always been embodied in the parent–child relationship. On reading the writings of Lloyd de Mause, we can see that taking care of children has not been the usual state of affairs in the history of mankind. De Mause opens the foreword to his book *History of Childhood* (1974) with the categorical statement, "The history of childhood is a night-mare", and then, chapter after chapter, describes the horrifying traditions and scenes from everyday life in which children have been murdered, used, abused, neglected, beaten, maimed. He writes:

> Parents—in particular mothers, who bear the most responsibility—both in the past and in the present, strangle, choke, suffocate and stab their children to death because at that moment they hate these children, their presence becomes unbearable, they represent a threat to their mental balance, to their innermost being". [*ibid.* p.107]

He goes on to say: "Genuine empathic love for children, in the sense of wanting to help them and educate them as an independent person, is in fact a historical acquisition of late" (*ibid.*, p. 112). De Mause's explanation of this is based on his concept of the child as "a poison container", by which he means the projection on to and into the child of the parents' negative feelings. The container is "a receptacle into which disowned parts of one's own psyche may be projected, so that these feelings may be manipulated and controlled in another without hurting oneself" (*ibid.*, p. 109). These texts and others (Badinter, 1981) force us to think again about the theoretical backdrop to psychoanalysis and to challenge the universality of the desire for a child supposedly rooted in human nature.

And even when the dark side of motherhood is not the dominant feature, it is always necessary to explore more deeply the feelings of hatred that a mother may experience towards her child—in the wish to kill her offspring during a conflict-ridden pregnancy, in the ambivalent affects that arise during every pregnancy (Lartigue, 2001, p. 113), in the transgenerational mandates that forbid love for the child and in the destructive demand to become a mother whatever the cost, with consequent subservience to superego mandates. There are notions both of impossibility and of excess in the expectation of the motherly function (Leisse de Lustgarten, 1999). In our culture, the wish to kill one's offspring may be expressed in different ways. Rascovsky (1985) has explored the death wishes of parents towards their children, and claims that this feeling plays a significant role in generating destructiveness in human beings.

Not all wombs are fantastic, as Cachard (1981) appropriately points out. In many cases, the woman presents a façade—that of a pregnant woman who is delighted with her baby—when she feels the pressures of social ideals, and suppresses her feelings of rejection and despair. In other cases, rejection is openly expressed.

Behaviour that evidences an excessive attachment to the child by the mother may also be a part of a Thanatos-related process. Such behaviour not only encourages pathological symbiosis, but also interferes with the process by which the developing child becomes an individual in his or her own right. This excessive attachment has been clearly outlined by Greenson (1968) in his description of the transsexual pathologies that stem from deficiencies in the process by which a son moves away from his primary identification with the mother figure.

On the other hand, those individual and social representations that sing the praises of the mother have at the same time a cruel and demanding downside when they consider her to be the main agent in the production of mental disorder in the child. Considered almost as the paradigm of completeness, the mother in imaginary representation is supposed capable of bringing up her children faultlessly and flawlessly; she transmits education, mental organization, and even takes on the exercise of the paternal function in cases when the actual father is absent. That kind of responsibility puts an overwhelming representational burden on the shoulders of the mother-as-signifier.

The mother's pregnancy in the construction of psychoanalytic theories about women can be explained in terms of the social and cultural context of social representations in which the maternal *locus* is simultaneously idealized, phallicized, praised, and condemned—all within the framework of unconscious hate and envy.

As Welldon states

> Mothers are expected by society to behave as if they had been provided with magic wands which not only free them from previous conflicts, but also equip them to deal with the new emergencies of motherhood with skill, precision, and dexterity. [(1988, p. 18]

Mothers are ordinary human beings born female, with their ambivalence, their bisexuality, their loves and hates, their shortcomings, and their achievements.

Mothers of the newer generation, partially freed from the demand to externalize unconditional love for the foetus, can express more fluently not only their fears concerning the actual birth process and the subsequent upbringing of their children, but also the overload and weariness they feel when faced with the intense demand to show unfailing dedication to their task. The ambivalence of their affects, the expression of the desire not to have children, can be manifested with much less resistance than in previous times.

No longer alienated by the superego obligation according to which all women should declare that they love becoming pregnant, giving birth, and raising children, some women can express their desire to renounce the reproductive function, without feeling themselves to be in bad health, selfish, and inhuman as a result. Also, they can express the absence of any desire for a child even while they are pregnant, and their annoyance at the transformations that are taking place in their body, etc.

The structuring of the mind: mother and woman

There is a significant association in some major psychoanalytic theories between femininity and motherhood. The vulva–vagina is the door through which the penis enters and also the one through which the child comes out. The vaginal canal and the birth canal share the same anatomical and imaginary space. The thinking behind this kind of theory made a very close link between woman and mother. Even though the reproductive process in women depends on major bodily changes, such as becoming pregnant, delivery, puerperium, and breastfeeding, this does not justify the exaggerated role attributed to motherhood in the organization of the mind.

According to Freud, psychic growth in girls requires the installation of the penis–child equation somewhere along the road from the pre-Oedipal stage to the Oedipus complex. The substitution of the father's wanted and envied penis by the wish for a child (Freud, 1924d, 1925j, 1931b) represents a theoretical axis that has important clinical consequences, a cornerstone or Freudian thought regarding women and femininity.

When referring to the Oedipus complex in the girl he writes (1925j)

> But now the girl's libido slips into a new position along the line— there is no other way of putting it—of the equation "penis–child". She gives up her wish for a penis and puts in place of it a wish for a child: and *with that purpose in view* she takes her father as a love-object. Her mother becomes the object of her jealousy. The girl has turned into a little woman. [Freud, 1925j, p. 256, original italics]

Later he states:

> The wish with which the girl turns to her father is no doubt originally the wish for the penis which her mother has refused her and which she now expects from the father. The feminine situation is

only established, however, if the wish for a penis is replaced by one for a baby, if, that is, a baby takes the place of a penis in accordance with an ancient symbolic equivalence [. . .]. Not until the emergence of the wish for a penis does the doll-baby become a baby from the girl's father, and thereafter the aim of the most powerful feminine wish.

Her happiness is great if later on this wish for a baby finds fulfilment in reality and quite especially so if the baby is a little boy who brings the longed-for penis with him. [. . .] In this way the ancient masculine wish for the possession of a penis is still faintly visible through the femininity now achieved. [1933b, p. 128]

Becoming a woman, being structured as such, requires, from the Freudian point of view, acquiring what we could call a *maternal psychic organization within the framework of a phallocentred theory*. As a representation in the mind, the equation penis–child lies at the very heart of the maternal figure; the mother can thus hide her covert wish for an illusory penis-phallus under her manifest love for her child.

Melanie Klein introduced the idea of an early Oedipus phase in childhood: penis, breast and vagina take on powerful fantasy value in the unconscious, while femininity and the wish for motherhood are closely bound together. She writes: "In the female position, the girl is led to internalize the paternal penis due to her sexual desire and her wish to have babies" (1945, p. 343).

As psychoanalysts in clinical practice, we must ask ourselves what takes place in the female psyche in cases where a woman does not want (overtly or not) to have children, or where her desire is merely formal, i.e., in order to conform to social expectations. What theoretical axes can be used to think about and guide our practice when faced with this particular expression of desire and with the wish *not* to become a mother?

These clinical issues are valid both for heterosexual and for homosexual women.

Non-motherhood can always be taken, *a posteriori*, to be a covert form of pathology. Psychoanalysis may construct or discover some unconscious reason that explains this lack of maternal fulfilment on the basis of conflict. This retroactive interpretation, however, is not always valid, and implies a presupposition (or biased view) according to which *health = wish for motherhood*.

The pathology or the mental health of women—the structure of their states of mind—are in many cases both quite independent of any desire for maternal fulfilment. On the other hand, motherhood may be expressed in a sublimated manner. A woman may treat another human being as her child, or she may project the child function on to her job, her friendships, her husband, or someone else's children. Social motherhood (Alizade, 1998, p. 183) is the exercise of sublimated motherhood in the arena of society and culture. The motherly function is manifested through acts of solidarity such as caring for and becoming involved with a fellow being. It is exercised both by men and women, and implies what I have come to call the establishment of narcissistic movements of transcendence, or tertiary narcissism (Alizade, 1995, Chapter Five).

The non-maternal psychic space

How can the psyche of women be thought of outside the realm of motherhood? Or, better, is there a psychic *locus* that can be represented independently from the function of procreation?

Non-maternal psychic space implies that the mind is partly independent of bodily functions, that freedom of choice is possible, that there is creativity in the way one shapes one's life, that the human subject is culturally integrated, and that the reproduction mandate of the species is no longer the only priority.

I would argue that psychic processes ought to be defused; when this filters through to clinical practice, it will substantially diminish the attribution of pathology to the fact that a woman has no particular wish to have a child. Both currents, maternal and non-maternal, participate in the formation of neurotic symptoms; it is only when the individual is in good mental health that they come together harmoniously.

I have described psychodynamic processes outside the maternal environment when proposing the idea of structural femininity (Alizade, 2002) and the resolution of the Oedipus complex in women (Alizade, 1992, 2000). Without subtracting from the importance of the phenomenon of motherhood for the psyche of women, I consider it crucial to explore the areas of the mind that are not tied up with that experience or are free of the psychic, social and biological determinants of motherhood. This implies an even more in-depth exploration of the non-maternal psychic space.

In connection with the need for attachment in women, their dependence, their need for the Other, their need to give themselves a body many times in a repetitive or compulsive fashion (Alizade, 1992 [1999, pp. 51–59]), I would suggest that there is another *psychic tendency or process* in which autonomy, self-possession, inner freedom, detachment from objects, and the need to see themselves as persons in their own right predominate. Both tendencies are deployed to a greater or lesser extent in every woman, and impact on the priority that she gives to the possibility of being a mother. In the attachment current, anything left over from the pre-Oedipal phase is expressed, the intensity of which has been extensively described in women, while the detachment axis is instrumental for the resolution of the Oedipus complex and the exercise of post-Oedipal freedom.

The predominance and resolution of this second psychic current precipitates the woman into the final stages of the Oedipus complex. These closing stages counteract the excessive dependence and the suffering of waiting mentioned by Schaeffer (2002, pp. 40–41) related to the penis, the child, the couple, and their various substitutes.

In my clinical work I have observed on occasion a patient's mind-set move from the repetitively compulsive wish for links in such a way that true transformation occurs; thanks to what I would call a new somato-psychic act, the woman is released from emotional insecurity and the excessive wish for some other person to alleviate separation anxiety. Penis envy no longer plays a leading role. A new psychic space opens up—I would hesitate to claim that this space lies "beyond the phallus" (an expression that Lacan [1972–1973, p. 69] found amusing) but, in any case, it is a territory unaffected by the vicissitudes of the penis–phallus complex. A truly feminine register is established thanks to the mental development of this area, triggering in women a movement of self-appropriation and de-alienation that dispels the ghosts of abandonment, emotional deprivation, and dependence on love. The woman finds a territory of her own, one that is not built

ST CHARLES COMMUNITY COLLEGE LIBRARY
WITHDRAWN

on the foundations of envy and the appropriation of what she, in fantasy representation, could not have; it is built on the exploration and recognition of what she does have and feels that she is. This is a movement of assertion, reflection, and self-knowledge. By partially freeing herself from envy and alienation she discovers— indeed, uncovers—new psychic potentialities that were hidden under the seemingly endless Oedipal conflict. A non-maternal space opens up, a space of her own, a space for the self, a space for solitude, a space for the woman-as-such, a space in which solitude in the company of her own self and femininity constitute a common ground.

At the level of object relations, the woman leaves to one side her urgent demand addressed to the other and focuses on a demand addressed to herself, which as a mirror image may be projected on to other women, frequently of her own generation. The inter-women space (Alizade, 1992 [1999, p. 132]) of sublimated Oedipal homosexuality thus reveals itself. It is a time of recognition, of gender assertion, of discovery of new forms of symbolization.

When this mental movement takes place, the predominance of phallic envy (penis–maternal womb, etc.) fades, and female castration loses its significance as a threat. It is not nearer or further from the penis–phallus complex; it addresses a whole new dimension. This psychic *locus* or female order (Alizade, 2002, pp. 32–33) gives relevance to the experience of deprivation, and brings the woman as a human being closer to becoming familiar with finitude. The Oedipal path ends with the learning of a "No" on the psychic flesh, a propitious "No", one that provides serenity and acceptance—a "No" that brings the subject closer to wisdom.

The woman can become more detached and experience less anxiety, she can treat herself as her own master, and to some extent she may lose what Chodorow (1999, p. viii) calls the "self in relation" that seems to dominate her personality. She then becomes capable of developing a part that is for herself alone, a self in relation to herself, a symbolic farewell to mother and father, to penis and phallus, in order to lay the foundations for mental growth on the freedom of a positive, liberating de-narcissistic process. This post-Oedipal capacity to be alone leads to the willing acceptance of being open to life experience.

A clinical vignette

In some women the maternal current dominates, in others, the detachment and autonomy aspect. Neurosis and other pathologies have mixed forms in which symptoms and defences interact. For some women, such as in the case of Mary, the wreckage of their Oedipus complex allows them to accept their particular non-desire for a child and to act accordingly, for the sake of their mental well-being and in line with their feeling of responsibility towards the Other—in this case, a potential child that they did not feel willing or able to educate and support.

The absence of any wish to become a mother is usually both a protective defence and the expression of the positive development of a psychic current.

Both aspects can be seen to be at work in Mary.

I have presented some of Mary's clinical material in a previous paper (Alizade, 1992). Here, I shall simply summarize some aspects of her history, in connection with her desire not to be a mother.

Mary was not wanted as a child; her father had tried to induce an abortion by taking her mother on a fast motorbike ride along a bumpy road; also, he had punched the mother in the stomach—but it was too late: Mary was destined to be born. She had no brothers or sisters, but often heard the retelling of stories of many abortions by her mother, abortions that had occurred both before and after Mary's birth. When she was a child, she lost her playmate, who drowned in a swimming pool almost before her eyes. In one session, she reproached herself for not having prevented that accident. She even reproached herself for being alive, while her brothers and sisters had been aborted. Her father frequently insulted her and scared her. As a teenager, she requested counselling, having made two attempts at suicide.

Her analysis, which lasted for some seven years, was successful. Mary had a very good capacity for processing and working through, and was very open to messages from her unconscious.

The idea of having children frightened her. She was afraid of having an abortion (or several abortions, just like her mother), and did not feel emotionally prepared for bringing up another human being. Nor did she feel any desire to become pregnant. In her moments of negative transference, she projected on to me the image of the terrifying father who would make her abort. At other times, I became the incarnation of a demand from the superego, forcing her to have children in order to comply with the superego social mandate. In her sessions, she expressed feelings of guilt, linked to her wish not to become a mother. This absence of any desire to have children was a self-protective measure against primitive and sinister anxieties, difficult—if not impossible—to work through. Many of her dreams alluded to dead foetuses and to violence and perversity against children, violence that she herself had suffered in her own childhood. Mary feared the transmission from generation to generation of these negative feelings, as well as the awakening of early, deadly experiences. Herself a survivor, Mary wanted so much to feel entitled simply to live.

As her analysis progressed, Mary was getting closer to the final movement of the Oedipus complex; she began to feel much happier, and in her mind she was much more autonomous.

Two years after her analysis ended, Mary married and sent me a long letter, in which she told me that she had undergone a tubal ligation procedure, so as to ensure that she would not become pregnant. She felt sure that her decision was the correct one, and she told me that she was happy in her marital life.

When this decision is evaluated in the light of her past history, the surgical operation can be seen to be in no way pathological. On the contrary, it was a healthy and protective act, which enabled her to escape from Thanatos-related catastrophic ghosts and enjoy life, freed from the actual trauma of a gestating body. Mary, by having her tubes tied, closed up in her body the traumatic core of the deaths of her siblings—this refers both to the actual abortions that her mother underwent and to the loss of her putative brothers in her political activity as a militant. She loosened her identification with the actual maternal function, and by this surgical act banished all possibility of allowing death to spring out of her own body. As a preventive measure, she neutralized her reproductive potential. She did not want to become pregnant, give birth to children and bring them up—nor did she want to abort. Through this reparative process the womb became a safe place, and its representation—now freed for all time from the threat of pregnancy and abortion—became a calming one.

Mary's mental growth allowed her to express her rejection of pregnancy and to put those feelings into action. As she developed as a person in her own right, with her own wishes and desires, she became able to express these, while taking on board her limits as well as her creative potential.

The action that Mary took is evidence of a deep-rooted desire for life, operating on her physical body an organizing psychic mark, thereby ending the perpetuation in fantasy of the sinister elements of her past history. She courageously exercised her non-desire for a child, in order to preserve her wish to live.

CHAPTER SIX

Why do you want to have a child?

Estela V. Welldon

What makes a woman, specifically a modern woman of the twenty-first century, long for a child? What are the motivations, conscious and unconscious?

In a Western romantic tradition falling madly, deeply, passionately, dangerously in love was a fact of life associated with sexual intimacy, probably leading to conception and the birth of a child. A child used to be the evidence of a man and a women falling in love and desperately wanting to have a being who represents the consummation of a dream. Falling in love was not necessarily connected with procreation, but the production of children was a question in which several generations were vitally concerned, not just the couple in love.

Ironically, as technological advances are on the increase, possibilities for sexual intimacy are decreasing and procreation no longer depends on relationships, rather on decision-making. And that decision is increasingly the responsibility of a woman alone as women become autonomous, more independent, and self-sufficient. But as we know, any decision made without consultation with others carries dangerous undertones associated with domination and control. This is especially so as the possible age for giving birth increases and is strongly associated with anxieties associated to impending menopause.

I refer in this chapter to the unmentionable; that motherhood, regardless of cultural or sociological reasons, could at times, be used unconsciously as a vehicle for perverse designs. The woman unconsciously "knows" that in becoming mother she will be in complete and total control of a new being who will be at her mercy. Unexpectedly, later on, her perception as an actual mother may be that this new baby controls and persecutes her.

Women today have to reconcile to cultural and social advances, specifically advanced reproductive technologies that could facilitate and even encourage unconscious omnipotent and narcissistic fantasies.

I shall refer to them in order to understand better the complexities attached to our communal responsibility for mothers and children; by recognizing and acknowledging not only the wonders, but also the abuses that motherhood can inflict, in a hidden way, and our complicity in not acknowledging them.

As previously stated (Welldon, 1988) why is it so difficult to conceptualize the notion of "bad" or perverse motherhood, though the evidence is that male perversion is often the result of early faulty mothering? There is an insistence in emphasizing all virtues of motherhood, to the dangerous degree of a complete denial of the possibility of negative conscious and unconscious motivations. These are sometimes present in pregnancies and later acted out in inappropriate and hostile attitudes from mothers to their babies. For example, we can describe the "dead mother" (Green, 1972), the "good" and the "bad" breast (Klein, 1946) or the stepmother in negative terms but never allow the possibility of a bad mother.

The only way society is allowed, either from within or without, to mention the existence of the bad mother is by making pathetic jokes about the mother-in-law; she is the one to be criticized, mocked, and ridiculed. A split is perpetuated and we are unable to acknowledge how the bad and the good can coexist and are integrated in the maternal function. In Kleinian terminology this translates as very primitive archaic fantasies that act as defences to interfere with societal achievement of a depressive position.

There are a few voices using psychoanalytical constructs to express some of the inner clashes women experience when facing pregnancies and motherhood. Pines (1986) has studied extensively how women can use their bodies, especially the reproductive system as vehicles for the expression of unconscious conflicts. She asserts that some women who have had fantasies of pregnancy may be disappointed, when faced with the birth of a real baby, the baby's demands representing his need to be seen as a separate object reflecting "mature object love" might result in a "calamity". The birth reawakens an awareness of mother's own unmet needs when they were babies. Motz (2001), from her extensive clinical experience of working with forensic patients, and in particular with violent mothers, goes further in explaining how difficult is for such mothers to accept any notion of separateness from their babies. She describes how the desire to have a baby corresponds to a feeling of being empty, with the baby filling up the experienced void. According to her, this emptiness may relate and mirror an earlier experience of emotional deprivation and depletion: the absence of an internalized good object. She describes extreme cases of maternal physical sexual and emotional abuse and even infanticide, where motherhood has become a perverse vehicle for power.

Sometimes women's longing for babies is contaminated or permeated by other wishes or reassurances about their fragile gender identity. We listen attentively, and our first concern is to differentiate between two possibilities: do they want to have a baby or do they want to become pregnant? Pines (1982) notes the "marked psychic distinction between the wish to become pregnant and the wish to bring a live child into the world and become a mother". The former comes very early in life. The female core gender-identity includes a pre-oedipal identification with mother but some young women have been unable to obtain this positive identification with mother and unconsciously they want assurances that the insides of their bodies are intact and able to produce beautiful babies. They fall pregnant and, quickly, either terminate their pregnancies, or decide to give the baby away from birth since the required goal of conception has been achieved. The reassurance of having the insides intact by creating a healthy baby is short-lived because, despite the fact that the reassurance has been created from within, it functions in an external way. Hence, the inner need to embark on further pregnancies returns, reflecting the power of an unconscious sense of gender inadequacy. This is a similar process to that of promiscuity in that both are doomed to failure; because they are linked to the frustrating and damaging experiences they have had with their own mothers when they were infants. Promiscuity and "compulsive pregnancy seeking" are illusory attempts to create object-relationships with a mother whom a woman feels has been unable to nurture her properly. She is now, compulsively and indiscriminately, looking in men and pregnancies for what she missed in her contact with her mother; this could be a real mother and/or a symbolic father/mother. Promiscuity and pregnancies can be seen as attempts to resolve early conflicts with mother, especially those related to frustration and anger. We have to recognize our own participation, or collusion, in this process because care for their welfare is available when pregnant, but concern is immediately withdrawn when they are no longer pregnant. Clearly, our focus of concern was the baby and not the mother, leading to further feelings of loss and emptiness.

Pregnancy and motherhood are central to any woman, and she has to follow her own choice. Chodorow (2003) importantly asserts that "For the individual woman, having children should be a choice rather than an assumed destiny". In the present day there are possibilities for choice, since following the family pattern is no longer automatically expected as it was in earlier times.

Many women are troubled by being unable to make a decision regarding having babies, when overwhelmed by their strong ambivalence. We know that there are inner biological and psychological strivings, present at all times, but which are more forceful at different stages of the woman's development. The "inner space" and the "biological clock" are different phenomena but their effects intertwine. In adolescence the inner space tends to be the more important of the two, in relation to fantasies about pregnancy, while later the biological clock becomes more dominant. These choices at times don't seem to be so apparent, and some women attend for professional help because they feel trapped, either in their professional success or because of the lack of a partner suitable for the purposes of fathering a child. Such women feel fulfilled in their professions and it is difficult to give up familiar positions that have taken a long time to achieve. They feel torn between their "non desire" to change, to remain still and independent and a wish to succumb to a desire to be transformed, to let their body be taken over, and to nest a growing being; to change blood for milk (Alizade, 2002) and to germinate.

Women, in contrast to men, have, until recently, not received public recognition as well as the domestic comforts of marriage. On the other hand, they have relied for their self-confidence on the domestic front, in which they exert and, at times, abuse their power. It is actually a vicarious sense of power with implicit frustration and sometimes bitterness that can lead to hidden violence. A man's abuse of power can be more easily or quickly detected, but a woman's may go unnoticed for a long time, directed as it is towards her children within the home.

Motherhood, in the eyes of a group of women who are disappointed and undervalued in their gender identity and feel insecure in their own femininity, is the magic answer that will resolve all doubts and will provide them with confidence about their sexuality and gender identity. They feel powerless; they have often been subjected to humiliation, physical and sexual abuse. There is low sense of self-esteem, reflected not only in frustrated interactions with others but also in their incapacity to achieve any sense of autonomy. Openly and candidly, they express a strong need to have a baby, which they see as the only way to provide a secure and affectionate bond for themselves. In their minds and expectations the baby's existence is to gratify mother, and they feel cheated, frustrated, and angry when faced with the baby's demands. The mother regresses to her own deprived childhood, identifies with the aggressive mother, and may easily attack the disappointing and depriving child (Steele, 1970).

I have written extensively elsewhere (Welldon, 1999, 2003) about some specific and drastic predicaments encountered by these severely emotionally deprived women when they become mothers. Frequently they collapse emotionally because of the previously unanticipated heavy demands. They are psychologically insufficiently equipped to deal with the considerable biological, emotional, and physical responsibilities. The envisaged paradise becomes in itself a bit of hell, as they succumb to "horrid" feelings towards their children and act them out. This can escalate even further when they are referred to a psychiatrist for the assessment of their maternal abilities. They enter real hell if the outcome is the taking away of their children. Interestingly, often unconsciously, there was some awareness of this possibility and they experience a sense of relief, since they feel the child will be protected from their own hostile impulses. Social Services become the recipients of their anger because, as opposed to their parents, they are aware and consistent in helping with the baby but they were not available to take care of their own needs as babies.

In Winnicott's (1953) terms, the "transitional object" is used by the pervert to be invented, manipulated, used and abused, ravaged and discarded, cherished and idealized, symbiotically identified with and deanimated all at once. This is exactly what I believe takes place in the perverse mother's mind and through her manipulations of her baby. In other words, the baby becomes for such a mother her "transitional object". This could become even more acute if she has managed to have a baby by reproductive techniques other than by getting pregnant through sexual intercourse, since she is the only one in power.

Many of these women do seek professional help because they have hurt their children, even to the extent of sexually abusing them. They come to us voluntarily, self-referring, precisely because of their tremendous loneliness, despair, and inability to get a hearing for their problems. They want to understand why they experience the compulsion to commit inexplicable acts that, although secret, fill them with an overwhelming and increasing shame.

Other women who have been able to achieve positions of public power come to seek professional help because of increasing uncertainty about having babies. Frequently they can voice this ambivalence but, at other times, have unconsciously sabotaged themselves by having had many abortions, infections, and subjecting themselves to contraceptive measures that have left them infertile. Technology tries to catch up with these problems and to offer choices with the far-fetched goals of the production of "factories" of babies. In our immediate culture the "creation" of motherhood could become the replacement for the adult achievement of intimacy using technical devices.

At other times, women come to therapy with a clear view of wanting babies; they seem not to have any ambivalence in their "decision", only to discover that unfortunately they have, biologically speaking, left it too late, the "too lateness" corresponding to an unconscious mechanism described by Chodorow (2003); in other words, a regretted delaying, with the possible outcome of infertility.

The social pressures relating to other achievements add to the pressure on women today to delay motherhood, colluding with a woman's ambivalence or resistance, As therapists we have to face, in these cases, the possibility of a tacit collusion, since the nature of psychotherapy is the working over lengthy periods of time that could easily be clashing against the biological clock and so interfering with a genuine desire and a healthy motivation to have a child.

A woman came for help related to her strong wish to have a child. She was an intelligent, perceptive, sensitive, warm and sensible woman of thirty-six who had spent much time and energy in her career. She had a good network of relatives and friends and access to many of their children, with whom she began to spend longer periods of time as she became aware of her sense of enjoyment being with them. She had had a long-term relationship in the past, which broke down after her male partner fell in love with somebody else, leaving her emotionally devastated and unable to pursue a new relationship. She had gone through her bereavement for this separation. To start with, in her therapy she had to work with her ambivalence projecting on to me her own reluctance at having a child as a single parent. She had assumed that I and her relatives would be strongly against it, and began a search for suitable partners who never materialized. Time was running out and she eventually decided to go for donor insemination. This was three years ago; she had a healthy baby and has been able to divide her time between her work and her maternal duties. She feels relaxed and fulfilled and continues with her therapy. Recently she met a man who may be a suitable partner, although she no longer feels a sense of urgency about it. I am aware that this may be one success in many other terrible outcomes for both mothers and children and it is not my intention to suggest that course of action for single women, but feel my duty to report it, since I had my own initial reluctance and doubts.

An added factor to be sorted out is that of women who are in their mid and late thirties who are not only anxious about becoming infertile, but are also narcissistically concerned at more visible signs of ageing and assume that a child would facilitate rejuvenation.

There are also, at times, tremendous fears of finding themselves barren, or unable to produce healthy babies, corresponding to projective fantasies of being the recipients of mother's envious attacks on their capacity for reproduction (Klein, 1957).

Women and their position in society, in general, and in family, in particular, are representative of modern society. Therefore, I shall address some of the sociological and cultural changes that have taken place during the past fifty years in the Western world, and that have seriously affected women's lives and the place of the family in the present day. Prior to the 1960s the family was central, with women in a pivotal position, automatically expected to create a family and to have children. In the post-1960s family was regarded almost as an abomination by the feminist and social radicals. For example, in the UK, Laing, in his famous *The Divided Self* (1959), viewed the family as a system of bourgeois subjugation, associating it with severe mental problems, specifically with schizophrenia. His colleague and associate, David Cooper, wrote *The Death of the Family* (1971), which was taken as a cult book by students and the media. They were hostile to the notion of family, and the media, through popular magazines, did everything to persuade their young women readers that their mothers were fools, since family equalled patriarchy, and patriarchy equalled the oppression of women down the centuries.

Feminism presented a challenge to the most archaic and effective splitting process in the world, that is between woman and man, body and mind. It was traditionally believed in Judeo-Christian doctrine that the body was woman's monopoly and the mind was man's. In the book of Genesis, Adam and Eve are assigned roles linked to morality, power, and sexuality, which have become stereotypes. Their essence is that Adam is the master, the one with the intellect, though weakened by the seductress, the sexual Eve. This is well expressed in the great Masaccio frescoes in Florence. After cleaning it was noted that the usual fig leaf was missing. According to Baldini (1990), "Masaccio's innovation is that Adam is not covering his sex, he is covering his face. His sin was not physical; it was the arrogance of his thoughts. Instead, the naked Eve conscious of her nakedness, covers her breast and pudenda, for her sin is that of the flesh whereas Adam's sinful folly is in his mind".

In the mid 1970s we were confronted with the "Superwoman", a term coined by Shirley Conran in her book of the same title, wittily used to describe her domestic ineptitudes. This label is used in connection with a woman who is not only a high achiever, but also has many children. It is never used to describe someone in low-paid employment, however hard they work. Nor is it ever used to describe a childless woman. The "super" element describes not the activity but the earning capacity; the "woman" not the gender but the reproduction.

And now let us return to some other women's predicaments that are associated with the myth of motherhood and to the "Super-woman syndrome". These are women who appear to be successful on the surface and are seen by those around as having a wonderfully fulfilled life. However, deep inside they feel unhappy, unfulfilled, frustrated, and unable to confide their despair to anyone; such is the enormous gap between their own inner reality and the fantasies the world has about them.

Some of these women have private family incomes but others are women who have achieved significant positions of power and wealth through their own efforts. Some derive from economically poor backgrounds, and they are forever frightened of ending up being subjects of the welfare state, just like their parents and grandparents were. In other words, they are self-made women with no previous experience of being familiar with wealth. They feel legitimately proud of their own achievements, but also very scared of losing it all if distracted in other directions. They are women in their early and middle thirties who "have everything", including a great degree of freedom in the choice of their relationships and the option to have children. However, this choice is sometimes undermined by the fact that work and professional accomplishments have taken much of their time and energy and have, in a way, limited their capacity for intimate relationships.

Very few of these women experience a sense of inner freedom and are sufficiently self-assertive to allow themselves to have a suitable partner who could be consistently caring and loving, but not necessarily more powerful and/or prosperous and successful. Their demand for equality clashes with the desire for a "parental", authoritative figure as a partner. Obviously, this makes it more difficult to find a suitable one.

The result is a prosperous and economically wealthy isolation which makes such women yearn for another kind of intimacy: the creation of motherhood. So, as they grow older they want children, their biological clocks are ticking very loudly, and they are not prepared to miss out on this fundamental aspect of their lives. As assessors, when such women present for professional help it is essential to make a distinction between an authentic need for children, which could be an important and enriching part of their lives, and the omnipotent and greedy need to have access to everything in life, including children. At times, the child, in their minds, becomes the manifestation of ultimate success and the replacement, or substitution, for a more complex adult intimacy with a sexual partner, and an expression of their contempt for men. For them, artificial insemination is not a last resort; increasingly it looks to them like the first and best option. Thus, child-bearing can become, literally, de-coupled from traditional sexual and—perhaps more importantly—familial, relationships.

During the course of psychotherapy with women who seriously want to consider the possibility of having children, when faced either with physical problems to do with fertility or psychological difficulties in achieving peer sexual relations, I have been surprised at the variety of outcomes, which have materialized only after much exploration and working-through of emotional needs. Some came to the conclusion they did not want to have any children. Others were strengthened in their relationships, enabling the couple to endure all kinds of different tests and intrusive medical investigations, only sustained by their clear conviction that they wanted to have babies. Still others decided on single motherhood, surrounded by accepting and supportive relations and friends after many doubts were worked through.

At times, the wider choice provided by technological advances, becomes a bitter power that brings much distress and suffering.

In a women's workshop, one of the women told us how distraught she was that, only a week previously, she had to have a termination of her six-month pregnancy. We all were shocked, having experienced, three months earlier in the previous workshop, her delight and pleasure in her pregnancy: a girl, she already had a son. She then told us, amid much pain and tears, how she had learnt from an amniocentesis test that her unborn daughter was affected with Down's syndrome. She became extremely anxious about the implied decision, which involved career prospects, employment, and special care for the child. She worried about her husband, and her three-year-old son, and how this birth would affect the family as a whole and each individual member. Finally, she made the decision for termination. As she was talking, some women were visibly affected by her pain and tears, but others were very angry, even full of rage at her "egotistical" decision.

I was quite shaken by the deep realization of the difficulties and responsibilities attached to the biological, psychological, cultural, and sociological implications that new technologies have revealed for the first time in history. The role is a very lonely one. This woman, who was so eagerly awaiting her first daughter's birth, had been shattered by knowledge provided by technological advancement. It could be said that these advances have added a new dimension of responsibility in dealing with life and death. The reversal of these hopes and dreams into sickness and death were devastating, and other women who had been witness to her early happiness were now in angry disagreement with her decision. These proved to be therapeutic, since the split in the response of other participants mirrored her own ambivalence towards her decision. They unanimously agreed that such an intense abreaction of emotions and opening up of ambivalence and mixed feelings would have been impossible in front of men. The woman in question had a kind of omnipotent fantasy that since she alone had created an abnormal child, she was the only one to have the power and authority to end this child's life.

In summary, there are added complications in our present-day society: the technological reproductive advancements that take a predominant place in controlling positions about parenthood and, as such, affecting and strongly influencing our children's future identity. Joan Raphael-Leff (2003) asserts: "the child of enigmatic self-origins may feel lost, consumed by a constant need to seek without knowing what" and "the child born out of donation, like many adopted babies, is always inserted into a place of absence— occupying a position of replacement for that which cannot be".

Advances in reproductive technology offer hope to many, but also bring previously unimagined dilemmas into sharp focus. The urge to have children continues, and it makes special demands on human ingenuity. New reproductive technologies have made it possible for individuals to create families in different ways.

Some problems, or conflicts, encountered with new fertility technology are linked to a complete time distortion; for example, recently in the UK, Bunting (2004) reported a mother giving birth to babies conceived twelve years earlier. These embryos had spent the first eleven years of their life deep-frozen. This practice could become routine, as women and men want to determine the timing of starting a family and use frozen embryos as an insurance measure against rising infertility rates. This process of embryo-freezing disconnects conception and gestation, just as surrogacy delinks the genetic and the gestational mother. There will no longer be a linear process in conception and birth; on the contrary, the pattern of procreation will be whimsically decided.

We have to adjust our understanding of "mother" to cover three distinct categories—genetic, gestational and carer. For example, women in their fifties living alone could choose to become mothers for the first time and will have the greatest influence in our society. These highly educated women will be sick of the "glass ceiling" and lack of personal flexibility in big organizations, and will set up business from their own homes and become the front-runners of the entrepreneurial economy. Medical advances mean that such a woman can delay having children until her early fifties and she will be able to decide whether to have a boy or a girl. She will be uncertain about cohabiting, since it would limit the choice of genetic stock. She can use her pregnancy as a defence against fear of death, ageing, etc., and this use of a baby may result in tremendous disappointment when she none the less ages and becomes frailer. She is responding to strong narcissistic needs in which there is no space or consideration for the baby's needs, including the chance to have grandparents, since she, herself, is in grandmother years.

If previously I was passionate about understanding the position of mothers when they were suddenly left feeling powerless and out of control, I now envisage a new problem of power and control, with a potentially dangerous dynamic. It can lead to disorientation, confusion and omnipotence to be in possession of such a degree of technological control of reproductive choices. Is giving life in such libertarian fashion corresponding to a denial of death? The ethical issues are immense. As psychotherapists we are limited to help only those women who are aware of their distress in facing these difficult areas and to liberate them from agonizing conflicts in their own identities. At other times, as "experts", we may be called upon to describe the motivations for the choices they have made, and even, in the rarer cases of child abuse, account for harm that mothers have, often unconsciously, inflicted.

CHAPTER SEVEN

The place of motherhood in primary femininity

Emilce Dio Bleichmar

The dilemma of primary femininity

T he concept of primary femininity has, from the start, been controversial, since it opposes Freud's approaches to femininity as a late avatar of the Oedipus complex (1931b, 1933a). From the conception of an inborn femininity by Jones (1922, 1935) and Melanie Klein (1932) concerning the prenatal knowledge of the difference between the sexes, until recent works stating that ". . . the concept of primary femininity entails an assumption that the girl develops some mental representation of genital femaleness at an early age" (Mayer, 1985, p. 345), all authors based their proposal on the equivalence between vaginal sexuality and femininity (Aslan, 2000). As Elise (1997, p. 493) points out, *primary* supposes identity, and it would be the vaginal feeling and the recognition of her genital organs—vulva and vagina—that stands as the rock of her primary femininity (Tyson, 1994, p. 452). In turn, the debate, both in its early years and nowadays, focuses on proving that in the pre-Oedipal period the representations of the girl's body revolve around what she is and not around what she lacks; that is, challenging the idea of femininity as castration (Mayer, 1995). But whether primary or secondary, what it is or what it is *not*, as long as *being* is concerned we are aiming at the self's identity, and beyond any doubt, it is assumed that it is the representation of the genital organs that grants such an identity.

A different line of thought—no less controversial—is the one initiated by Stoller (1968a, 1976) building on the ideas of John Money, who, through experiences with hermaphroditic children, proved that identity may have nothing to do with biology, but instead with the gender allocation made by physicians and later supported by parents and relatives. Gender—that is, femininity/masculinity—in Stoller's work refers to the fact that the ego identity, the self's feeling of being a girl or a boy, is based on the words that he/she hears, and the beliefs held by their parents on their child's body. *Gender, a grammatical concept differentiating words into masculine/feminine, was chosen by Money to highlight the power of the interpersonal dimension in the building of the differential identity between men and women.* Where, then, is the value of the body and genitalia in the structuring of differential identity? From an evolutionary perspective, in a second stage, which for the girl may coincide with the vicissitudes involved in the classical castration complex, also very challenged with regard to its universality, the representation of her genitalia do not alter an already-established identity around her femininity like her mother's. The novel factor introduced by Stoller into evolutionary development is that this early pre-Oedipal femininity period is free from conflicts involving the phallus. The observation of the gracefulness, unconcern, and easy manner of many little girls seems to prove Stoller right.

Dichotomic thought still prevails in psychoanalysis, and thus Elise points out:

> "Femininity" floats between two realms: 1) an attempt to speed a sense of self that inherently has to do with being a biological female; 2) a culturally based experience imposed on the child through early object relations and, thus, internalized in the psyche

and her proposal to leave this deadlock behind is that: "the term primary sense of femaleness [should] indicate mental representation of the female body that develops in the first years of life". She adds:

> This concept is not the same as core gender identity, as used by
> Stoller and Tyson, which involves the imposed learning of sexual
> category and gender-derived psychological traits . . . his definition
> leads to confusion, however, because most clinicians think that core
> gender equals sex equals body.

And finally she proposes: "In order to exit from this maze, we need
to separate and individuate from Freud" (Elise, 1997, p. 500).

I agree with Elise *vis-à-vis* her suggestion concerning individuation from Freud, but such suggestion does not elucidate whether
the representation of one's body is or is not central to the configuration of one's identity. Is it possible to have a subjective sense of
self without gender? When infants enter the interpersonal world
and recognize their parents and are, in turn, recognized by them,
and when this recognition begins to configure their representation
of themselves, they are not seen or considered in a neutral way. And
so, the girl becomes "little Mary, my darling girl, mummy's girl".
When the girl looks at her mummy and her daddy, she sees two
different bodies requiring her; they are in fact different human
bodies but the difference does not lie in the genitalia in sight, but in
the differentiating features that make up a feminine or a masculine
person, without the prevalence of the genital aspect.

Just as it is difficult to conceive a narcissism of the Ego where the
Ego does not presume itself as an object, how can we conceive a
plain ego for little Jack, Jack senior's son, or for little Mary, mother
Mary's daughter? Is it not time we started thinking that the Ego is
always a precipitate of identifications with a mother or a father in
which gender plays a decisive role? While it is theoretically valid to
hold that the femininity–masculinity pair has an origin and an existence before the Oedipus complex, and that self-eroticism is sexuality released from the unity of the ego before its constitution, the
statement that there is a femininity–masculinity before or after the
ego is not as legitimate, *since the ego from its origin is a gendered representation of self.* That is to say, gender is one of the attributes that
constitute the ego from its origin. *The ego as an image of oneself, the
ego-representation of Laplanche, or the ego imagery of Lacan make up the
relevant domain of the gender concept.* In its transposition to human
sciences, Money & Ehrhardt (1982) warn of the fact that grammatical gender does admit a neuter status of a wider or narrower scope
in each language, but human gender does not.

Stressing the impossibility of conceiving a neutral ego in human experience leads us to establish the role of the other, of parents, of adults surrounding the child being reared. For the parental couple, and with the advent of the new ultrasound technologies, the foetus already has a sex, and it is the shape of the external sexual organs of the foetus that triggers what John Money has defined—and which I consider the best definition of gender to date—as: "the dimorphism of answers in view of the external sexual characters as one of the most universal aspects of the social bond" (Money & Ehrhardt, 1982, p. 30).

Money points out that the gender scheme coded in the brain after birth is as powerful as the scheme coded by means of the foetal hormones in the prenatal period, and that it may become as immutable as in the case of a mother tongue.

> Speaking of development, identification and complementation in gender coding are like listening and speaking to language acquisition. For instance, children who are raised bilingual can improve the internalization of both languages if the people around them do not speak only one of the languages, although the child does listen to them in only one language. In order to receive attention, be listened to, and secure an answer, the child has no choice but to speak the language of the person listening to them and not mix it with the second language. *The identification mechanism is as important as complementation for identity* [Money, 1981, p. 71, my italics]

Money brings up the example of a family that had to reassign the boy's sex as female when the child was seventeen months old. The father retells the following story:

> "during the week, when I get back home, all of us go upstairs, play a record and dance. For a while she looked at her brother and imitated him, but I took her in my arms and we danced. Now she wants to do so the whole time ..." Tradition requires the girl to dance with her father, who complemented a role in which she identified with her mother. The mother dancing with her son complemented his role, in which he identified with his father. [Money, 1988, p. 72]

Before the human being is born, there is a process of gender assignment through the fantasies and expectations of femininity–

masculinity, when parents imagine their baby as the son who will lead the family business or the woman who will accompany them in their old age (these fantasies are not related to the child's sexuality, but clearly to their gender). Later, this process will be constantly intersubjective; the adult's conforming look is supplemented with the child's wish for identification with the double of his/her own gender, and the differentiation and complementation with the different other.

Ontogenesis of femininity–masculinity: the mother and father representations

When discriminating between the human world and the inanimate world, a central role is played by the fact that the sequences in which people interact are fragmentary: each person supplies part of the total behaviour—the child reaches up and the adult wraps him/her in an embrace—while the instrumental behaviour with objects always implies performing a complete sequence. This "completeness" feature in the experiences with objects and the "incompleteness" feature in the case of personal interactions foster the development of two different kinds of symbolization processes, one based in action schemes and the other in interaction patterns (Wolf & Gardner, 1981).

The organization of the first symbols keeps the trace of its roots in the action and interaction patterns. There is a trend to define such organization in terms of role structuring; that is, the capacity to understand, represent, and signify the functions of people and objects in action and interaction sequences (Riviere, 1991). It is when the child can separate the activity from the person performing it that the symbolic game begins, the capacity to act "as if" they were the mother or the father. The roles of people and the functions of objects provide the building blocks for symbolic processing.

Thus, we must conclude that the first differential representations generated by infants in terms of sex/gender are those of mummy and daddy, representations that include the parents' bodies but in terms of the activities and attitudes that generate a dimorphic response in the child, as illustrated in the activity of the girl dancing with her father.

The value of intersubjectivity in the understanding of gender or primary femininity

The current conceptual models provide us with tools that may help overcome the deadlock and the confusion. Intersubjectivity plays a key role in Lacan's proposals concerning the desire and the imagery of the Ego (1966), Kohut's statements regarding the structure of Self (1971), Laplanche's formulation of the value of enigmatic messages in the implantation of sexuality (1987), in pathologies such as phobias (Dio Bleichmar, 1991c), and in the intergenerational transmission of attachment patterns (Fonagy, 1999). In connection with gender, we have proposed a multimodal intersubjective model (Dio Bleichmar, 1991a, 1995, 1997) within which the psychoanalytical concept of projective identification plays a fundamental role. In her clinical practice, Klein witnessed—although she held it theoretically as an intrapsychic process—the powerful structuring effects on early relationships produced by the projection on to the other. Hence, the addition of identification to the projection concept: it is not a mere projection by the subject, but also the identification with the object, and the subsequent performance in the real world based on what is projected. The concept helps to illustrate the process by which adults, to a greater or lesser degree, configure children's identity.

In the asymmetrical structure of the adult–child relationship, parents constantly enact their fantasies around femininity–masculinity, as precipitated from the history and experience of both, which will work as the pattern based on which the young human being will structure his/her gender identification and complementation. The projective identification process does not deploy in the adult with the motivation stated by Melanie Klein in her writings (to hurt, control, or possess the other), but to shape their children in their own image, or as complements, or as opposites (many parents consciously enact ways of relating that are the complete opposite of those they experienced in their own childhood).

The adult identifies in the newborn's sexed body his/her own unconscious fantasies about femininity–masculinity of his/her own history, such as fears of helplessness or of being doomed to dependence, multiple stereotypes that are constantly seen in the history of men and women.

Within the framework of the intersubjective paradigm, a *sex/ gender system is* implemented in order to understand human development, since what triggers the fantasy is the sex of the body. Still, that body is never only anatomic, but stems from the subjectivity of an adult who will endow it with the gender attributes of its specific group or culture from its conception. *The fantasy of gender is a mandatory component of the fantasy of a child* that the parents have. It will unfold and impress on the newborn's body and will be present in the relationship for life.

The gender fantasy is part of the preconscious–unconscious mind's contents enacted by means of the specific actions of a more or less dichotomic nature scattered in any child's childhood. A three-year-old boy falls and hurts his knee. He is received by his mother and grandmother who, celebrating his fall, say to him: "Boys always have their knees full of scars because they walk a lot in the streets and they climb everywhere!" And, thus, a meaning of masculinity is implanted on him and is recorded as a differential opposition to what is not proper for a girl. Femininity–masculinity is built on intersubjectivity and interaction. There is no fantasy without a gesture, or a gesture that is not generated in representation. Femininity–masculinity are representations in the minds of adults, conscious and preconscious meanings like those of the boy's mother and grandmother, and unconscious contents—fantasies of femininity–masculinity—secluded in harder-to-reach layers. But unconscious fantasies are also passed on from generation to generation through discourse or action.

Primary femininity as an ideal ego—the ego ideal

The mother in the core of femininity

In the girl's evolutionary development, a privileged situation takes place in the constitution of a feminine ego from the beginning of intersubjective recognition since the attachment figure is her peer. The attributions of femininity that parents may confer on that sexed body gives rise to the attachment—a very powerful attachment indeed—of the valuation and idealization by the girl of her equal, who adopts such a key position, affectively and instrumentally, during her life. The identification with her mother and the constitution of an ideal Ego–Ego Ideal in her own image is guaranteed by the structure of the relationship itself. I believe that this dimension is not highlighted enough in the proposals concerning primary femininity.

Personally, we think that *the girl's primary femininity is structured around the maternal function*, the wish to take care, to deploy role behaviours whose narcissistic and attachment cathexis focuses on the rehearsal and the anticipation of maternal activities. In turn, the latter generate the specific development of cognitive–affective attributes that have a feedback on the wishes and extend them, since the efficacy of achievement strengthens motivation. A *femininity, the core of which is not genital anatomy or genital arousal, but an early staging of motherhood through the complex parents' sex/gender network*. This organization of subjectivity sets a first meaning of the human distinction between equal and different, between the ego and the *alter*, grounded on what looks different to the girl regarding the parental aspect. A set of attributes characterizes the mother as different from the father: behaviour, aspect, clothing, sensory qualities, and among them the secondary sexual characters, but not the genital characters or their functions. This perspective has some forerunners in psychoanalytic literature; Kestenberg (1956) emphasizes that an early maternal stage precedes the phallic–oedipal phase, while Bergman (1987) and Silverman (1987) are authors who include motherhood as part of the girl's early femininity.

Dolls and dolls' houses remain the girls' favourite game, and the division of work and activities by gender is set early in childhood by means of the playthings offered to children. It is after the gender studies that reflection set off *vis-à-vis* the cognitive and affective effects of such an early dichotomic orientation of human activity. When the girl plays with her dolls, she enacts—with swapped roles—her relationship with her mother and the adults taking care of her, a care which is branded maternal. In its playful structure it is a role-play, and the girl, systematically and universally, takes the place and the value of a mother.

In this ludic format, the girl actively enacts a preliminary of the purest form of femininity and reproduces, step by step, the main activity of most women: the vital cycle. The girl will have children as her mother has, and will take upon herself the maintenance of life through the playful rehearsal of taking care of family members. The human species' preservation instinct is reduced to a minimum;

a newborn could not survive if left to his/her own devices. What in animal life is ensured by "specific action", in the human being is an adult's function, and in the history of humankind a mother's responsibility; it is *heteropreservation* (Bleichmar, 1997).

Freud considered that the wish for a child from the father completed the organization of female sexuality, very far from the notion of a child as a desire for attachment, intimacy, and responsibility for life and well-being. The status of the child in female subjectivity, if we follow the path set by young girls' games and fantasies, seems to be the paradigmatic expression of the first meaning of femininity for the girl, and a strong core of her early identity established through identification with the gender double. It is a two- or three-way process, if you will, since the processes of implantation of femininity initiated by the parents introducing similarity and complementarity are added to the girl's identification motion.

Thus, motherhood becomes one of the early cores of the female Ego Ideal, and one of the contents and objectives of her narcissistic system, providing self-esteem and efficacy to her representation of her being as female. Additionally, motherhood feeds one of the motivations that, due to its intensity, differentiates genders: the desire for attachment, for intimacy, for affectivity that leads women to degrees of love dependency that cannot be justified (Dio Bleichmar, 1991b, 1997). Freud pointed out this difference when he highlighted that the fear of losing the object was a regular feature in female subjectivity.

What remained invisible: gender demands of the female superego towards taking care of life

Freud held that the feelings of jealousy and envy tended to be more powerful in the subjectivity of women, and Melanie Klein stressed the intensity of the persecution anxiety of girls and women inside their bodies as a consequence of the attacks on the maternal body. But how have these apparent feelings of a hostile nature been explained? Both Freud and Melanie Klein underscored the instinct, affective component: more intensity and degree of hate between daughter and mother or between mother and daughter, an effect of the penis envy. What remained invisible are the consequences of the maternal role; the fact that the mother stands as a guarantor of early heteropreservation may generate feelings of responsibility, persecution, and guilt *a propos* the possibility of not measuring up to that mandate. We should ask ourselves if between man and woman the difference is such in economic terms—an intensity of charge—or in structural terms. The sanction for a transgression or the mere self-recognition of the hostile impulse in women takes place owing to a double coding system: related to morality and to gender. Just as there are moral codes with different degrees of severity and punishment, there are different degrees of severity and punishment for hostility in intimate relationships for men and women. Female violence is not tolerated, is not legitimated, and generates in the female aggressor profound feelings of guilt, whether conscious or unconscious.

If the Freudian superego refers to sexual rules, the female superego sets rules on taking care of life and well-being in the love relationship. If a woman deserts her children, she is branded as "denaturalized", since she is flaunting a mandate that is considered so by nature: "Thou shall be a mother or thou shall be nobody", could be the female gender mandate (Levinton, 2000). Very few works in psychoanalytic literature circle around the female superego (Jacobson, 1976; Bernstein, 1983; Paschero, 2000), which is contradictory to the many theoretical proposals describing features in the realization of motherhood in which mothers may run the risk of being lethal or pathogenic—a phallic mother, a schizophrenogenic mother, a "freezer"-mother, an intrusive mother, an invasive mother, a seductive mother. Faced with each of these categories, what position is taken by the woman running the risk of falling within them? We could say that while not much work has been done on the role played by motherhood in women's feelings of guilt, in literature categories placing the guilt on mothers abound (Dio Bleichmar, 1995).

Motherhood in the content, strength and structure of the female superego

In her brilliant work, Bernstein (1983) distinguishes three aspects when studying the superego instance: content, strength, and structure. Regarding content, ideals and prohibitions, the universality of the incest taboo is a pivotal issue in psychoanalytic theory, its universality involving both sexes, but in connection with taking care of and deserting children, the universality and the strength of women's superego leaves no place for doubt. Bernstein states that strength refers to the efficiency with which content is regulated. Structure is related to the organization or articulation of content. Maybe it was around structure that Freud believed he saw a weakness in the female superego, and that in fact it is the inherent conflictive nature of the female identity, the ancestral difficulty to reconcile, develop, and manage to work in a balanced way her different motivation systems. As Eliacheff and Heinich (2002) point out, much of a mother and little of a woman, much of a woman and little of a mother, much of an executive and little of a woman, much of a mother and no professional life. Conflict, renouncement, and guilt are ever-present contents in female subjectivity. ". . . Women are more likely to experience conflict in choosing which of the contents will be given dominance, and they are far more likely to experience guilt (no matter what their choice)" (Bernstein, 1983, p. 189).

CHAPTER EIGHT

Reconstructing Oedipus? Considerations of the psychosexual development of boys of lesbian parents*

Toni Vaughn Heineman

T his article examines the ways in which a psychoanalytic perspective may illuminate the behavior and underlying developmental dynamics of children of gay and lesbian parents. Families headed by gay and lesbian parents demand reconsideration of a theory of oedipal development based on heterosexual parents. If we understand that triangulation—the move from dyadic to triadic object relationships—depends on two primary processes-the child's acceptance of the immutability of generations and the child's recognition that children are excluded from the world of adult sexuality–parental gender or sexual orientation assumes less importance. The emergence of conscience from a multi-faceted process of identification with both parents is consistent with this view of triangulation as a developmental phase. If we expect to offer help to the children of gay and lesbian parents we must create a theory of healthy development that includes them.

*An earlier version of the article was first published in 2004, in *Psychoanalytic Psychology*, 21: 99–115. Copyright © 2004 by the Educational Publishing Foundation. Adapted with permission.

Introduction

While this paper has had many beginnings over the last few years, its original impetus grew from a family visit to welcome the newborn son of our friends Nancy and Susan. As we drove away, our then ten-year-old son mused from the back seat, "I wonder what they'll want him to be—whether they'll want him to be like them and be with a man, or be like them and be with a woman?"

This question astounded and sobered his parents in the front seat. We had grown up in a world of closeted homosexuality and, until well into adulthood, had had little reason, either personally or professionally, to consider a universe that did not assume the heterosexuality of parents. Not only would we not have been able to ask the question as succinctly—at his age, we wouldn't even have thought to ask such a question.

My incentive for pursuing this inquiry stems, in large part, from my recognition that I did not even begin to have an answer to my son's very intriguing and legitimate question. Often I have thought I've begun to find a way into questions about how a male child parented by two women might experience himself as a sexual being in relation to his parents and the world. More often than not, I have found myself lost in the confusions and contradictions offered by my own musings and the theoretical constructions and deconstructions offered by professional writings and conversations with colleagues.

Triangulation

In an effort to step outside the heterocentric assumptions and theories that have shaped and continue to influence our ideas about children and families, I have posited a model that recognizes the essential elements of this pivotal developmental stage without reference to the parents' sexual orientation or sexual object choice. However, this does not exclude sexuality; it simply demands that children recognize and accept their parents as living in the world of adult sexuality. This world, from which the child is excluded, can and does include men whose sexual partners are women and those whose partners are men. It includes women whose romantic eyes are for men and those who long for and seek romance with other women. It is a model that recognizes that our inherent bisexuality is expressed in different ways by parents and their children.

From dyadic to triadic relationships

In examining the ways in which a psychoanalytic perspective may illuminate the behaviour and underlying developmental dynamics of children of gay and lesbian parents, I am limiting my focus to a theoretical consideration of the movement from dyadic to triadic relationships in boys of lesbian parents. When we move away from a heterosexual family configuration we encounter multiple possible variations, including, but not limited to, boys being raised by women and boys parented by men; lesbian women or gay men parenting sons and/or daughters. I hope that by limiting my inquiry I might provide more clarity than if I were simultaneously to consider multiple variations in family structure.

Triangulation is the pivotal developmental phase of psychoanalytic theory; we tend to mark developmental time and conflicts as "pre" and "post" oedipal (Schafer, 1995, p.198). Although we have learned that the complexities of human sexuality have their beginnings in the earliest months of life, we also recognize that it is the pre-school child's shifting orientation towards triadic relationships that marks his awareness of his sexual self in relation to his parents and their sexuality. Therefore, without discounting the influence of parental gender (Chodorow, 1978) on early development or the adolescent re-workings and expanded integration of sexuality into self and object representations, parental sexual orientation and object choice would seem to have a heightened saliency during the child's initial conscious awareness and integration of his parents' sexual relationship.

The richness in our understanding of human development arises from the confluence of actual and imagined parents in the child's interpersonal interactions and internal relational world. However, psychoanalytic writings sometimes contain confusing, interchangeable references to the actual parents of the child's day-to-day life, the child's internal, individual, and idiosyncratic parental constructions, and the more abstract, universal, mythological parental representations. This tendency to merge references can create difficulties when reading with an eye to applying these theories to non-traditional families.

For example, does it matter (and if so, in what way(s)) if the parent who returns home from the end of the working day is a woman greeting another woman? Is this reality so different from the abstract, collectively held notions of family consisting of a mother, father, and children that the theories based on those ideas do not apply? If the child's day-to-day reality differs in this basic way, will he feel himself excluded from, rather than embraced by and included in, the myths and fairy tales that contain and convey these representations of heterosexual triads and shared developmental conflicts? Alternatively, are the universal elements of developmental growth and change captured in and extrapolated by myth, shared fantasy, and articulated theory of triangulation so powerful that they will, to a greater or lesser extent, represent and shape a growing child's ideas about, and experiences of, his sexual self in his family and the world, regardless of the configuration of his actual family or the sexual orientation of his parents?

Consider this mother's description, posted in an internet chat room for lesbian mums, of the play of her five- and six-year-old children:

> So I don't think their play reflects their own family all the time, just social experience. You know, they don't make doll houses with two moms, or two moms and one dad. (Although we've been tempted to remove the "father figure" and replace him with another woman, although sometimes they take the farmer from the farm set and make a family with two dad's [sic].) The only time it gets confusing is when they play "Mom and Mom", which also happens. Then when one of them says "Mom" three people answer, then they'll say "Not you! I meant [pretend mom]."

While the description of the play is somewhat confusing, it seems to suggest that these children's play is not bound by the facts of their family, but allows for imaginative exploration of families that include fathers.

I would suggest that this reflects not just the social influences of a heterosexual world on children of homosexual parents, but the unconscious recognition of the developmental importance of a different third, usually represented by the father in the stories and theories that describe, rather than determine, the powerful tension between the dyadic and triadic paradigms of human relationships. Couples—whether experienced in the engrossment of the parent–infant pair, the adoration of young love, the mutual work and joys of parenting partners, or the intimate bond grown from years of shared memories—provide us with a sense of belonging, and exclusivity. Triadic relationships demand an opening up of the dyad to make psychic space for a third, and for the creation of new and special dyadic interchanges. The internal, potential space of triadic relationships can be maintained only when each point exerts sufficient tension to avoid the actual or virtual collapse into a twosome that either physically or psychologically excludes the third. For example, when a couple decides to bring a child into their relationship, the creation of a triad offers the possibility that their relationship will be enriched by the exclusive dyadic relationship each of them develops with the child as well as their shared experience of parenting. However, if the child, for whatever reason, absorbs too little or too much psychic energy in relation to the parental couple, the emotional currents of the family will be dyadic, each pair operating in parallel to the others.

The psychological paradox of triangulation is that triadic relationships simultaneously exclude and include a third in relation to a twosome. I would understand the story of triangulation as a powerful theme in the conscious and unconscious lives of children whose world is filled with parenting couples and their children. This is a theme with numerous variations arising from individual differences in experiences of self and family. Although the children of gay and lesbian parents may respond to the possibilities of triadic relationships in different ways, these may chiefly represent new variations on the very old theme of the psychological negotiations demanded by developmental changes in parent–child relationships.

The parental complex

In "A special type of choice of object made by men: contributions to the psychology of love" (1910), Freud introduced the term

"Oedipus complex", which, at that time he used synonymously with "parental complex". We cannot completely set aside all of the meanings, associations, and feelings that the term "Oedipus complex" has taken on in our individual and collective minds over the past ninety years. Therefore, I am going to adopt this earlier, less meaning-laden term, "parental complex", to denote the child's complicated and conflicting sexual desires and rivalrous feelings in relation to the parental couple.

The little boy's shift from his narcissistic, possessive attachment to his mother[1] to a recognition of her as an object of his sexual desire is paralleled by his recognition of the parental couple. He comes to see these two lovely and adored creatures not merely as two parents in relation to him, but as partners in relation to each other. As the egocentrism of his world-view lessens, he can begin to entertain the notion that they have a special relationship with each other that excludes him. Prior to this, the child lived at the centre of the universe; to his mind, the vectors of emotional exchange in all relationships included him. Now he must come to know that there are exclusive exchanges of loving and knowing communication that move between those he loves. His parents inhabit the world of adult, genital sexuality—a world that is closed to him because of his physical, sexual, and emotional immaturity. As a child, he is neither a desirable nor adequate sexual partner. Along with this blow to his self-esteem, he must also come to terms with the immutability of generations—he will always be a child in relation to his parents.

The parental complex makes rather extraordinary emotional and cognitive demands on a little fellow, which in turn promote his psychological and intellectual growth. Cognitively he moves from the world of concrete operations to the "preoperational stage" in which he can begin to use symbols and increasingly representational mental processes (Phillips, 1981). This growing capacity to *think* frees the child from the world of action and the actual. He can begin to consider his own thoughts, as thoughts, and to recognize that his ideas and views may differ from the thoughts and motivations of others (Fonagy & Target, 1996). This period ushers in the child's capacity for reflection—about the world around him and the world inside him. He becomes increasingly sensitive to the differences among the internal worlds of those he loves, and the world of intimate relationships that exclude him.

Traditional psychoanalytic theory offers the suggestion that the parental complex is resolved through the boy's identification with the person he perceives as his rival for his mother's sexual attention. The identification comes not only from his love for this parent, but out of a fear of the parent's castrating retaliation for the little boy's aggressive wish to displace his mother's lover and assume the role of her exclusive sexual partner. More recent theory enables us to understand that the identificatory processes that allow the little boy to bury his incestuous wishes in the world of infantile repression are complex and involve incestuous wishes towards both parents as well as identifications with aspects of both parents.

The distressing aspects of this newly acquired knowledge can lead to temporary regressions as he attempts to manage and integrate these difficult and competing feelings. However, developmentally, there really is no turning back; even though it can provide some temporary relief, regression to an earlier world-view can never completely erase what he has come to know about his parents and his place in their world. And, while problematic, his discoveries also offer the excitement of genital sexuality and the possibility of relationships in the world beyond the family. A child's successful move from the infantile grandiosity of dyads into the world of triadic relationships, acceptance of an external reality that cannot be manipulated or governed by magical thinking, and the internalization of a relatively reliable, relatively benign conscience, constitutes an extremely tumultuous journey. It is not surprising that children in the throes of this developmental phase often show transient symptoms in response to their heightened distress and efforts at mastery.

Until now we have understood many of the developmental conflicts of this period as stemming from the little boy's attempts to come to terms with his parents' heterosexual love for each other. However, the characteristic emotional dynamics may not be confined to children and parents in traditional families. When one lesbian mother talked about her of feeling of awkwardness in response to her young son's asking her to "rough me up", I was reminded of my feelings of envy at the rough and tumble play that came so naturally to my sons and their father. In a pinch, they would turn to me as a substitute, but it never seemed to work quite as well. In contrast, a lesbian mother described her responses to her four-year-old son's demands for more exuberant physical contact. She reported silently wondering, "What do we think we're doing . . . two women trying to raise a boy?" as she arranged to have regular "wrestling matches" with him. However, she found bringing some the pleasures of the athletic activities of her childhood and adolescence into their relationship deeply satisfying.

Triadic collapse

Answering the question of "Who is Mother?" often arouses anxiety and discord in the parenting couple as they struggle to come to terms with their conscious and unconscious ideas of motherhood and to situate their family in a heterosexual world. (Benkov, 1998; Crespi, 2001; Mitchell, 1996). Developmentally, the question has particular saliency for a little boy with two female parents as he moves towards recognition and acceptance of a "third" who captures his mother's sexual attention.

In lesbian families where the child's primary parent is clearly designated, the psychological stage is set for the child to use the remaining parent as the necessary "other" who can occupy the third point on the triangle when he moves towards mastery of the parental complex. In particular, the parents' definition of themselves as either "two mothers" or a "mother" and an "other" may influence the manner in which their children negotiate the transition from dyadic to triadic relationships. Women who have not sufficiently resolved their own conflicts over the loss of a dyadic relationship will have understandable difficulties in helping their child(ren) manage the feelings and negotiate the conflicts inherent in triadic relationships.

These difficulties are often painfully enacted during the dissolution of a family headed by a lesbian couple if one or both parents cannot operate in the matrix of triadic relationships. We know that children of gay and lesbian parents can suffer even more egregiously than children of heterosexual parents because in many instances they do not have equal protection under the laws that govern families. Unless both parents are legally recognized as biological or adoptive parents, one parent can, quite effectively, simply remove the other from the child's life.

Whether in or out of the courts, the efforts of one parent to eradicate the parental status of her lesbian partner assert that there can be one and only one mother and that the mother–child relationship must be protected and preserved above all else. A belief that this is the only relationship that sustains the child often lurks beneath all of the appropriate rhetoric about the importance of supporting the child's healthy development, including the promotion of the child's relationships with another parent. The parent who believes herself to be the true parent, i.e., the mother, often offers tacit support for the child's relationship with the other parent. However, her conviction that this child has one and only one parent typically shows itself not in her words, but in the obstacles she places between the child and the "other"—the disavowed parent.

Particularly if the "other" mother has been the more nurturing of the two parents, her parental status may be completely disavowed by the self-assigned mother. The "other" may be described as merely the "nanny" or "babysitter" who served at the mother's behest. The child's attachment for her might be acknowledged as important, but transient, in the same way that the child's affection for an important caregiver or teacher might simultaneously be granted and minimized. Alternatively, the child's attachment is sometimes described as more apparent than real—actually out of compliance with the other's needy demands for the child's affectionate attention. Not surprisingly, this description often reveals the self-assigned mother's projection of her own desperation and hopelessness in regard to commanding her child's freely loving attention. In the first instance, the disavowed mother is portrayed as someone who is not a "real" parent; instead she is seen as the intolerable other who threatens the dyadic relationship of the mother–child pair. In the second instance the child's relationship with the other is characterized as pathological—a dangerous liaison that demands destruction.

In cases where the self-assigned mother sees herself as being the more nurturing of the two parents, the disavowed parent is often portrayed as distant, disinterested, and emotionally unavailable to the child. While the actual parental status may not be overtly denied, the disavowed parent is frequently characterized as an intruder into the mother–child relationship. The child may concur in the description of the disavowed parent's interference in the special bond, asserting that spending time with her merely takes precious time away from his time with his self-assigned mother. In these families the implicit or explicit references to a stereotypical heterosexual family configuration is striking. If any importance whatsoever is granted to the "other" by the mother, it is usually in the disavowed parent's role as an (overly strict) disciplinarian and/or as a person who might offer connections to the world of athletics or stereotypically male activities. In these instances, the continual message is that the disavowed parent is not only not a "real" parent because she lacks the special, intuitive, maternal connection to the child, but a dangerous intruder into that relationship. In families such as these, the notion of two parents collapses into the primacy of the mother–child relationship in which there can be one and only one mother.

If we now return to a consideration of the essential elements of the parental complex, it is clear that a self-assigned mother is, for whatever reason, imprisoned in the world of dyadic relationships and threatens to hold her child hostage to her psychopathology. She insists that she alone can know and accurately reflect her child's mind. Her child is the apple of her eye[2] and, while she may overtly support his developing relationships with another parent, friends, and other adults, the insidious, unconscious message is that he must have eyes only for her.

This is not meant to suggest that this problem characterizes or is particular to lesbian parents. It is meant to underscore the importance of giving children in these situations a chance to establish and maintain triadic relationships. The ongoing interaction with an actual "third" guards against the child's collapse into the mother's unconscious dyadic world. It is essential that children of gay and lesbian parents, along with the children of heterosexual parents whose relationships dissolve, have a chance for access to two (or more) parents. Mental health professionals are in a pivotal position to educate the community—particularly those in the judicial system—about the developmental importance of the third in helping the child to move into the matrix of triadic relationships that provides the foundation for multiple and complex relationships with peers and other adults.

Conclusion

This brings me back to the question that prompted this excursion into the triadic world of a boy with two female parents. What will they want for him? "Will they want him to be like them and be with a man, or be like them and be with a woman?" The question captures both the multiplicities of identificatory possibilities and the idea that sexuality can be as much about similarity as difference (Chodorow, 1994; Dimen, 1995). It assumes, I believe correctly, that parents want their children to identify with them and, by implication, that children, regardless of their parents' sexual orientation or expression, will want to find points of similarity while establishing an independent identity.

However, this returns us to comparative thinking. Heterosexual parents not only assume but desire their children's heterosexual identification with them. The agonies of homosexual children's "coming out" to their heterosexual parents attests to the intensity of feeling when the expectation of sameness is not met. In contrast, gay parents frequently expect, and sometimes wish, that their children will be straight (Drucker, 1998; Gottman, 1989; Mitchell, 1996). Costello (1997) disputes the contention that there are no differences between children of heterosexual and homosexual parents. "There is copious evidence that the children of gay parents are distinguished from their straight counterparts because they do not tend to adopt the same sexual identity as their parents" (p. 68). Although most children of homosexual parents identify themselves as heterosexual, it is not surprising that they report more homosexual experimentation than the children of heterosexual parents (Tasker & Golombok, 1997). Lesbian parents may offer their children a range of identificatory possibilities, at least in the area of sexual object choice—perhaps wishing for their children to be different from them, while being open to their being like them in this regard.

Perhaps when we can put aside the heterocentric need to keep proving that the children of gay and lesbian parents are no different from, i.e., just as healthy as, children of heterosexual parents, we may find some interesting and important distinctions that will greatly enhance our understanding of the psychosexual development of all children. We need to pay careful attention to the effects on the child of the lack of an adult male figure in competition for his mother's affections and to consequences of the having two female parents as the primary figures for identification. If we encounter sons of lesbian parents whose aggression is particularly heightened or diminished, we must take care not to conclude too quickly that this stems from his parents' lesbianism, and equal care to consider fully the effects of having two female parents. Freud based his theories of oedipal development on the assumption of generic, good-enough parents. We must start from the same position when considering the development of children of gay and lesbian parents, by assuming that they are capable of triadic relationships and able to embrace both similarity and difference. From this vantage point we will be in a better position to understand both healthy and troubled development in these families.

We may find that children of gay and lesbian parents need to develop different psychological strategies, both conscious and unconscious, to come to terms with the demands of the parental complex. By attending to children's reports of family romance fantasies, observing their play, listening to their stories, and the stories adults provide for them, we will learn something about how they understand and internalize the representations of self and family. When we no longer need to demonstrate the overriding mental health of children of gay and lesbian parents, then we can accord them equal rights to the conflicts, inevitable disappointments, hurts, triumphs, and struggles of human development. We know that development is not an easy or painless process; if the children of homosexual parents have struggles that are different—whether a little or a lot—from what we are used to, we need to know about them. We must adopt a truly analytically affirmative stance, from which we allow ourselves to observe and attempt to understand what these children have to show and tell us about how best to help them master the developmental tasks of childhood and adolescence.

Notes

1. Mother is used to refer to one or more actual mothers along with the child's internal representation of mother.
2. When writing this I mistakenly, but accurately, typed: "Her child is the apple of her I".

CHAPTER NINE

Maternity and femininity: sharing and splitting in the mother–daughter relationship

Florence Guignard

Introduction

C onceptualizing the specific features of the mother–daughter relationship from a psychoanalytic point of view means that we have to refer constantly to what we can learn from our clinical work and to distinguish at all times between manifest and latent, visible and invisible, phallic and genital, maternal and feminine; this is the only way to confirm or to invalidate the metapsychological hypotheses that are still being worked out.

On the biological side, the role of gender identity in instinctual drive organization (Guignard, 1997a) should be noted; on the social side, the part played by the prevalent group mentality (Bion, 1961) and its characteristic features in the complex problem-set that accompanies parental cathexis of an infant boy as a distinct from an infant girl must also be taken into account.

Unlike boys, girls have to change their love object if their Oedipal development is to proceed. The upheaval generated by the discovery of her love for the father puts a daughter in a situation of dangerous rivalry with respect to the original love object, her mother.

The mother is the first identificatory object for both daughters and sons—the boy will have to change his identificatory object, but for the girl, the mother is also the reference marker for her sense of identity through all the stages of her development and throughout her life as woman and mother.

That pattern constitutes, at one and the same time, the strength and the fragility of feminine development and impacts on the relationship that a woman establishes both with men and with other women.

Of all intimate relationships, that between mother and child (boy or girl) is the one that is most firmly and permanently rooted in the physical or bodily domain. Given the prohibition against incest, it is also that relationship which, as far as the mother is concerned, comprises the highest level of requirement as to renunciation and sublimation.

From a psychoanalytic perspective, any discussion of the sexual dimension in the mother–child relationship always carries with it the risk of "splitting" the theme being debated: for the adult woman-and-mother, the Other's body is always twofold—on the one hand, that of the man/lover and, on the other, that of the foetus-then-baby-then-child-then-adult.

That is why any psychoanalytic discussion of women's psychosexuality is fraught with difficulties: how are we to understand and describe the manner in which a woman apportions her drive-related cathexes between the feminine, maternal, and autoerotic spheres?

The infant daughter and her mother

The mental space of the "primary maternal sphere"

For the infant daughter, the original mental space is what I refer to as the "primary maternal sphere" (Bégoin-Guignard, 1987; Guignard, 1995). This is where the binding of the instincts referred to by Freud (1950a) takes place, as well as the development of the ego's initial relationship and identity organization (Guignard, 1997b) in accordance with the mother's capacity for reverie (Bion, 1962). This space is established in terms of the Oedipal pattern of a mother-of-a-daughter, which is quite different from that of a mother-of-a-son. In addition, the internal group mentality of this mother-of-a-daughter is very different, as is her representation of her relationship with the *socius*.

The mental space of the "primary feminine sphere"

The specific nature of the mother–daughter relationship becomes even more prominent when, in the wake of the primary maternal dimension, comes what I call the "space of the primary feminine sphere", a part of mental space that is organized in terms of the primary triangulation of object relations and identifications. This mental space includes the primary feminine phase common to children of both sexes that Melanie Klein describes (Klein 1932); in that phase, the influence of the genital drives increases significantly and the infant identifies with the mother's desire for the father and his penis. This identification with the mother's feminine desire significantly increases the infant's capacity to introject.

For all infants, boys and girls, the space of the "primary feminine sphere" is what enables them to break free of the mutual projective identification between mother and baby that is a feature of the "primary maternal sphere". It is the *locus* of identification with the other's desire for the Other—and, above all, with the mother's feminine sexual desire for the man/father. It is also the *locus* of the experience of absence and of the diversification of negative aspects through confrontation with the primal fantasies of seduction and the primal scene. The fate of mourning processes and of the individual's introjective identifications depends on the appropriate organization of this primary feminine sphere, as does that of the economic equilibrium of psychic bisexuality in terms of the individual's belonging biologically to one or the other sex. The loss of the omnipotence that gave the infant the impression of being the mother's unique object leads the child to identify simultaneously with the "maternal mother" as a lost object and with the father as the object of the feminine desire of this "mother with a new face"—the sexual mother.

The early Oedipal stage

As soon as the early stages of Oedipal triangulation are established (Klein 1928)—they derive immediately from the primary feminine phase—the young girl has to come to terms with her Oedipal destiny in her relationship with her mother; this forces girls, unlike boys, to change their love object. The upheaval created by her early passionate interest for the Oedipal father (Guignard, 1996a) brings in its wake two principal consequences:

- the young girl finds herself opposing, in a cruelly dangerous way, her primary love object: the mother;
- the different stages of her Oedipus complex—the early stages, then at age three–four years, the Oedipus complex at puberty and, last but not least, the Oedipal situation in motherhood— mean that she will have to cope with difficult mourning processes and have to work through her identification with the lost object, i.e., the mother of primary love who now additionally becomes the sexual mother, the one who deprived her of her omnipotent status as the sole love object of the maternal mother.

Thus, at every stage in the girl's development, and throughout her life as woman and mother, her own mother is the identificatory reference marker. This pattern makes both for the strength and for the fragility of feminine development and of the relationship that women have with respect to one another.

The destiny of primal fantasies in girls

Given that a girl has the same sex as the mother who gave birth to her, the primal fantasy of going back to intra-uterine life—the function of which is to deny the expulsion of birth (Guignard, 1996b)— comes up against a specific set of problems involving the fantasy of castration that have to do with the denial of belonging biologically to one's given gender. Unlike in the case of boys, these issues cannot crystallize around the denial of the feminine dimension, the classic unisex expression of which is the image of the phallic mother (Guignard, 1993).

Mutual projective identification between mother and infant, which structures the primary individuation of infants of both sexes—the primary maternal sphere—is thus, from the outset, in girls, marked by an infinite set of mirror-images: the mother's unconscious Infantile dimension (Guignard, 1996c) includes a representation of herself as a young girl, so that both are experienced as being "the same". It is in this specific pattern that the extraordinary cathexis of the contents of the maternal body, as discovered and described by Melanie Klein, takes its place.

While the young boy is supported in his desire by his drive towards penetration linked to his male genitals, the young girl is forever oscillating between individuation, which leads to envy (Guignard, 1997c) of the riches that the mother possesses, and regression to a quasi-mimetic projective identification. The endless mirror-imaging between the mother's Infantile dimension and that of her daughter means that the latter's individuation runs the risk of being constantly called into question, especially if the mother's Oedipal structure—in particular, her paternal identification and cathexis of man-as-lover—is defective.

The hidden destinies of femininity and maternity

As I have said, it is in the primary feminine sphere that individuation processes take place, together with the discovery of the evidence in the mother's face that she has another desire. This discovery thus suddenly reveals to the infant the existence of a third person—and, at the same time, the difference between the sexes. Thus, the "too little" of the maternal woman very quickly finds an echo in the "too much" of the sexual mother.

On three occasions in his writings, Freud (1905d, 1919e, 1924c) based his description and investigation of masochism on what he called feminine masochism. I think that he may have been forced to think along these lines by the oscillation of individuation processes in young girls that I have just mentioned. I had earlier (Guignard, 1985) suggested that the Moebius strip might be an appropriate representation of the links that exist between masochism and femininity, and I have tried to conceptualize how masochism, mourning, and trauma may be related (Guignard, 1997d).

In women, the organs of sexual pleasure and of those of reproduction share the same anatomical fate with respect to the fact that they are hidden from sight. Yet the hidden destinies of femininity and motherhood can be seen to be different as soon as we look at them from the point of view of drive-related cathexes and of the mental representation of these organs that women themselves have.

The psychoanalytic treatment of women patients has taught me that the unconscious drive-related cathexis of their reproductive organs—uterus, fallopian tubes, and ovaries—and of those of sexual pleasure—vagina, clitoris, and labia—follows quite different paths. There are also quite significant differences as regards their respective degrees of representability.

Thus, in this wide range of modalities by means of which adult sexuality may be cathected, the psychoanalytic material of young women who are still childless and who have as yet no plans to have children shows that, unconsciously, they experience their uterus as being completely undifferentiated from that of their mother. Consequently, they unconsciously cathect the maternal uterus—to a very high degree and with a great deal of ambivalence—as the *locus* of a desire that must for ever remain prohibited. This is expressed on the one hand as a form of projective identification through hypochondriac anxiety over their own periods, for example, and, on the other, as a persecutory focus in terms of their mother's gynaecological changes (and especially hysterectomy). These gynaecological misadventures are experienced as an attack against them personally, not only in terms of fear of retaliation for their own envious attacks on the creative capacity of the maternal womb, but also as the unjust destruction of a *locus* that, in fantasy, still belongs to them.

Thus the young girl's desire to steal the contents of the maternal body (Klein, 1932) has also to do with denying the loss of the uterine container, which is just as coveted as a *locus* as for its actual contents.

This pattern plays a significant role in the functional prevalence of the identificatory mechanisms—hysterico-projective and introjective—that lie at the heart of the mother–daughter relationship.

When all goes well (Guignard, 1984), the young woman's first pregnancy enables her to give up her desire to possess the maternal womb and leads her to reappropriate her own uterus or even to create some representation of it. The whole point about this is that this new cathexis occurs in the woman who becomes a mother at the precise moment when her womb ceases to belong to her as a potentially autoerotic organ linked to her sense of identity, because it is inhabited by a foetus that belongs to the following generation.

When women patients talk about their body, it becomes clear that this generation gap—characteristic of the axis along which drive-related cathexes of reproductive organs takes place—plays a significant part in their economic equilibrium, caught up, as every woman is, between genital cathexes and maternal cathexes of their sex drives.

Certain forms of female homosexuality could be seen as an expression of the primal fantasy of going back inside the maternal womb. The sexual pleasure of homosexual women has in such cases to do with their fantasy cathexis of the maternal womb, as well as with the diffusion of drive-based excitation towards their own organs of sexual pleasure.

The neck of the womb—the anatomical locus of the destiny of guilt feelings

Maternal and feminine dimensions are anatomically linked together at the frontier *locus* that we call the cervix, or neck of the womb.

In women, guilt feelings associated with sexual desire do not have the same origins as those that are linked to the desire to have a child.

With respect to a woman's pleasure, guilt feelings concerning sexual desire are related to the importance of the introjective impulse that that pleasure sets free. For a short time, that process does away with all limits: those of gender, through narcissistic elation; those of the sexes, via projective identification; and those of generations, through the momentary merging of drive-related cathexes concerning both uterus and vagina.

As for guilt feelings related specifically to the desire to have a child, they are in my view rooted in the repression of the primal fantasy of going back inside the maternal womb. That repression is maintained with the help of splitting and denying the expulsion that took place at birth.

When one walks across the Himalayan high plateau, after a welcome rest at the summit of a mountain pass,[1] the custom is to run towards the next valley while gleefully pronouncing a some-what violent rallying-call that goes something like "To hell with the place that belongs to the past! Let's run on, with no regrets, towards the future!"

I would willingly use that Tibetan "saying" as a metaphor for the primary repression of the primal fantasy of going back inside the maternal womb. The maternal womb is indeed the emblem *par excellence* of the difference between generations, and it cannot be ignored. The sex drives cathect it on a massive scale; this cathexis is quite different from that of the vagina, and it mobilizes in every human being, male and female, no matter what his or her age, the desire to give a child to the mother (or to the women who represent her) as well as the unconscious guilt feelings that such a desire arouses.

Maternal/feminine: the switch-over

In order to establish a balanced psychic bisexuality, children of both sexes have to accomplish introjective identification with both the primary maternal dimension and the primary feminine one. However, in the case of girls—given their future as women and possible mothers—these introjections have a much more specific importance as regards their bodily ego.

My hypothesis is that, unless she has recourse to some perverse solution or other, the adult woman-and-mother's cathexis of the maternal and feminine dimensions functions quite naturally in a switch-over or flip-flop fashion, and is marked by feelings of guilt.

Motherhood and femininity, as actual facts in external reality, amount therefore to an illusion of having integrated in the mind the dimensions implied by the maternal and feminine spheres.

Moreover, there are three obscure objects of cathexis: in the first place, the womb; second, that other *locus* (much debated as to its rightful place in the list of erogenous zones) called the vagina; and, finally, the pregenital *locus* (so easy to talk about because of its unisex quality) that is the anus. These three are in such close geographical proximity that confusion cannot but be the result; in addition, the representations of how these different organs are cathected by the sex drives are condensed.

Anality is a defence more readily employed by boys and by men, from the perspective of their unisex infantile sexual theory that lays the foundation for the masculine castration complex. Hypochondriasis and depression are defences more usually employed by girls and by women because of their primary identification with the maternal reproductive organs; that identification seals off primary castration with the expulsion that takes place at birth.

Repudiation of the feminine sphere as a rejection of the mother's sexuality

When I look at my own clinical experience, I find it impossible to say which is the harder to represent, the feminine dimension or the maternal one. I would tend to say that this non-representable aspect has to do with the frontier, the *neck*, the mountain pass . . . in other words with the boundary between maternal and feminine—that boundary is non-representable precisely because it borders on incest with the mother figure. In any case, it is this non-representable frontier that makes it both possible and necessary for the adult woman-and-mother to switch rapidly and in both directions between her feminine and maternal dimensions.

Perhaps, in fact, men find it easier than women to maintain the non-representability of the frontier between maternal and feminine within the limits of their refusal of the feminine sphere as a whole (Schaeffer, 1997). Given the fact that motherhood breaks through that frontier in all of its bodily reality—though the vagina is the obligatory channel, it draws aside to let the newborn through—women have no choice but to re-establish that frontier as far as psychic reality is concerned. This is probably the form that rejection of the feminine sphere takes in women.

"Everybody has his or her own way of looking at things", as the saying has it. Acknowledging the difference between the sexes implies that we accept the fact of our belonging biologically to a specific gender and, consequently, that we give up the idea of belonging to the opposite sex. This in turn requires that we abandon the infantile sexual theories that derive from omnipotent magical thinking.

In "Analysis terminable and interminable" (Freud, 1937c), Freud considers what he calls "repudiation of femininity" to be a "bedrock"; our acceptance of belonging to one biological gender or the other comes up against that "bedrock" because, by definition, we have to accept that another gender also exists. In accordance with the unisex infantile sexual theory that structures the castration complex in men, Freud describes that repudiation as a demand, in both sexes, for possession of a penis.

In my view, the economic reason for "clinging" to a theory that focuses solely on the penis lies in the "generation gap" that is related to the cathexis, in fantasy, of the womb—because it gives rise to a certain number of problems. That cathexis unites indissolubly, in the unconscious representation of the female body by the woman herself and by the Other, both the primal fantasy in which going back to intra-uterine life acts as a denial of birth *and* the primal fantasy of castration as a denial of belonging biologically to one specific sex.

I would therefore define the repudiation of femininity (or, as we would put it perhaps nowadays, of the feminine sphere) as being more precisely a rejection of the mother's sexuality. This is indeed a bedrock, and it acts as the biological foundation for the Oedipus complex and for the incest prohibition.

This rejection is approached differently by girls and by boys. For the young boy (and, later, man), rejection of the feminine sphere has a major structuring role to play in shaping the castration complex as a defence against the "too much" quality of the discovery of the mother's sexual desire for the father-and-his-penis; that discovery may threaten the boy's basic sense of identity as a male, given the vicissitudes of his Oedipal rivalry with the father.

For the young girl (and, later, woman), rejection of the feminine sphere has a secondary structuring role to play in the shape of the demand for a penis, which, to all intents and purposes, is a metamorphosis of the desire to have a child by the father. On that particular point, I would agree with the order in which Klein placed these elements: the desire to have a child comes first, the desire to have a penis being subsequent to that. The girl's (and, later, woman's) demand for a penis is thus a defence against the "too much" quality of the discovery of the father's sexual desire for the mother-and-her-vagina; that discovery may threaten her basic sense of identity as a female, given the vicissitudes of her Oedipal rivalry with the mother.

From that point of view, the switch-over movement in women's cathexis as regards the maternal and feminine dimensions is another solution that enables the contradictory impulses of the desire for a penis and the repudiation of femininity to be preserved, split-off from each other in an actively neutral kind of way.

If we were to try to picture this, we could perhaps say that when the maternal aspect takes precedence over the feminine one, then "closure" prevails over "opening-up", and "control" prevails over "defeat" in Schaeffer's conceptualization of these terms—the unconscious cathexis of the uterus takes precedence over that of the vagina. When the feminine aspect prevails over the maternal one, these patterns are reversed.

Mother and daughter: between sharing and splitting

Throughout a girl's development, the use of identification as the prevalent mode of relating between mother and daughter occurs almost without any limit; this is because of the attraction that this process has as the primary mode of relating, then, later, as and when the Oedipus complex has to be worked through. The absence of any limits is a dangerous situation, which may be alleviated to some extent if the mother's Oedipus complex is properly structured, especially in terms of the positive cathexis she makes of her sexual life and of the censorship of the (male) lover (Braunschweig & Fain, 1975).

When a woman gives birth to a daughter, she can counter-cathect the pain of delivery with the thought that one day her daughter will experience the happiness that she herself is experiencing at that precise moment. Before the infant daughter learns to talk, the infinitely-repeated mirroring of projective identification sets the seal on the link between mother and daughter in a short-lived condensation between feminine and maternal dimensions.

On the other hand, the maternal dimension may well be less powerful between mother and daughter than between mother and son. For example, I have noted that women who breast-feed their children tend to wean their daughters more quickly than they do their sons. This could be because of some tendency to Oedipal jealousy in the mother as regards her daughter, a tendency that gets caught up in the infinitely-repeated mirroring of projective identification that I have just mentioned.

Finally, with respect to this already complex pattern, the virtual infinity of mirror-imaging involves more than the two generations that are biologically concerned. The mother unconsciously projects her own mother or older sister on to her daughter, while she experiences her son more in terms of her father or a younger brother.

Receptiveness towards maternal and feminine aspects in male and in female psychoanalysts

For several years now, I, together with Dr D Arnoux, have been researching the specific characteristics of the countertransference response of male and of female psychoanalysts as they deal with the transference material of their male and female analysands.[2]

Here are some of our comments on the manner in which the maternal and feminine dimensions are responded to in psychoanalytic treatment:

- The defensive processes of male and of female analysts are structured in accordance with the reassertion of their gender identity. Their blind spots have to do with their own Oedipal rivalry with the analysand (male or female). Whatever the pathology presented by the patient, these blind spots are different in male and in female psychoanalysts; that difference is again modified depending on whether the partners in the psychoanalytic relationship are of the same sex or not.
- The psychoanalyst's sense of identity is threatened more when he or she is of the same sex as the analysand. The reason seems to be that the triangular Oedipal perspective is destabilized in this kind of situation. The integration of the twofold difference—between the sexes and between generations—is thus insidiously held in check, because the defences used against this are identical in both members of the psychoanalytic partnership. The principal irresolvable contradiction that is the bedrock of denial of the feminine dimension does not have the same impact on the male psychoanalyst's receptiveness as on that of a female psychoanalyst. Their gender identity is not

challenged in the same way; this is the case whatever their respective theoretical and clinical references.

- The relationship between, on the one hand, male and female psychoanalysts and, on the other, their internal parental objects changes depending on whether the male (or female) psycho-analyst is working with a male (or female) analysand. It follows, therefore, that the paternal and maternal transference is not dealt with in the same way by male psychoanalysts and by their female counterparts.

- Male and female psychoanalysts do not have the same recep-tiveness when it comes to the *maternal* focus in the analysand's material, again depending on the sex of that analysand.

- When listening to what is expressed in the male or female analysand's material concerning the *feminine* focus in the trans-ference with respect to his or her mother and the homosexual or heterosexual erotic desires that are felt towards her, the psychoanalyst's countertransference identification with the paternal figure is very different and depends on the sex of that psychoanalyst.

- A male psychoanalyst will find it easy to grasp, in what his female patient says about her mother, the manifest expression of Oedipal rivalry; however, he will tend to underestimate the underlying anxiety as to her sense of identity that she experiences when attacking the Oedipal mother (because the risk is that, in so doing, she may destroy the object of her primary cathexis and the very foundations of her sense of identity).

- On the other hand, though a female psychoanalyst will find it easier to pinpoint that identity-related anxiety in a female analysand, any issues involving her own sense of identity will be stirred up much more forcefully than in the case of her male counterpart whenever she has to be receptive towards and interpret the Oedipal rivalry of a woman analysand.

- When a female analysand talks of her relationship with her siblings, a male psychoanalyst will tend to decode this mater-ial in terms of penis envy, whereas a female psychoanalyst will focus more on the wish to steal the internal babies of the mother-in-the-transference.

It is striking that this "preferential focus" quite clearly transcends the various theoretical references of the psychoanalysts taking part in this workgroup.

Conclusion

In the Ivory Coast Guro,[3] a man traditionally takes as his wife a woman who belongs to a "foreign" and perhaps even "enemy" village. Young girls leave their home village very early in order to live in their husband's village. Once there, they become part of the "wives' group" which, all generations taken together, has much less power than the group comprising the daughters and sisters of the menfolk of the village, the "daughters' group". Many rituals are structured around this dichotomy between the female inhabitants of the same village, and verbal assaults on the "wives' group" run from mere jokes to the cruellest of insults. One day, in one of those villages, Ariane Deluz—an ethnologist in the *College de France*, with whom I have worked for many years now—saw a man who, during his mother's funeral, had an acute nervous breakdown: in his despair, he refused to accept the funeral ritual according to which his mother's body had to be taken back to the village in which she was born and buried there by her uterine nephews. The ethnologist reports that, faced with that man's distress and pain, the two antagonistic groups of women—"wives" and "daughters"—came spontaneously together to help to contain the suffering that the man/orphan was experiencing, making sure all the while that the funeral would carry on as planned: in the face of the man-child's distress, their feminine rivalry was put to one side so that their maternal quality could come to the fore.

In Ingmar Bergman's film *Autumn Sonata*, it is the infant, or indeed the foetus, who is the object of the most secretly violent conflict between mother and daughter.

Some daughters—as in Bergman's film and among the Guro— have to put some geographical distance between themselves and their mothers before they can become pregnant; others, on the contrary, cannot see themselves having children when they are far away from their mothers. I recall one woman who, very happily married, lived in various foreign countries at some great distance from her own family; for twenty years, she suffered from psycho-genic sterility. Just a few months after she returned to the country in which her mother lived, she found herself pregnant, without any need to have recourse to medical assistance.

A daughter's sense of identity is a subtle mixture of sharing and splitting with respect to her mother. And since every mother is or has been herself a daughter, and every daughter may well become a mother, that mixture is constantly having to be modified; these modifications switch back and forth between their feminine and maternal aspects. That is why they appear so suddenly and turn out to be so fragile; their potential for explosion is considerable.

Fortunately, faced with this explosive fragility, the man/father stirs up the tremendous power of the Oedipal cathexis that the girl/daughter directs towards him. These are the cathexes that structure what is called the "hysterical" basis in girls, a major point of reference for every woman's normal development. But, as Kipling used to say, that is another story . . .

Notes

1. There is a play on words here in the original French. "Neck of the womb" is "col de l'utérus", and the same word "col" also designates a mountain pass. [Translator's note]

2. The results of this research project are due to be published in English in the *Bulletin of the European Federation of Psychoanalysis*, and in Italian in the *Journal of the Italian Psychoanalytic Society*.

3. I am grateful to Ariane Deluz for sharing with me the data that I present here.

CHAPTER TEN

The parents, the baby, and the high-tech stork

Fanny Blanck-Cereijido

Introduction

T he new reproductive techniques (NRT) may offer women and couples who have difficulty in conceiving a fresh possibility that could change the course of their lives, by helping them make a hitherto-frustrated dream come true. Procedures range from simple hormone regulation to interventions that consist of fertilizing the egg in a test-tube for the gestation process to take place in another woman's uterus. Thus, in so far as they are an attempt at solving a problem, NRTs are a valuable resource, but since they generate a series of new situations they in turn raise fresh questions that have to be thought through in all their implications.

Deriving from the use of these techniques, there are issues that have to do with the weakening of conditions for filiation, the question of maternal identity, and the challenge to the concept of the desire to have a child. The choice of such procedures also leads us to ask ourselves why these women accept, seemingly without question, the painful physical implications and how they confront the resultant ethical issues. It also involves reflecting on the psychic

consequences of children coming into the world under such conditions, both for the parents and for the children themselves.

Of course, the effect on the woman's physical body, and on her
and her partner's psyche, depends on the nature of the technique
involved: the situation when spermatozoa and ova from the father
and mother are used is different from that in which material from
an unknown donor and a surrogate mother are employed, this
latter case being the source of ethical and even legal problems. The
different techniques may be summarized as artificial insemination,
in vitro fertilization (IVF), and surrogate embryo transfer (SET) in
cases of surrogate maternity.

Different civilizations seem to share a firm belief in the so-called
woman = mother identity (Blanck-Cereijido, 1997). In such societies,
the desire and the destiny of women have taken support from the
myth that their only legitimate fulfilment is through motherhood:
the woman-as-mother obtains satisfaction in taking care of her children. The *woman–mother–nature* equation relates to a phallocratic
order that places women in such a position, and consequently gives
each child a mythical image of absolute desire and satisfaction that
comes from another—in other words, absolute maternal desire.
This would imply that women are outside the symbolic order, in the
universe of instinct, outside culture, following a crude "law of the
species". Nothing could be further from the psychoanalytic way of
thinking, which defines the emergence of subject and desire as a
feature specific to human beings. The desire and the experience of
mothers are major elements that have to be taken into account in
examining such beliefs and in understanding the personal and
social reality of what being a mother involves.

In this sense, Janine Chasseguet-Smirgel (1964) states that the
helplessness with which the human child comes into the world
necessitates such a prolonged dependence on the mother that the
hostility caused by this situation brings about, as a way of defence,
the assertion of phallocratic theories. The need that the child feels
for his or her mother therefore becomes the woman's only mission
in life: procreating and loving her child. This same need for care
and protection turns the mother into an all-powerful being, hated
or idealized, yet at the same time wanted and desired.

Cases of surrogate maternity, or multiple fertilization, make us
wonder who takes the mother's place, and whether the traditional

associations of the term "mother", as the person who gives birth to and raises a child, may be maintained in the face of these technical and legal developments. Is the mother the egg that includes the genetic code, the womb that nourishes and contains, or the person who provides maternal care? (Blanck-Cereijido, 1996). And in this sense, will the concept of "mother" still be linked to that of gender? The concept seems to fall apart, as does the concept of maternal instinct. Is it an inborn instinct?

I shall try to answer these questions in the following paragraphs.

Motherhood and the symbolic order

The NRTs have been developed thanks to scientific and technological breakthroughs, at a time when the family system is being called into question and weakened. Nowadays we often come across single-parent families, homosexual couples, children living with the new partners of their fathers or mothers. There is a connection between the reproductive liberalism of biotechnologies and the freedom of relationships between the sexes and their ways of symbolization.

Lévi-Strauss (1949) claimed that the kinship system is an instrument designed to reproduce the social order, which is generated on the basis of universal biological data: there is a process that goes from biological paternity to line of descent—men and women procreating create a succession of generations. Each kinship system is a particular solution that illustrates one of the different but logically possible combinations arising from such irreducible biological data, which express the essential otherness of each person from birth onwards. The knowledge that each of us is created in the sexual relationship between a man and a woman is a factor that gives structure to our states of mind through the working-through of the Oedipal situation—or at least this was the case until the end of the twentieth century. What will happen with the child born as a result of NRTs? Our task is to look and listen in order to find some answers to that question, investigating how the unconscious deals with such situations.

In every culture, procreation is an operation in which the symbolic order plays a part. While the difference between the sexes, the prohibition of incest and the paternal metaphor define us as human species, these conditions must not be looked upon as sacred. It is the order that exists at present, but it is not the only possible one. When analysing the symbolic function, psychoanalysis runs the risk of simply buttressing prevailing perspectives instead of analysing them (Tort, 1989).

Motherhood in mythology and in history

We know that the desire for a child depends, to a large extent, on the culture in which the mother lives. This is so true that, when reading my first notes on the subject, dating back to 1994, I find that the increasingly frequent use of NRTs changes their character, granting them a different psychic place as they become more and more socially accepted. Another example in this sense is divorce, which over the past years has changed from being a stigma to an ordinary, accepted fact in Western society.

In biblical times, being a mother was so crucial, and the meaning of a woman's life depended to such a great extent on having a child, that Tamar, upon the death of her successive husbands Er and Onan, ended up contriving a scheme so as to be fecundated by her father-in-law Judah (Genesis: 38). Quite different was the situation of middle- and upper- class women in France and England during the seventeenth and eighteenth centuries: they handed over their babies to be taken care of and suckled by maids. This could perhaps lead us to think that, by acting in this way, they were trying to avoid any close emotional involvement with their newborn baby, in view of the extremely high rate of child mortality at the time. Badinter (1987), however, believes that such an argument is a fallacy. She develops the idea that suckling and raising a baby was seen as something inferior and degrading, and that was why the well-to-do classes handed their children to wet-nurses, who took them to live in their own houses and treated them with neglect, which was in fact the true reason for the high mortality rate. Her opinion is supported by the fact that this rate was lower in working-class babies, who were looked after directly by their own mothers.

It is only after 1750 that we find motherly love mentioned; thereafter, women began to be encouraged in their role as mothers.

This change seems to have occurred, to a large degree, because it was necessary for children to survive, since the death rate of human beings in Europe at the time was considerable.

From the twentieth century on, women have found a place in diverse occupations, interests, and professions, and it is not rare for them to reject or delay maternity when faced with a choice between their career and having children.

Motherhood in psychoanalysis

For Freud (1925j), anatomy does not imply destiny; he derives the categories of feminine and masculine as originating from the symbolic order, inserting the question of the difference between the sexes into the problems of culture. This psychoanalytic position began with "The three essays" where, in the chapter on perversions, Freud (1905d) grants sexuality a subjective status, since he holds that the aims of instinct may be reached through diverse objects and means. From then on, all developments referring to the concepts of need and desire, of the erogenous body, take us away from what is empirically observable as a theoretical basis. In this way, sexual difference is organized around the threat of castration and not on anatomic reality. The girl, in her wish to obtain an equivalent of the male penis, replaces this wish with that for a child, and she turns to her father to obtain a child from him. Thus, it is the *penis = child* symbolic equation that places the girl in a feminine sexual position, and the Oedipus complex leads the little woman-to-be to repress her primitive love for her mother and turn to her father.

Of course, we think of identification with the mother, first in a dyadic context and later in the Oedipal one, as an element referring to the early wish for motherhood, in which the need to make reparation to the mother may play a role. But I think that it may be understood as a desire to be like the mother and have what she has, and not necessarily to procreate and raise a child.

The girl's feminine identification starts at birth, and is determined by her name, the expectations surrounding her, and the way she is treated (Blanck-Cereijido, 1983). This identification is more firmly structured around age four, largely depending on her mother's femininity—in other words, on how harmonious and pleasant she experiences her role as a woman. The mother, through her own transgenerational links and Oedipal construction, relays the values and beliefs of her own, as well as the father's, ancestors. The father is also involved in the process by which his daughter accepts her gender, in so far as it is possible for him to cathect her as a little woman and to make contact with her feminine aspects, as well as with those of his wife and of his own mother.

Just as after the Oedipal renunciation the young boy enters latency, a waiting period that will allow him to grow and acquire a penis like his father's—thereby placing him in a situation in which he can build a love life in the future with a woman other than his mother—so must the little girl work through her castration complex for the sake of hoping for a child. However, every woman has to put up with an additional loss, since she will have to surrender her child to society for him or her to become integrated into the prevailing culture (Saal, 1991). If the part this child has to play is that of making the mother whole by being kept back by and for her, instead of being conceived as another person in his or her own right, the child's development will be psychotic.

The wish for a child and its vicissitudes

The powerful biological tendency towards having a child appears to be laid down, as it were, by the Other, by language, by family, and by society. The human desire for offspring is also a result of the woman's identification with her own mother, and of the desire to fulfil the potentiality for an identity of her own. Also, it positions the parents in an historical perspective, in which they convey to their children the biological and cultural heritage of their own parents and ancestors. In addition, human life searches for meaning in the continuity bestowed on it by procreation, thereby mythically continuing one's own life through future generations.

We can see, then, that the wish for a child appears in the woman during the gender determination process. At first it has a strong narcissistic feature, which implies that the wish for pregnancy and the wish for a child will not always neatly overlap. The possibility for object love to arise later may give the child a place as a separate object, loved as such, with a human shape, name, and destiny, in an intimate, rich, and rewarding mother–child relationship.

The development of femininity and the desire for a child felt by a woman and her partner may have to take on board situations involving unconscious conflicts that may hamper female and male fertility. The woman may find it difficult to give up her masculine dimension or her omnipotence. The need to see herself as her mother's equal leaves her in a dangerous situation, where she may feel attacked inside her own body by aggressive and potentially pathogenic fantasies of retaliation.

Conceiving a child makes a woman feel more relaxed about her inner self, her identification with her mother, and her projections for the future. Sterility leaves her with no such guarantee, and introduces the notion of her own death, of finitude, through the absence of offspring.

In psychoanalytic clinical practice, difficulties concerning procreation frequently express hysterical mechanisms or somatization, based on disorders of an Oedipal nature; among these are the rejection of the fantasy of having a child by her father, the consequences of not having worked through penis envy, or some particular effects of the former relationship with her mother and conflicts related to her ability to engender.

Women who are identified with the phallocratic ideal and subjected to the dictate that their only destiny is motherhood are able to endure any process of aggression to their body that is inherent to fertilization. In addition, the search for wholeness and for guarantees regarding internal integrity may constitute one of the conditions that leave the woman immobilized with a relentless demand for pregnancy that accepts no substitution. Such women will stop at nothing in order to obtain fertilization, whatever the method involved. Their bodies will suffer any sacrifice in pursuit of that ideal, because it is the only goal worth reaching.

The situations in which these women become immobilized in this way are frequently highly traumatic, and in this sense they are the outcome of ambivalence concerning the mother as an omnipotent character. Often, the "couple" formed by the physician and the woman-who-wants-to-be-a-mother pursue arcane and obscure paths in the disheartening cycle covering ovulation → ultrasound → tests → hormones → artificial fertilization → implant of an embryo that was previously developed *in vitro*. In all of these

situations, the *unheimlich* and the primitive fantasies of a fragmented body thrive and dominate.

New reproductive techniques

The consideration given by our culture to the use of artificial technology varies from admiration for the efforts made by a mother to
procreate, to condemnation of what it considers a narcissistic, selfish search for a child of her own, instead of adopting one of the
million orphan or abandoned children who are already alive.
Besides, the consideration these techniques deserve varies, depending on country and social class. Colleagues at the Population
Council of Mexico have told me that they have no experience in this
matter, since their problem is contraception.

The techniques range from an artificial insemination treatment
with spermatozoa from the couple to others that involve using and
disposing of embryos, other women's uteri, *in vitro* fertilization
with spermatozoa from already-deceased husbands, and preserv-
ing impregnated eggs in liquid nitrogen. These cases raise ethical
and even legal issues.

Turning the problem of sterility into a simple question of
medical technique and finding its solution by way of the body,
without listening to what the individual person has to say, subverts
the approach to the conflict, and is a defence against the unconscious difficulty, attacking the link between mind and body. In this
sense, according to Tort (1989), having recourse so rapidly to
medical technology in the treatment of infertility is a manic defence,
which helps to disregard the recurrent unconscious elements that
are involved.

If we consider that sterility is a symptom with its own individual history and meaning, the plea for a child and the difficulties that
that entails must be listened to in what each particular person has
to say; it thus becomes necessary to listen to the woman concerned
and to keep in mind that it is possible to accompany in her desire a
woman who does *not* want a child.

Let us suppose that the final decision is to have recourse to one
of the new reproductive techniques. These procedures give rise to
a multi-faceted set of problems; for example, even in the case of a

sterile couple whose pathology is not obvious as such, countless questions arise, due to the multiple causes for sterility and the variety of procedures they can choose from (Tubert, 1991). One possible difficulty could be related to the point that, in fact, the artificial solution may frustrate an unconscious desire not to have children. We also know that artificial insemination is used by women who do not have any problem with respect to conceiving as such, but who want to conceive without the participation of a male partner (Cereijido, 1990).

If we now focus on the child conceived through these techniques, the question comes to mind as to what place the "test-tube child" holds in the family: can it be equivalent to the place that a baby born in a "natural" way would have held?

The place held by the test-tube child depends on how the parents cathect that child, and on their desire. Thus, it is possible for such children to integrate themselves satisfactorily in the family, especially if they have been truly desired and conceived jointly by both members of the couple. In fact, all children are adopted, in the sense that they must be accepted, taken care of, and loved by their parents, and this applies to their own children and to children otherwise conceived. However, we do not yet know what psychic and social effects may be generated by circumstances that up till now have almost never been encountered—such as being the child of a dead father's spermatozoa, or of an ovum and a spermatozoon nested in the womb of the mother's mother. As analysts, we do not yet have clinical instruments or sufficient experience to appreciate the consequences entailed by the production of children by means of these new reproductive techniques. We believe that the dangers for the parents stem from fantasized omnipotence, from the close proximity of omnipotent phantasies to actual reality, and from the psychosis-generating potential of these experiences, since they may lend weight to the fantasy of conceiving children with God, with the father, or even with the mother. For the resulting children, these dangers may lie in confusion concerning their identity, or in the fact that their birth exposes them to being treated as objects, belonging to the world of concrete reality of their parents, and removed from genealogy and from history. Of course, these outcomes depend on the personal and family structure, and on the fantasies of the parents.

Finally, it is necessary to take each woman, each couple looking for help from the new reproductive techniques, as a special case, with subjective particularities, which raises new ethical and even ideological problems. Listening to them is a challenge, and our difficulty may lie in approaching each individual case without prejudice, whatever our own beliefs or standpoint may be.

CHAPTER ELEVEN

Motherhood and work

Herta E. Harsch

T he full-scale arrival of women to the world of work was one of the greatest social changes of the last century. In the twenty-first century, the conflict between motherhood and work will remain central in the lives of women. This article looks at this issue from a psychoanalytic point of view, elaborating on underlying unconscious processes. The first section discusses women confronted with the question of whether to work, bear a child, or both. The psychoanalytic theory of femininity is drawn upon to cast light on the conflict between motherhood and work. The second section of this paper examines the mother's concerns about the potential effects of maternal absence and surrogate mothering on the mother–child relationship as well as the child's development. The theoretical models drawn upon here include the concepts of primary maternal preoccupation and triangulation. The case material stems from the long-term psychoanalytic treatments of adults.

Job or child?

Public discussion regarding the compatibility of motherhood and work has been fuelled by the fact that the birth rate in Germany is one of the lowest in the world (along with those of Italy, Spain, and Greece). One-third of the women in Western Germany remain childless. For university graduates the childlessness rate approaches one-half. The birth rate dropped suddenly and dramatically between the mid-1960s and early 1970s, a period that saw the arrival of the pill, the feminist movement, and the first post-war economic crisis. This was the generation born after 1942; more men remained childless than women (as is still the case today). The early childhood of this generation coincided with the war and the post-war years. This suggests that there was little impetus for family life and the desire to have children that is unconsciously influenced by childhood experiences, particularly the early mother–child relationship.

Renowned women psychoanalysts have advanced groundbreaking theories on the development and transmission of motherliness. Common to all psychoanalytic theories of femininity since the 1920s is the assumption that motherliness is based on the unconscious identification with one's own mother. Klein (1932) traces the trans-generational transmission of motherliness to introjective and projective identification that occurred during the very early mother–daughter relationship. The mothering one receives is the basis not only for one's own motherliness but also for the desire to have a child, in turn leading to the continuity of a particular mothering style through the generations.

The psychoanalytic theory of the trans-generational transmission of motherliness (from grandmother to mother to daughter) was initially based on individual cases. Empirical investigations covering three generations have since confirmed its validity. Researchers of infant development like Stern suggest that very early interaction with the mother instils preverbal relational knowledge and maternal competence in the infant. Facing the decision of whether to have a child oneself reactivates relational experiences with the mother. Successful psychic separation from the parents is a crucial factor for competent parenting.

Pines (1993) emphasizes that the early experience of being mothered creates an internalized maternal representation that serves as a lifelong model for the daughter. Adolescent daughters face the dual task of identifying with their mothers, while at the same time separating from them in order to develop an independent female identity of their own. Writing about involuntary childless-ness, abortion, and pregnancy, Pines shows that in women's deci-sions to have children or not, unconscious identifications with mothers are reactivated and early conflicts associated with them may be reinforced. If an ambivalent relationship to the mother has not been resolved because good and persecutory maternal objects and self-objects have not been integrated, the daughter may remain in a state of infantile dependence. For women (and men), the unconscious identifications and counter-identifications, concealed behind conscious rationalization, can have a crucial bearing on the decisions for or against having children. Extreme idealization or devaluation of the mother, the desire to outdo her, and fear of envy or revenge from the maternal introject can make it difficult for a daughter to assume the maternal role.

In the following clinical examples, I describe two patients who made divergent choices between job and motherhood. Ms A, a thirty-eight-year-old computer scientist married for thirteen years, had decided in favour of a career, against having children because, "One needs to invest a lot of time in looking after children." I was surprised at her forthright attitude on this point because ordinarily she was indecisive, uncertain, and lacking clear ideas. She was an extremely attentive daughter who revered her mother. Her rejection of motherhood was the unconscious expression of disappointment with, and hatred for, her mother.

Ms A was her parents' first child. Her mother continued with her job and left her daughter with the grandmother every day, although the latter had not wanted to take the child because the grandfather required constant care. The double experience of being burdensome to others became a basic feeling for the patient. She implemented her longing for mothering by mothering her own needy mother, experiencing herself as indispensable in that relationship. Ms A had the fantasy that motherly love must be total and sacrificial to the point of self-abnegation. Accordingly, she was convinced she could never be a mother. Her relationship with her partner was symbiotic and dependent; there was no place in it for a child.

Unlike Ms A, thirty-seven-year-old Ms B decided in favour of children and against working. She had the same profession as her mother and, like her, had three children. But in a counter-identification with her mother she gave up her job after the birth of her first child. Unlike her own working mother, she was determined to spend as much time as possible with the children. Ms B had been looked after by a series of nursemaids because her mother, readily dissatisfied with them, dismissed them. During the early years, Ms B was happy with her children, but then she became increasingly depressed, fearing that she had manoeuvred herself into a hopeless position. She had been unable to separate from the maternal introject and from her mother in reality. Every day, Ms B's mother called for a report on everything concerning the children and then gave precise instructions on how her daughter should behave. It was an unconscious repetition of Ms B's childhood situation: her mother retained her original role, while she herself had identified with the nursemaids whose care for the children had been devalued.

Both patients made their decisions on work or children against the background of an unresolved conflictual identification with the internalized mother. In their analyses the main theme involved the need to separate from the ambivalent maternal introject and the establishment of an independent female identity.

Job and children

The number of working mothers has increased continuously since the end of the nineteenth century, again with a quantum leap in the early 1970s. This is true of all western countries. Before 1970, most mothers of pre-school children in the USA stayed at home; since the 1970s only a minority has done so. At present, almost two-thirds of the mothers in the USA return to work a few months after giving birth. For child care they seek individual solutions: grandmother, father, another relative, in-home non-relative, child-care in a home or centre. In Western Germany today, one-third of mothers with children under three go out to work, almost exclusively part-time. Only 3% of the infants attend a child-care centre. In the vast majority of cases, grandparents take care of the baby. Fully employed mothers still spend 60% of their infants' waking time with their children. From birth to kindergarten or elementary school, mothers have to reconcile job and family, frequently suffering from strain, partner conflicts, feelings of guilt, inadequacy, and chronic lack of time. This chapter concentrates on infancy, a time in which separation and parenting change weigh most heavily.

Surrogate care for infants is not a modern phenomenon; it has been practised for 4,000 years (Harsch, 2001). In many societies it was normal for mothers to look after their children with the help of others. At various times in history there were social developments in which substitute care took extreme forms, with mothers having little or no contact with their children.

Today, pregnant women and mothers of infants are faced with the problem of reconciling motherhood with work. The crucial issue here is how much maternal absence is tolerable for the child and the mother–child relationship. The alarming studies by Spitz, Bowlby and others indicated that long separations from the mother without satisfactory replacement are a prime risk factor. However, this did not indicate whether and when maternal absence with substitute care for some hours during the day could be traumatic. Relevant studies on factors supporting or threatening mental health may throw some light on this area. These are prospective or retrospective long-term cohort studies such as the well-known investigations undertaken in Hawaii, Minnesota, New York, Berlin, or Mannheim. They indicate that high risk factors include severe psychosocial childhood problems such as poverty, severe neglect, chronic parental conflict, or the severe illness of a parent. But brief maternal absences are not mentioned as risk factors. All the studies referred to the presence of an emotionally supportive mother or another person as a major factor protecting against mental disturbance, but no mention is made of the requisite amount of availability.

Since the 1950s there have also been empirical studies on the development of children of working mothers. As they differ in methodology, they are not comparable, nor is there uniformity in their findings. In the 1980s, attachment researchers began studying the effect of day care on mother–child attachment in the first year. Initially, the consequences were found to be detrimental, but later studies failed to confirm this (Clarke-Stewart, 1989; Howes, 1999). The National Institute for Child Health and Human Development (NICHD) conducted a long-term prospective study on 1,300 children. Its findings suggested that "child care by itself constitutes neither a risk nor a benefit for the development of the infant–mother attachment relationship" (NICHD, 1997, p. 877). Maternal sensitivity proved to be the crucial factor for mother–child attachment and infant development. The term refers to a mother's ability to perceive signals from the infant, interpret them correctly, and respond to them. This concept has points in common with Winnicott's holding, Stern's affect attunement, and Bion's containment. The investigation also revealed correlations between sensitive mothering, fewer hours in child care, and higher quality care.

Empirical studies indicate that the question of whether absences of the working mother are detrimental to the infant cannot be answered with an unequivocal yes or no. An assessment of the effects of early surrogate mothering needs to take a number of variables into account. The complexity and interrelations in this field can be better understood with the aid of psychoanalytic theory. Especially helpful in this respect, in my view, are Winnicott's concept of primary maternal preoccupation and the psychoanalytic theory of triangulation.

In his article "From dependence towards independence in the development of the individual" (1963), Winnicott suggests that toward the end of pregnancy and for a number of weeks after birth, mentally healthy mothers display a state of heightened sensitivity in which they are preoccupied with the child to the exclusion of all other interests. He calls this state "primary maternal preoccupation" (Winnicott, 1956). Through projective identification with the baby, the mother knows how the child is feeling and is able to adapt to its needs. The child undergoes the experience of a secure holding environment. This period of sensitive adaptation lasts only a short while and soon the mother will be back to her office or writing novels, says Winnicott (1963). The first stage of "absolute dependence" is followed by the stage of "relative dependence", during which the mother gradually reduces her exclusive attunement and returns to leading her own life. Winnicott believes that the development of the child corresponds more or less exactly to the mother's return to independence.

For babies, severe holding deficiencies at the absolute dependence stage can cause unimaginable anxieties of total collapse, endless falling, and permanent dying and the fear that there will never be contact again (Winnicott, 1970). For mothers, absence for a number of hours or absorption in other things during the stage of absolute dependence with afforded attunement to the subtlest signals from the infant at the primary process level, will make their adaptation to the child more difficult. The effects of brief periods of separation during the relative dependence stage will depend on various conditions. Of essential significance are the experiences mother and infant have been through together. If attunement during the absolute dependence period was successful, the child will have developed trust in his holding environment. At the same time, there will be an increase in the mother's confidence as a mother and in her ability to regain independence. She will sensitively adapt the times and durations of her absence to the needs of the child, share and bear its sadness at her departure, and on her return show that she understands how the child felt while she was away. But if a mother has doubts about her own motherliness and believes that someone else would be better for the child, then the infant will sense this from the way she gives it into another's care. The child may develop the feeling that he has become too much for the mother to bear because he has been too greedy or too difficult.

The infant also registers whom the mother chooses as caregiver and senses the relationship between them. Hardin and Hardin (2000) established that when mothers deny the child's emotional attachment to a nanny they are unable to validate the child's loss of a caregiver. Disturbances in the relations between mothers and caregivers are often the reason for frequent changes of caregivers or child-care homes. The well-being and health of infants in child-care centres is significantly better when there is mutual esteem between mother and caregiver. A secure mother-attachment leads to a secure relationship between infant and caregiver, while a close relationship to the caregiver improves that with the mother.

In my publications on surrogate mothering I have discussed the relationship between mother, caregiver, and child in the light of the concept of triangulation. Triangulation is a fundamental principle of life. The dyadic mother–child relationship is triangular from the outset through the mother's inner representation of the father. If her capacity for triangulation is high, it will support the gradual internalization of triangular structures in the child. During the first few weeks after birth, the infant is increasingly able to perceive others as well as the mother, and to develop a relationship with both simultaneously. Early dual mothering is a triangular constellation. The child's ability to come to terms with this constellation depends on the relationship between mother and the other. The cardinal factor is the mother's choice of caregiver. Frequently she unconsciously selects someone to whom she either gives no chance or who gives her no chance in her relationship with the child. Parenting by mother and father is different from caregiving by two women. Normally, a maternal or sibling transference will take place between two women, one that unconsciously reactivates old relational conflicts. The result may be envy, rivalry, and devaluation (Harsch, 1990, 1994). Dual mothering succeeds when the mother integrates the surrogate with her family, approves of the surrogate's relationship with the child, and experiences her own involvement with the child as protected and encouraged by the caregiver (Hardin & Hardin, 2000). Like the father, a substitute mother can assist in the healthy resolution of symbiosis, supplement and enrich the child's relationship experiences. Successful cooperation will depend on the triangulation capacity of the mother and the caregiver. Detrimental is a constellation where the child is never looked after by both together but only in alternation, like shift-workers. A concerted approach and communication about the child and his state of mind during the other's absence are of crucial importance.

I shall now illustrate these points with reference to two patients whose children were born during analysis. Ms C, a married woman, was twenty-six when she came to treatment. She had two abortions and a previous miscarriage. She had also discontinued two university courses. Unconscious guilt and punishment anxieties underlay her self-destructive inclinations. She had not separated from a highly ambivalent maternal introject, and her dependence on her real mother was extremely strong. At the end of the first year of analysis, Ms C had resumed her studies and gained new confidence in her abilities. Despite being on the pill, she became pregnant during her second year of analysis; unconsciously, she wanted to bear a child in the protective context of treatment. Her daughter, Julia, was born during her third year of analysis. After the infant's birth (with interruption of analysis for three weeks) she reported vehement conflicts with her mother, who questioned her ability to function as mother. There were also disputes with her husband who found it difficult to come to terms with the developing mother–child symbiosis. During her sessions, Ms C left Julia with the father and supported his contact with the child. This gradually led to a close father–daughter relationship. Three months after the birth, Ms C started preparing for her examinations. She was unwilling to interrupt her studies; they had done a great deal for her stability. When Julia was six months old, Ms C started attending the most important seminars at university. She was absolutely sure that no one except her own mother would be suitable to look after Julia when she was away. Thus, she gave her mother a share in the child that she unconsciously thought she owed to her. Julia loved her grandmother, and Ms C accepted this without doubting herself or her significance to the child. Ms C's analysis continues. Her conflict between motherhood and work no doubt will continue for some time though it appears that she will cope adequately with it in the future.

Conflicts between work and parenthood are by no means limited to women. Accordingly, I want to report on Mr D, a thirty-one-year-old who became a father a few months after starting analysis. Years before, Mr D had interrupted his studies because of severe depression and work inhibition and worked as a waiter. He became a loving father, developing an intense relationship with his son, Frank. Mr D resolved to resume his studies as he wanted his son to be proud of him. When Frank was a year old, Mr D's wife began working part-time. Frank was to spend his mornings at a child-care centre. Mr D was worried about the impact of day care on the boy. Though he could not interrupt his studies, his schedule was flexible. The parents took a long time to find a centre where they formed a good relationship with the main caregiver. Frank was the youngest child in the nursery. His father took him there in the mornings and initially stayed there with him. During the long process of acclimatization, Mr D observed Frank and evaluated his state of mind and accordingly determined the length of his stay.

Mr D's mother had always been at home in his childhood, but had been largely insensitive to his episodes of separation anxiety. During analysis, establishing contact with feelings of loneliness and abandonment in early infancy, Mr D was able to empathize with his son. In my countertransference, I occasionally had difficulty coming to terms with my own fears that Frank might suffer harm. Mr D consulted the caregiver every day when leaving Frank and again on picking him up. Frank was described as a reserved child, quietly observing what went on around him, as is typical of children with a secure mother attachment entering a child-care centre. He took a long time to become livelier and join in the other children's games. His contact with the main caregiver was good and he was able to allow himself to be consoled by others if she was absent.

The example of Mr D indicates that the "new fathers" can play a crucial role in the conflict between motherhood and work. Internalized relationship experiences conditioned by the mothering they received are instrumental to fathers becoming proficient at mothering. Studies have shown that children develop well when their fathers are early primary caretakers. But the new paternity also involves new difficulties because the father's participation in baby and infant care requires a marked capacity for triangulation on the part of both parents. The initially clear distinction between "fatherly" and "motherly" is becoming blurred. Complication may ensue in the form of competition regarding which parent is the better mother.

Outlook: the new mothers

During the past thirty years there has been a huge increase in the number of working mothers. If daughters experience their own mothers as able to find a satisfactory solution for the work–children conflict, they will identify with this model. The new mother-ideal is that of the working woman deriving satisfaction from an ability to fulfil both life aims: an independent, socially and vocationally active woman who is a sufficiently good mother. Despite the double strain and vocational disadvantages involved, satisfaction is based on a subjective feeling of success in achieving the goals one has aimed at: motherhood and work. Subjective success is then a career that can be reconciled with the private sphere.

The generation of children now growing up has internalized a different mother and father image. Hitherto, psychoanalytic theories have assumed that the capacity for achievement and sublimation is based on paternal identifications. This overlooks the identification of girls and boys with the maternal competence in dealing with both work and children. It would be desirable for the dual-guilt syndrome besetting the older generation of working mothers to recede in the next generation. Instead, it will be necessary to expand our knowledge of how the detrimental consequences of separation and surrogate care can be avoided. With this issue psychoanalysis has a significant role to play.

CHAPTER TWELVE

The bodies of present-day maternity

Leticia Glocer Fiorini

Introduction

W hen we discuss motherhood in the twenty-first century we must take into consideration the ramifications of creating life in a non-conventional way. This in turn leads us to reflect on the vertiginous progress of bio-technology as an expression of present-day culture. Psychoanalysis is being challenged on its very frontiers. We need to consider the full implications and limits of these technologies, as well as their impact on analysts and patients. This puts the psychoanalytic method to the test.

The objective is to delimit the new relationships between technology, the human body and subjectivity; to investigate the impact of these new reproductive techniques on body representations, on traditional representations of the female body, of sexuality, of motherhood, and on the role of men and women in procreation.

The effects will depend on the particular features of each case and the specific characteristics of the techniques used. I emphasize the differences that exist between the simplest techniques, involving both members of a heterosexual couple, and the most complex ones, in which several bodies participate (gamete donor, surrogate womb, nursing mother). We must now add cloning, already established in the social imaginary and getting closer to becoming a reality.

I will not discuss the ethical dilemmas at stake in circumstances such as, for instance, cryopreservation of embryos, twins with deferred births, the use of a dead father's sperm and other techniques. These issues call into question our concepts of life and death, the frontiers between generations, and the laws of kinship.

But we must also consider *context*. These technologies are associated with a transformation of the relationship between the sexes and entail important changes as regards the nuclear family. They include multiple family relationships not strictly tied to gender roles such as homosexual couples and even one-parent families. Another remarkable change to be considered is that of motherhood being prolonged beyond the limits of the biological clock.

We face complex questions with no pre-established solutions and only fragmentary and partial answers.

Technological bodies. Construction and de-construction

We must bear in mind that, historically, motherhood has always involved the body of only one woman. There is a basic unity—a Moebius strip—between nature and culture, between bodies, desires, and fantasies, that feeds the idealized myths of motherhood. The new techniques of reproduction question this unity. This will highlight the contrast between the ideal and idealized body of motherhood—a unitary and complete body—and the multiple bodies that may be involved in the technological gestation of a baby.

We are dealing with complex issues, paradigms of a new maternity. This kind of maternity creates a gap with respect to natural essence, while at the same time the bodies involved appear to acquire special strength. In other words, these technologies move further and further away from nature while, paradoxically, bodies and biology are present to an excessive degree.

We are faced with artificially constructed bodies that challenge the laws of nature and cause some degree of ontological discomfort. Medicine and biology alone cannot solve this kind of problem. For instance: who is the true mother? The ovule donor, the surrogate mother or the nursing mother? The protagonists of such technological adventures are traversed by these ethical, legal, and psychological dilemmas. New frontiers have appeared between what belongs to the self and what is truly the other person's, between internal and external.

I am therefore focusing on the irruption of various bodies and the sheer power of their realness, together with their potentially disturbing or upsetting effects on the psyche. We must keep in mind the fact that these techniques propose alternative methods of procreation with the interplay of multiple combinations of bodies.

Mothers as well as children become the products of a construction that is simultaneously a de-construction. They are parts of bodies that, paradoxically, must generate a fictional unity. We are dealing with imaginary bodies strongly rooted in a heightened reality that are difficult to symbolize.

The intrusive and disturbing characteristics of these procedures lie at the root of paranoid anxieties and feelings of being threatened. They are related to splitting processes between donors, surrogate mothers, and nursing mothers.

On the one hand, they evoke the anxiety involving the primary object. We know that the uncanny has to do with the earliest relationship between mother and child: something that is both highly familiar and yet intrinsically possesses a sinister, mysterious aspect (Freud, 1919h). The question of origins generates both fascination and repulsion (Glocer Fiorini, 1998).

On the other hand, some specific issues concerning biotechnological maternity involve the manipulation of multiple, material bodies. The notion of a constructed child may have beneficial effects that satisfy parents' desires, but an anxiety that is impossible to put into words may lie in the background of this kind of maternity (Duvignaud, 1981). These effects may have different sources. First, the transgression of the rules of kinship, of the differences between generations and of the frontiers between life and death that some of these techniques involve is not innocuous. Second, anxiety and ancestral dread may arise now that it becomes possible to conceive a child by artificial means, a child whose origin involves unknown parts of other bodies. This may generate a feeling of "uncanniness", which in the Romance languages goes under the highly evocative name of "disquieting strangeness".

The psychic effects of these technologies highlight the contrast between idealized conceptions of motherhood and the terrifying myths relating to fantasies of neogenesis associated with the social imaginary.

When conventional body limits are erased and other, intensely-real bodies participate, an interplay of contradictory wishes, rivalries, and hatreds is generated among the actors of these sagas. Their convergent and divergent wishes become intertwined.

To my mind, we must explore the specific kinds of conflict, fantasies, and psychic splitting, in so far as they involve body fragmentations and combinations, that are characteristic of these technologies. As Elliott (1992) points out, we have to traverse the imaginary register in order to make new conditions of symbolization possible.

Clinical illustration

In this context I will refer to a dream of a thirty-nine-year-old woman patient. She was unable to become pregnant, and she consulted me because her physician had suggested assisted fertilization with an ovule donor and sperm from her own husband. For several months, she was tortured by anxiety and doubts (shared by her husband) that were extremely difficult to work through.

In the dream the patient is holding a baby in her arms. Little by little, and almost without noticing it, the contact with the infant makes her feel horror and strangeness, even though she sees no significant change in the child. That feeling becomes more and more intense, and finally the patient wakes up terrified. We spent several sessions working through this dream, and one of her associations led to the film *Rosemary's Baby*. Paranoid anxieties were clear and were associated with a third person. In the film, a satanic sect produces a diabolical baby by putting a teratogenic substance into the protagonist's food.

This seemed an interesting line that led us to think in terms of an unknown space. We related her anxieties to the intrusion of a non-symbolized third party: in this case, the donated ovule and its genetic material. Her associations referred to an unpredictable, dangerous, ambiguous, and diabolical Other. More than a year later, the couple decided to accept the assisted fertilization technique that had been suggested. The procedure was successful.

During her pregnancy the patient alternated between intense paranoid anxieties (Dr Frankenstein's creation was in the line of her associations) and moments of peacefulness and optimistic expectation. A girl was born and the mother–daughter relationship progressed positively. After a few months their relationship became affectionate, spontaneous and more and more consolidated, and paranoid anxiety diminished significantly. In a certain sense, she had adopted her child.

The analytic working-through of the material concerning this baby, constructed via a foreign, concrete intervention, allowed us to recognize a dual aspect of my patient's desire: the original desire for a baby that led her to consult me and the desire that vacillated because of the incorporation of an unknown donor, with its meaning of a "threatening Other". In other words, the construction of a desire over and above another desire.

Bodies, fictions and cybernetics

To go further along this road, I suggest we think about current technological maternity in terms of the premonitory and anticipatory categories of science fiction, and of present and future notions of cybernetics. For this purpose I will take as a model the technologically constructed artificial bodies of both disciplines. These may be considered contemporary narratives concerning bodies; bodies that are both concrete and virtual.

We are dealing with fictions and stories about bodies that evoke other possible representations of mothers, fathers and children. These fictions, since they go beyond the traditional means of reproduction, propose: (a) alternative ideas of procreation, gestation, and delivery in non-conventional ways; (b) the intervention of an alien third party, which could be an insect, an extraterrestrial creature, a machine or a virtual combination—a threatening Other that mirrors our fears and anxieties; (c) different conceptions of the sexual difference and (d) a redefinition of the relationship between love, sexuality, procreation, and the place of gender in these issues.

As a result, a multiple and fragmented model of the female-maternal body is generated. This leads us to think in terms of a re-combination of bodies and parts of bodies to make the desire for a child possible. This model also refers to a maternity that is always possible, though with the ever-present risk of ignoring, splitting off or denying either limits or impossibilities. We are confronted with proposals that could involve taking absolute control of reproduction—and hence of life and death—thereby completely ignoring the boundaries of time and space (Tort, 1992).

The child born of the new reproductive techniques may be considered, in a metaphorical way, to be a cyborg, a cybernetic being lying at the intersection between machines, bodies, and fiction. Further, the image of a constructed child is related to the image of a mother created by the combination of different bodies. An imaginary register emerges between *"collage" mothers and cyborg children*. These figures may well have an impact on subjectivity.

The issues that I have outlined highlight the contradictory aspects of these techniques.

We therefore need to think about possible new forms of psychic representation and to investigate the kind of subjectivity generated in the context of these new reproductive techniques.

In addition, these technologies based on fragmentation and dissociation challenge the concept of a unitary subject and, in this sense, are linked to postmodernism. Social determinants also have an impact: we are immersed in a consumer society, with its mass media and its overdeveloped technology, that pervades the production of subjectivity.

Another aspect of these techniques is that they emphasize the reproductive role of women: this "incubator effect" carries the potential risk of generating indiscriminate pregnancy proposals that fail to take into account the psychic availability of each woman as a person in her own right. These innovations may paradoxically strengthen the idealization of motherhood. In this sense, there is a gender issue relating to potentially excessive manipulation of the female body, with the aim of strictly complying with natural mandates (Glocer Fiorini, 2002).

All these issues force us to re-think the meanings and roles of bodies. In psychoanalysis, the concept of body is a complex notion. The body is simultaneously partial and unified; the component drives give it its partial aspect, while ego functions unify it. It is an image and a signifier (Lacan, 1949). It signifies and is signified. It is a surface and an inscription; material reality and image. It is symbolic, but also difficult to symbolize. It is the hard core of concrete reality, a frontier concept, and consequently a conflict-ridden one (Glocer Fiorini & Giménez de Vainer, 2003).

We know also that the idea of the body has different meanings for men and women. A woman's body has a strong involvement with reproduction, which is not exactly the case for the male body. New reproductive techniques emphasize these aspects.

The body is also an Other for each of us. During pregnancy it acquires a life of its own, accompanied by anxieties and various fantasies. In this sense, the body as an Other is over-cathected when other bodies, other cells, or other genes are involved.

The material quality of bodies and their combinations produce either a "mother effect" or a "child effect". But we must emphasize that this excessive presence is frequently associated with difficulties in the process of symbolization. We are dealing, therefore, with a kind of presence that can shift towards a non-symbolized absence.

Freud (1923b) maintained that the ego is above all a bodily ego. It is constituted through contact and through the mother's eyes as she contemplates her infant, the mother being the primary other. But what may be the effect on the way in which the mother looks at her child when she, the maternal other, is infused with another Other, strange, ambiguous, and unknown? Such a situation could almost inevitably generate anxiety and doubts as to the origin of this child who carries material parts of that strange Other.

How can an identificatory structure (Freud, 1921c) be established, in view of the multiple contributions that the look in the mother's eyes may comprise? And what are the marks that may be permanently inscribed in those bodies?

In such cases, how is self-identity constructed, how is the primal scene organized, how are the fantasies of fatherhood constituted and how is the family romance structured in the process through which the self becomes truly a subject? And with regard to the parents: what is the relationship between fantasies about the intervention of a third person and persecutory anxieties or different kinds of somatization?

I wish to emphasize that, thanks to these alternative methods of procreation, bodies shift from supposedly "natural" reproduction to other levels. Strange bodies, parts of bodies, intrusive all-powerful fragments begin to circulate (Bukatman, 1994). They are bodies inhabited by technology. This fact generates new meanings, alternative narratives that are in turn referred back to the body and its psychic representations. In this sense, we need to emphasize that, *for the drives, the erogenous body is always partial, but that there is another type of "partialness" that is characteristic of this kind of technique.*

Multicentric maternity

In such a context, is it possible to accept a foreign element, when it is doubly foreign? When the always inevitably unknown child of one's own is superimposed on the unknown and non-symbolized third party, as materialized in the person of the gamete donor? Recognition of otherness involves a double challenge. On the one hand, it requires, above and beyond narcissistic ambitions (Freud, 1914c), the necessary recognition of the child as an Other by accepting his or her difference. On the other hand, it obliges us to go beyond the menacing characteristics that are part of the Other as a threatening alien. There is an aspect of these excessive realities in which anything non-symbolized is experienced as traumatic. In this sense, that aspect is a metaphor for what is difficult to symbolize.

In an allusion to the beneficial aspects of parenthood, we could say that every child has to be symbolically constructed. Every wish implies a generative aspect, which leads us to reflect on the position of Eros. In an earlier paper, I discussed the idea of an expanded configuration relating to the desire for a child; not only as a substitution or as an effect of a fundamental phallic "lack", but in a productive, *poietic* sense, one that may generate a difference (Glocer Fiorini, 2000). In this context, by accepting the challenge these techniques force us to face up to, psychoanalysis may make the desire for a child possible.

The question is how to construct a symbolic difference, a child-as-Other (Glocer Fiorini, 2001), without denying the unknown element that originates in a concrete foreign other. This difficult path may lead to the acceptance of incompleteness.

I propose the concept of *multicentric maternity* as a notion that corresponds to current commonly-held beliefs and statements on the subject of neogenesis and technological procreation. These narratives express representations of femininity, maternity, reproduction, and female sexuality. They represent areas of intersection between fictional fantasies taken from literature and the cinema, cybernetics, and individual fantasies concerning procreation. They may help us to take on board new psychic representations and their limits.

If symbolization, however inchoate, is to be made possible, psychoanalysis must cut through these particular fictions and narratives concerning procreation and the relationship between the sexes. Technological realities make the pathways of symbolization more complex.

CHAPTER THIRTEEN

New reproductive realities: paradoxes, parameters, and maternal orientations

Joan Raphael-Leff

M otherhood in the twenty-first century involves many innovations that stretch traditional thinking. As clinicians we encounter these new manifestations increasingly in professional practices. Our psychoanalytic theories are expanding to encompass findings from other fields (neonatology, developmental and neurobiological research, cultural studies, and reproductive physiology) and to address new patterns of family formation, some aided by reproductive technology. Efficient contraception, safe abortion, and, recently, egg-freezing, create an illusion of control over reproductive functions facilitating postponement of motherhood, and it is estimated that some 12–20% of women in Europe have decided to forgo motherhood entirely. Others resort to lone motherhood. Radical sociocultural changes with diminishing stigma of unwed mothers and improved earning capacity of women have led to many chance pregnancies being sustained rather than aborted, with a very high incidence of women raising babies on their own, especially among teenage girls. In addition, over the past decades, many older women utilized reproductive technology to become pregnant in the absence of a partner. Infertile people and same-sexed couples have also been assisted to become parents, sometimes with the aid of donors and surrogates. Finally, routine use of technology during pregnancy, such as ultrasound, amniocentesis and other types of antenatal or even pre-implantation screening, prenatal surgery and selective foetocide, high-tech births and incubation of very premature babies, expose childbearing adults to illusions of control and, paradoxically, to catastrophic disillusionments leading to ethical dilemmas about keeping their babies alive or destroying them in reality.

As societies undergo rapid transformation and extended families are dispersed, we lose childrearing traditions. Mothers (and fathers, too) are now freer to follow their own unconscious representations and desires, for better or worse. I suggest that the rise in parental distress is due to a twenty-first century paradox: nuclear families foster intense dyadic relationships; however, smaller families and social stratification have also resulted in lack of contact with babies while growing up, providing few opportunities to resolve unprocessed early issues before becoming a parent. This, in turn, leads to a high rate of perinatal emotional disturbances. Due to lack of familiarity with newborns and little preparation for the powerful ordeal of parenting, primary carers of infants are overcome by "contagious arousal" with compelling reactivation of their own non-verbal infantile experience. Resonance with implicit feelings enables compassionate understanding of the baby. However, in the absence of a supportive network, the intense intimacy may feel overwhelming to an isolated mother. Furthermore, I suggest that although the needs of babies have changed very little over the millennia, over the past decades, female equality in education and occupational opportunities has altered maternal expectations. This renders baby-care requirements discordant with ambition for many mothers, and produces heartfelt dilemmas for others. These are presented later in the chapter as different orientations to mothering and their attendant perinatal disturbances.

I argue that one of the greatest paradoxes in the twenty-first century is that psychosocial changes and technological advances inaugurate new procreative options that foster unprecedented kinship patterns and raise powerful anxieties and disturbances. Conversely, these innovations also revive archaic desires and allow *actualization* of fantasies, such as sex-change or post-menopausal pregnancy, which hitherto were restricted to imagination.

Unconscious representations associated with new technological realities

If contraception disconnected the age-old link between sex and baby-making, assisted reproduction has made it possible to have babies without sex. The reproductive scene is now spun of the stuff of unbridled fantasy. The primal scene shifts from the parental bedroom to a laboratory, from two lovers in bed to sperm and egg in a Petrie dish. In fact, procreation ceases to be a two-person endeavour and may encompass three or four or, with cloning, even one. Virgin births are feasible. Would-be parents no longer need be of different sexes. Positive and negative Oedipal wishes can be given expression through "impregnating" doctors, or idealized anonymous donors, with few restraining reality principles.

Miracles abound in daily life. Fertilization outside the body is taken for granted, as are transplantation of long-stored, deep-frozen embryos. Identical twins may be born years apart. Multiple broods hitherto unknown to humankind occur as a side effect of fertility drug stimulation, often necessitating selective "reduction". Worries arise about long term consequences of these decisions—what, for instance, might be the emotional effects of arbitrary or discriminating selective abortion (due to anomalies or excess) on the remaining twin/triplet/quadruplet and on the ongoing maternal relationship with the survivor? How does a parent process an act so redolent with archaic omnipotence, conjuring up infantile fantasy of retributive attacks on the maternal womb and the primitive talion of sibling rivalry? Controversial cases, such as a pregnant woman's press-sponsored retention of all her doomed octuplets, or an expectant mother's decision to abort one healthy twin, similarly fire the public imagination, re-igniting nursery emotions. Family romance narratives are revitalized by the mysterious origins of donated gametes or embryos. Finally, infertility re-evokes childish humiliation for those unable to reproduce without intervention of a powerful authority, the fertility expert who knows how impregnating is done.

What are the psychic repercussions of these mind-boggling fantasies that are actualized daily? One way of evading their emotional impact is to rationalize the body as a machine which can always go into the "repair shop" to be fixed or adapted. Infertility is merely another defect when immutables such as sex, ageing, and death can be challenged at will by organ transplants, pace-makers, life-prolonging machinery and even whole-body cryo-preservation. An illusion is sustained that time itself can be physically controlled or even reversed. Wrinkles are erased, hair is dyed, and features restructured to match unconscious self-representations and erotic fantasies. The idea of health is promoted as a function of corrective additives or riddance—"detoxification" of noxious waste of hectic life-styles with "work-outs" to work off harmful excesses of food, drink, and drugs. Imperfections are altered by cosmetic illusions, botox, or nip and tuck surgery. Body-building and hair transplants can enhance masculine identity. A super-feminine body image is acquired by extending or contracting corporeal boundaries with breast implants or liposuction. Anatomical sex itself may now be changed with biochemical interventions and surgical advances. Paradoxically, all these innovations merely illustrate Freud's nineteenth-century understanding that, although irreducibly biological, the body is a psychosocial construction; a cocoon spun of intrapsychic desires, unconscious representations, and culturally generated symbols and illusions.

Reproduction in the twenty-first century

In our late modern society, there are seemingly no limitations. Postmenopausal women give birth. Generations blur as mothers act as surrogates to gestate their own grandchildren. Lesbian partners exchange their eggs. With *in vitro* fertilization (IVF) gay partners can simultaneously impregnate the same woman with their respective semen, creating bi-fathered twin offspring. The twenty-first century has seen the human genome fully mapped, human embryos cloned, and goat kids fostered in artificial wombs. Our lifespan has increased dramatically, and ageing processes are chemically slowed down. Stem-cell technology enables celibate men, dead people, and gay couples to "conceive". Paradoxically, although procedures are unprecedented, the fantasies themselves are ancient.[1] Transgressions of the constraints of *sex, generation, genesis,* and *generativity* may be sought to disavow human limitations—a triumphal flaunting of Oedipal and generative laws by realizing fantasy in reality (Raphael-Leff, 2000a). Yet these omnipotent breakthroughs have unknown safety and ethical implications. For instance, the effects of a missing fifty million brides in India— due to twentieth century female foetocide aided and abetted by ultrasound and abortion. Worldwide, inequities of cost and access restrict fertility treatment to wealthier, more astute patients, while adoptions draw on "surplus" babies in low income societies. These may have inadvertent eugenic ramifications. And, ironically, expenditure on infertility in western countries vastly exceeds investment in third world population control, where 90% of the world's babies are born.

The mysteries of natural reproduction, too, are rudely exposed, and even the secret moment of conception has been captured by Technicolour fibre optic filming. What happens to fantasy when the enigmas of the womb, so intriguing to Leonardo Da Vinci 500 years ago, are now routinely revealed to every expectant parent in live-action ultrasound? How does this affect their relationship to an imaginary baby? Paradoxically, the foetus whose features become so endearingly familiarized by three-dimensional sonogram is also the foetus endangered—condemned to extermination by this self-same prenatal screening when faulty development is disclosed. Furthermore, invasive antenatal tests, such as amniocentesis, themselves carry a chance of miscarriage as well as a risk of misdiagnosing a healthy foetus as abnormal. Like "foetal reduction" in the case of multiple pregnancy, by destroying imperfect babies, the medical model's bid for perfection meets an archaic fantasy in the parents, embedded in unconscious ideas of infantile omnipotence and triumphalism.

Technology of conception and gestation

Infertility strikes indiscriminately, and even the most robust individual may be adversely affected by psychological issues relating to the trauma of diagnosis; the change in body image and intrapsychic, psychosexual, and social/occupational effects of being unable to reproduce unassisted; the emotional consequences of invasive, bizarre, and largely unsuccessful fertility treatments; anxieties about the viability of resultant offspring and/or grief over irreversible childlessness and genealogical extinction (for clinical examples see Raphael-Leff, 2000a).

A further paradox of the twenty-first century is that, despite its very low success rate (<25%), people undergoing fertility treatment are fully involved with the whole risky procedure of conception from its earliest stage, thereby increasing the impact of failure. The woman injects herself daily with growth-stimulating drugs and regularly observes the growth of her follicles on the ultrasound screen. After egg "harvesting", she is informed about fertilization of the eggs in the laboratory, then, after two chosen embryos are inserted, the woman or couple will wait fearfully for two weeks for reassurance of their implantation in the womb. As a consequence, even extremely early miscarriage is accompanied by a great sense of loss of the multi-celled embryo. These are already babies with whom the mother, and father too, if he is around, are intimately acquainted from "dot" (see case study, Raphael-Leff, 1992). When the foetus(es) do survive, parental anxiety about their normality, owing to their mode of conception, persists long after the birth.[2] Equally disturbing for a woman can be the discovery, through early ultrasound, that she is carrying twins, one of whom then "vanishes" in subsequent scans, as it is reabsorbed. Technology now reveals a hitherto unknown very high incidence of twin conceptions, affecting the parental relationship to the survivor, born into their fantasies that one baby used up all the resources, "ate" the other and/or has stayed alive at its expense.

Technology and pre-term viability:

On the other end of the scale, scientific advances may have unforeseen negative results. Ironically, some contraceptive devices have actually contributed to infertility. Similarly, X-rays and drugs administered during pregnancy have resulted in severe deformities. Paradoxically, viability of ever-younger pre-term babies, and survival through special intensive care procedures of newborns with hitherto morbid conditions, introduce new types of handicap. For a high percentage of premature infants life begins with a Caesarean section, followed by prolonged incubation of several weeks' or months' duration. One can only speculate on the long-term emotional effects on these of newborns. These tiny scraps of human life bond with a machine. Although encouraged to participate in their care, parents are often too alarmed by the scrawny, doll-sized, thin-skinned "alien" attached to tubes and wired to electronic monitors and bleeping machinery. The discrepancy between the real baby and cherubic representations in pregnancy, disconfirms the mother's capacity to create a good and viable infant. Parental guilt, helplessness in the face of their baby's horrific predicament, and self-protective withdrawal are apparent to observers (Cohen, 2003). Paradoxically, in developing countries where high-tech equipment and even electricity are scarce commodities, pre-term babies are often "kangarooed" in skin-to-skin contact between the mother's breasts, with good rates of survival. In fact, very low weight babies have better physiological outcomes and stabilization than the same care provided in closed servo-controlled incubators (Bergman, Linley, & Fawcus, 2003).

Ethics and medical care

Health providers are often unaware of the long-term risks involved, even when a procedure seems relatively risk-free. For instance, a recently published epidemiological study carried out over thirteen years by the National Research and Development Centre for Welfare and Health in Finland, found that childbirth was protective against death by accident, homicide, or suicide in the following year. But suicide rates were elevated among women who had an abortion in the previous year, and six times higher in the 15–24 age group, compared to new mothers or women who had miscarried in the previous year (Gissler, Berg, Bouvier-Colle, & Buekens, 2005). Similarly, although some subfertility is decidedly due to psychogenic factors related to unconscious desires and internalized prohibitions, the rising incidence of infertility in the West is attributable to external factors. These involve environmental pollution, sexually transmitted diseases, and, in some cases, contraceptive measures (such as the copper-7 intra-uterine device (IUD)) or prophylactic treatments. Iatrogenic factors lead to disillusionment with medical care and clinical authority. For instance, the drug DES, administered to over two million women between 1940 and 1970 to *improve* the outcome of pregnancy, resulted in structural defects, psychiatric and psycho-sexual problems, and infertility in their coveted offspring. Likewise, a drug used to curtail nausea in pregnancy led to the well-docu-mented Thalidomide tragedy.

Reproductive technologies raise new ethical dilemmas in medi-cine, such as whether to destroy 3,300 "orphaned" frozen human embryos in the UK, as they remained unclaimed when the arbitrar-ily allotted five-year storage period ran out. Ironically, they were ultimately disposed of despite thousands of infertile couples seeking embryo donation. Similarly, although some subfertility is decidedly due to psychogenic factors related to unconscious desires and inter-nalized prohibitions, the rising incidence of infertility in the West is attributable to external factors. These involve environmental pollu-tion, sexually transmitted diseases, and, in some cases, contraceptive measures (such as the copper-7 intra-uterine device (IUD)) or pro-phylactic treatments. Iatrogenic factors lead to disillusionment with medical care and clinical authority. For instance, the drug DES, administered to over two million women between 1940 and 1970 to *improve* the outcome of pregnancy, resulted in structural defects, psy-chiatric and psychosexual problems, and infertility in their coveted offspring. Likewise, a drug used to curtail nausea in pregnancy led to the well-documented Thalidomide tragedy.

Reproductive technologies raise new ethical dilemmas in medi-cine, such as whether to destroy 3,300 "orphaned" frozen human embryos in the UK, as they remained unclaimed when the arbitrar-ily allotted five-year storage period ran out. Ironically, they were ultimately disposed of despite thousands of infertile couples seeking embryo donation. Similarly, in disputes over proposed unilateral use of a "joint" creation, legal debates have centred on psychosocial and moral rights—whether a woman is entitled to be impregnated with her own frozen embryo if estranged from her partner. Or indeed, whether it may be implanted in the biological father's new partner, following death or divorce from the ovarian mother.

In the ensuing confusions and philosophical quandaries, public and legal debates attempt to rethink old concepts and to define some of the new parameters of childbearing in the twenty-first century:

• What constitutes a "parent'?

- grounds for parenthood—genetic, gestational, social-intentional and causal accounts
- primary identifications—who is the "real" parent?
- What are the moral preconditions for procreation—rights and responsibilities?
  - Is everyone entitled to reproduce?
  - Is it ethical to reduce the costs of fertility treatment if a woman donates some of her eggs to another infertile woman?
  - Can a woman carrying sextuplets be obliged to abort part of her brood for the sake of the rest? If so, how are they to be selected?
  - May a surrogate terminate her pregnancy?
  - Are economic grounds a sufficient reason for selective "reduction" of twins?
  - Should first-cousin couples be required to have genetic counselling and pre-implantation screening?
  Can a woman be compelled against her will to have a Caesarean to aid her baby?
- Questions also touch back to paternal status:
  - May a man forbid his partner to abort?
  - Are anonymous sperm donors entitled to information about their offspring?
  - Should known donors be allowed visiting rights and/or be held liable for financial maintenance?
  - What are the effects of donor registration containing identifying information for future use by offspring wishing to locate their biological parent/s?
- Finally, who is entitled/obligated to make these life and death decisions?

All these entail serious ethical and emotional considerations to which psychoanalytic thinking, like philosophy, must make a contribution (some issues are addressed in Raphael-Leff, 2002).

Twenty-first century pregnancy and motherhood orientations

For today's couples or individual parents, these past decades are exceptional in retaining so few childrearing traditions, owing to geographical mobility, dispersal of extended families, and plurality of media presentations. The upshot is that in the absence of prescribed parenting practices, each mother is free to pursue her own orientation to mothering rather than following the set ways of her mother and grandmother. In fact, her own orientation may even change with subsequent pregnancies as her internal representations and external circumstances alter. The same applies to fathers. I suggest that it is useful to delineate these orientations, since the downside is that postnatal disturbances vary in accordance with discrepancies between these particular intrapsychic expectations and illusions during pregnancy and obstacles to their materialization (Raphael-Leff, 1986, 1997; Sharp & Bramwell, 2004). These orientations were delineated through findings from several sources—clinical work over the past thirty years in a psychoanalytic practice devoted to issues of reproduction. Ongoing thrice weekly observations of twenty-three mother–infant pairs in a large community centre play-group setting and qualitative research in small scale studies of expectant parents through the child's first years, with eighteen month intervals between consecutive samples. These findings have since been replicated in large scale longitudinal and prospective studies in different countries (Scher, 2001; Scher & Blumberg, 1992, 2000; Sharp, 1995; Sharp & Bramwell, 2004). Finally, cross-cultural confirmation and variations have also come from consultative work with numerous perinatal projects/workshops with over a thousand primary health workers (midwives, health visitors, community nurses, etc.) on six continents over the past three decades.

The first orientation is that of the *Facilitator*—a woman for whom mothering seems the culmination of her female identity. She relishes the "communion" with her baby during pregnancy and hopes for an unaided natural birth. In her view, she, the biological mother is uniquely privileged, primed by processes of gestation and breastfeeding to intuitively decipher and meet her perfect baby's needs. Her wish to maintain a representation of herself as the secure bountiful source necessitates her exclusive care. (If the baby was formed by egg donation, she may prolong breastfeeding as her special connection.) She adapts her life to mothering the infant (unconsciously identified with her ideal baby-self), seeking close proximity at all times, so as to be ready to receive and interpret his/her communications, thus maintaining an illusion of symbiotic merger, unconditionally gratifying his desires and, by association, vicariously gratifying her own.

This orientation is at variance with that of a *Regulator*, where a woman treats pregnancy as an uncomfortable means to getting a baby, preferably by Caesarean section. Mothering is regarded as one role among many in her life. Rather than adapting to her baby like the Facilitator, she regards her main maternal task as "socializing" the pre-social (asocial or antisocial) infant, and therefore getting him or her to adapt to the household/social order. To this end she establishes a predictable routine that also enables her to share care-giving smoothly. Believing that the young baby does not differentiate between carers, she introduces her co-helpers early, hoping to expose her child to a range of relationships rather than one overweening one. Shared care is possible since, in her view, mothering is a skill rather than a "vocation". It also reduces the mother's continuous exposure to the infant's primitive feelings, decreasing risk of contagious arousal, depletion, and the burden of sole accountability. In her view, the routine provides security, contributing to predictability in a potentially chaotic and disturbing situation. It relieves the mother from the threat of recognizing in the baby representations of her own repudiated baby-self and infantile needs.

A third orientation is that of a *Reciprocator*. Rather than either mother or baby habitually adapting to the other, each incident is negotiated on its own terms within a situation that is regarded as mutually constructed. This complex pattern is rooted in the maturity of recognizing the baby as a little person, similar in having human emotions yet different in being an infant. For a mother who has processed and integrated infantile aspects of her own experience, interaction is based on empathy and reciprocal exchange rather than enacted or denied primary identification. Inevitably, this also involves tolerance of uncertainty and acceptance of multivariate motives and healthy ambivalence in both carer and baby (rather than denying her hatred like the Facilitator, or fearing falling in love, like the Regulator). A fourth response is a "conflicted" one, where contradictory orientations vie with each other in the same carer towards the same baby. These may be unconscious reflections of differences between internalized parents, intrapsychic tensions between stereotypical representations of "feminine" and

"masculine" facets of herself, or more conscious ideological discrepancies, for instance between feminism and child-care ideals.

Disturbances in twenty-first century mothering

Finally, from unconscious representations underpinning practical
solutions to mothering, we come to an age-old topic. Increasingly,
civilization imposes sanitized control over physical and emotional
outpourings. However, all new mothers are confronted not only by
a baby, but one accompanied by primal substances. In hospital
births, some of these, like amniotic fluid, vernix, and blood, may be
cleaned away before the first encounter. However, a primary carer
cannot avoid close contact with urine, faeces, posset, and secretions
oozing out of the baby's eyes, nose, ears, and navel; the parturient
herself leaks colostrum, milk, and lochia from her own orifices. I
suggest that, coupled with exposure to the infant's primitive
emotions and her own hormonal fluctuations, the smell and feel of
these primal substances is extremely evocative, reactivating archaic
procedural memories from the mother's own infancy. For each
unprotected new mother, *contagious arousal*, as I've termed it, retrig-
gers unprocessessed preverbal feelings of being mothered and
unmothered—unconscious co-products of her own baby-self seen
through the eyes of idealized or denigrated care-giving imagos.
These internalized representations permeate her relationship to the
new baby, upon whom she projects her feelings. The extent to
which she can treat him or her as "new" rather than a replica of her
own past depends on the degree to which she has integrated or
disavowed early emotional processes.

I argue that, in the twenty-first century, reactivation of the new
parent's procedural experiences is heightened. Small nuclear families provide few opportunities someone to actively process these
unvoiced infantile feelings in the presence of successive siblings,
cousins, and other new babies before being given full responsibility
for her own newborn. Lack of support in motherhood from people
who have known her throughout her life exacerbates a mother's
sense of loneliness, regression, and identificatory confusion. While
some mothers are moved to empathize with the baby, others
become overwhelmed by passionate identification with the infant's

predicament or defensively repudiate any similarities with the baby. It is no wonder that postnatal disturbances are so prevalent— over 50% of western mothers (and at least a quarter of fathers) experience emotional distress during the early months, and another 12–22% mothers suffer severe disorders diagnosed by health carers. When coupled with childhood adversity and/or lack of emotional support from a partner or confidante, vulnerability is increased (Brown, Harris, & Hepworth, 1995). Current life events and economic problems raise the likelihood of distress even further.[3]

Disorders of early motherhood in the twenty-first century

In today's social climate, where for each parent individual preferences predominate over prescribed childcare patterns, and where little guidance and support are available, early motherhood is affected by subjective discoveries, personal disillusionments and emotional losses. Postnatal disturbances include not only *depressive* reactions (with guilt, anxiety, pervasive low mood, and sense of worthlessness) but also the much overlooked *persecutory* ones, including paranoia, phobias, and anxiety, or obsessionality and breakthrough of compulsive thoughts, or violent action and sexual abuse. These often manifest in infant disorders of sleep, feeding, persistent crying, behavioural disturbances both reflecting and contributing to family symptomatology. In extreme forms the former leads to suicide, whereas the latter may end in infanticide.

Western women have been schooled to expect equal career opportunities. Postnatal distress is rife as many a contemporary Facilitator feels depressed and anxious about separating from her baby to return to work, or guilt-ridden over jettisoning her work prospects to "indulge" her need to be a full-time mother to her needy baby (identified with her own baby-self). Some succumb to over-involvement with the baby, or experience high anxiety about separation. Others accuse themselves of failing to provide the perfect infancy, unconsciously fearing the effects of their own repressed hostility.

When her routine or self-control fails, a Regulator mother may fall prey to persecutory feelings of competition with, or envy of, her baby. If she is unable to distance herself by engaging in adult occupations, disturbance manifests in feeling cheated of her career, trapped and restricted by motherhood, and confined with a demanding, greedy, exploitative baby (unconsciously identified with repudiated aspects of herself). In the turmoil of early motherhood, both types of mothers feel unable to work through or to defend against these regressive forces.

I suggest that the pattern of each mother's postpartum distress reflects internal or external obstacles to her attaining her ideological orientation of care-giving (as defined by her own expectations during pregnancy designed to meet unconscious representations of the baby/her baby-self). Some mothers are also threatened by a compulsion to re-enact in the new family unconscious intergenerational effects of emotional deprivation, childhood abuse, and psychosocial adversity. Where there is a couple, enjoyment of parenting is determined by the quality of their relationship and the degree to which their respective orientations dovetail. For first time parents, the shift from dyad to triangle recapitulates the Oedipal situation. Depending on how this was originally resolved and how generative identity has been constituted, joint parenting takes on a variety of forms according to re-activated early experiences, unconscious identifications, and gender depictions (Raphael-Leff, 2005; and clinical example, 2000b).

Conclusions

In urbanized, post-industrial, twenty-first century societies, elastic cultural expectations and changing social attitudes towards sexuality and intimate relationships foster many forms of family formation, ranging through traditional, single-parent, extended, composite/"blended" and same-sex families, with diverse child-rearing practices and "para"-parenting arrangements. Within these, each partner also has an individual orientation towards pregnancy and parenting that may coincide or clash. Technologically assisted reproduction raises the stakes, rendering some babies especially precious. Isolation of the small nuclear family leads to unusually intense dyadic relationships with high and often unrealistic expectations of partner and infant, as modern life does not prepare people for parenting. Contact with primal substances and uncontrolled primitive emotions of the newborn may feel overwhelming, rendering a new parent vulnerable to reactivation of unconscious infantile feelings at the very time of greatest demand for adult capacities. This turmoil will be internalized by the baby, to be revitalized when he or she becomes a parent in his/her own right.

Luckily, the late nineteenth and early twentieth century evolved a "talking cure" that still holds true in the twenty-first century. When unresolved issues from the past threaten to break through in parenthood to be re-enacted with the next generation, psychoanalytic psychotherapy can interrupt the cycle of mindless repetition, uncovering sources of internal tensions and externalized components. Through recall and verbal processing in therapy, early conflicts and implicit emotional trauma come to be transformed into explicit memories that can then be thought about rather than enacted (detailed clinical example, Raphael-Leff, 2000b). In particular, perinatal psychotherapy alleviates distress during fertility treatments, pregnancy, and parenting, preventing establishment of pathological interactions with the new baby. The timing of therapeutic intervention—preconceptually, antenatally, and/or after the birth—is determined by the nature of the disturbance. Similarly, a choice between parent–infant therapy, family, couple, individual, or group therapy depends on circumstances and location of pathology in the family, and the course therapy takes—crisis-orientated, brief or ongoing long-term psychodynamic psychotherapy—is decided according to the transitional or chronic nature of the distress and fixity of the underpinning representations. Therapy thus offers an opportunity to work through some of the difficult issues of becoming a mother in the twenty-first century. By processing maternal desires, disillusionment, and the effect of their emotional disturbance on their own children, perinatal psychotherapy thereby contributes to the mental health of future generations.

Notes

1   Even the recent posthumous insemination granted by the European court to a widow bidding for impregnation with sperm mechanically removed from her comatose husband recreates a scenario last depicted four thousand years ago, when the legendary Egyptian queen Isis

conceived Horus by her dead husband/brother Osiris (Raphael-Leff, 1990).

2. Yet one study has shown that IVF mothers pay extra attention to their infants, who are found to be more playful in face-to-face communication, with seemingly no ill-effects of assisted reproduction (Papaligoura & Trevarthen, 2001).

3. For instance, the prevalence of postnatal depression in Khayelitsha, a township near Cape Town, is 34.7% (Cooper et al., 1999), almost triple that among the white middle-class population.

CHAPTER FOURTEEN

Parenthood and HIV/AIDS. An investigation of the INPer based on psychoanalytic and gender theory[1]

Teresa Lartigue

" . . . [C]hildren who are received in a harsh and disagreeable way die easily and willingly. Either they use one of the many proffered organic possibilities for a quick exit, or if they escape this fate, they keep a streak of pessimism and of aversion to life."

(Ferenczi, 1929, p. 127)

Introduction

T he global epidemic of HIV/AIDS has caused the death of some 21.8 million persons, of whom 17.5 million were adults (9 million of them women) and 4.3 million children. A cumulative total of 13.2 million minors throughout the world have been orphaned by AIDS, of whom 10 million are in Latin America (Magis, Bravo, & Rivera, 2000). UNICEF estimates that there are 100,000 infected persons in Mexico. An idea of the importance of this epidemic can be conveyed by the fact that for every minute that passes, ten persons are infected by the human immunodeficiency virus.

Of a sample of 392 pregnant women,[2] forty formed the group labelled "HIV/AIDS" since either they or their partner were infected with HIV. In our study, using the Life Histories Method (Martinez, 1996),[3] we were able to look into the representational life of these patients.

To record the testimony of women in order to be able to report on and narrate their history has become an increasingly strong tendency in recent decades, thanks to a combination of factors. In the first place, the rediscovery in the nineteenth century that the family is the basic unit of society, which makes it the central nucleus of a historical anthropology placing kinship and sexuality structures, and consequently the feminine dimension, in the foreground. Second, because history and documents concerning women are an integral part of the de-colonization movement in the Western world, ideas that were taken up again during the 1968 student movement, encouraging political reflection on exiles, minorities, silenced and oppressed cultures, with particular emphasis on the analysis of their relations with power structures. A third factor was the feminist movement, whose will to know has allowed the formulation of questions and theories in which decisive weight has been placed on the relationships between the sexes in diverse events and in the development of Society (Duby & Perrot, 1990).

After a detailed review of the life histories, testimonies, and narrations of these women,[4] time and again I found a common denominator in all: severe failures in the maternal and paternal functions, internalized in the psyche as traumatic events. These deficiencies could involve the death, abandonment, or separation of the parents, as well as the visible presence of domestic violence—in some cases going almost as far as filicide—and invisible gender violence. It is important to remember that the power structure in the family system implies domination, supported by diverse means such as coercion, punishment, abuse, or ill-treatment—this is the visible violence—or by submissive behaviour incorporated into family life as a "natural" way of organizing daily life; the protagonists are unaware of this, or if they are aware of it, consent to it, since it is "the natural thing to do": this is invisible violence (Berezin de Guiter, 2000). The visible, explicit violence can culminate in death or in different physical and mental disorders;[5] however, invisible violence is inherent to the constitution of families, implicit in the roles assigned to women and to men, as a function of "naturalistic" conceptions of their gender condition. It is also legitimized by society in its sex/gender structure, in which childcare and upbringing systems have their roots, as well as the methods for applying discipline in the home. "The invisible is not hidden, but disavowed, forbidden from being visible" (*ibid.*, p. 302).

My countertransference reactions were intense, tinged with feelings of indignation, anger, worry, and uncertainty; they oscillated at times between fantasies of salvation and of denial, rejection and paralysis. Sheer helplessness predominated when I realized how dramatic, how sinister the deadly repetition compulsion was over three or four generations, within the shadow of the dead.

To make explicit, report on and explain what happened in the childhood of these women infected with HIV is the aim of this paper; it is a first step towards the de-legitimization of this visible and invisible violence, which their parents before them had also suffered. It is also an invitation to think about what we can do to break the conspiracy of silence, of not writing about this illness, which has already come into psychoanalytic consulting rooms,[6] and is part of the real Mexico, the heart of Mexico with its 54 million inhabitants living in conditions of poverty and marginalization, where the women of the poorest countries pay the highest price to AIDS (Urrutia, 1994).

Parenthood

Freud opened the door to the study of this line of development (Lartigue, 1991, 1996) with "Totem and taboo" (1912–1913), which analyses the principles of unconscious functioning that underlie parenthood as a psychic structure. Parenthood, like culture, is seen as a foundational organization in each individual and every social group, internalized in a manner concomitant with its context and genealogy. Devereux (1965) maintains that the unconscious contains no concept of parenthood. I agree entirely with Leticia Solís (2002) who considers that parenthood is constructed in the intrapsychic apparatus as a product of intersubjectivity and transgenerational transmission. From this perspective, parenthood can be seen as a system of mental categories that include that of age and difference between generations (mother–daughter, father–son, parents–children), in addition to the category of sex and gender difference. This model introduces the notions of asymmetry, heterogeneity within complexity, as well as the elements that organize the relationships between parents and children. These principles are internalized by the members of the family group, forming a system of references that organize mental representations of the world and the self (Solís, 2002).

Thus, parenthood structures the parents' thinking about themselves and their baby; it also organizes the parents' and children's thoughts about the differentiating attributions and obligations of men and women, which make it clear and obvious that being a girl is not the same as being a boy. The mother cathects her baby before she can perceive him or her. Lebovici (1983) differentiates four types of baby before birth: the imaginary, the fantasy, the narcissistic, and the cultural or mythical baby. These multiple representations alternate with interactions with the real baby after birth, and contribute to the imaginary and fantasy dimensions of emotional communication between mother and baby. They involve the expression of the mother's unconscious conflicts and can generate misunderstandings, disharmony, or conflict in the relationship with the infant, who can become the depository or reservoir of her projections and conflicts. It is important to remember that the construction of the infant's representational world depends largely on the representations that the mother made of him or her as an imaginary baby. Further, this relationship is bidirectional, the baby constructing and "parentalizing" the parents while constructing him- or herself (*ibid.*).

According to Solís (2002), the parental ego is constructed in successive stages, on basis of four sources. The first is the ego ideal, based on primary narcissism and initial identifications with the subject's own parents—the infant's grandparents. The second is pre-oedipal relationships with their constitutional determinants, such as: the baby's condition of incompleteness, defencelessness, and dependency on another fellow human being for survival. The third is the superego, heir of the Oedipus complex, and the fourth, the *a posteriori* factors, by which I mean psychic temporality, not in terms of linear causality but in response to a deferred re-interpretation of traumatic events, as well as of libidinal or psychosexual development.

Recognizing the elements of the psychic legacy allows the individual to leave behind a passive situation and take an active position that consists in transforming the demands of the superego, a process that secondarily involves filiation to a line of behaviour, seen from a distance through the constructive creation of a condensed version of the subject's own history, which apprehends the function of infantile sexuality as it develops. Recognition of the perverse polymorphic sexuality of childhood becomes acceptance of the human condition, and also establishes the possibility of identification with the baby (Solís, 2002). Also, acknowledging the destructive potential, the internal force that operates silently in the id, or in an obvious way in external violence, allows us to protect our sons and daughters from the sadistic and Thanatic impulses that inhabit us. Benjamin (1998) stresses that our theory of the Unconscious teaches us that we cannot avoid identifying with our primary love objects, our progenitors; the defence mechanisms of splitting, foreclosure (*forclusion*) and displacement create a dangerous kind of complementarity, of non-concordance. Psychoanalysis and gender studies agree that the best option for becoming a subject capable of love, sexual ecstasy, and creativity is the development of identifications that allow us to readmit what had been rejected, in a self-reflective process during the analytic experience. Freud's journey through transference is a magnificent allegory of the process of learning about how surprising and yet familiar complementary relationships are (*ibid.*).

This brief synthesis makes it obvious that becoming a father or mother involves a whole series of experiences that begin in early infancy and depend on desire and unconscious fantasies, as well as on personality organization. The requirements are enormous, since mothers and fathers are expected to master capacities similar to those required to be psychoanalysts; or we could say that psychoanalysts are expected to have the same profile as "good enough" parental figures. We could ask, as Florinda Riquer (1996) does, whether mothers and fathers know these models, wish to follow them, or have sufficient capacity to do so, since a great number of women experience motherhood as a matter of fate, an imposition, or the unfortunate price to pay for sexual pleasure.

Preliminary findings

In this sample of thirty women interviewed during pregnancy and/or postpartum,[7] twenty-seven of whom were infected with the human immunodeficiency virus, it was confirmed that the principal manner of transmission is through sexual intercourse: 92.59% (twenty-five) were infected in this way. This group also confirmed the fact that women are more vulnerable to this type of infection (only 10% of the sample was not infected when the husband was), since propagation of the virus from man to woman is easier than the reverse, in a proportion of two to one. A tragic and distressing fact is that nearly half, 48% (12/25), of the patients were infected by their first sexual partner; in six of these cases, indeed, the virus was transmitted by their only sexual partner, the women concerned being in a monogamous relationship. Seven were infected by their second partner (all the partners died), and two others by the third. It is noteworthy that in two cases there was a clear prior intention to transmit the virus.

It seems that, for this group, it was impossible to have safe or protected sex, so that intercourse was followed by unplanned gestations in 50% of the patients, who became pregnant between thirteen and eighteen years of age. This obviously complicated the outcome of their adolescent process and transition to adulthood, also threatened by the diagnosis of HIV-positive. AIDS thus becomes doubly significant: in transforming the erogenous body into a suffering one, and in causing mental pain, given the possibility of the subject's dying within ten or twenty years, in the "prime of life". The patients, besides suffering rejection and stigmatization by family and friends, also experience great distress when they see their partner die. At the time of writing, fourteen men have died, three of them without ever having seen their son or daughter.

In the case of four patients with more than three sexual partners without protection, it is worth mentioning that one was a "street urchin", with a history of neglect, lack of care, and abandonment by her mother, together with physical and emotional abuse by her father and step-mother; this caused her to run away from home with her younger sister. Another case, a mentally handicapped woman who all too easily becomes infatuated, worked in a night club where she drank alcohol and "earned easy money"; unable to take proper care of herself, she could prevent neither HIV infection and other venereal diseases nor several unplanned pregnancies.

Transmission via contact with infected blood occurred in two women, one linked to an occupational hazard, since she worked in a chemical laboratory without wearing gloves. This woman, like the person I have just mentioned, came from a family living in conditions of extreme poverty. The second case shows a clear homicidal attitude towards a young woman who, when she entered high school, came into contact with adolescents "who were angrier" than she, and noticed that they seemed happy while under the influence of drugs. Her way of putting it was: "I wanted to feel happy even if it was only a sham", and so she began to use marijuana, solvent thinner, glue, cocaine, whatever she could get. Once, when she was sharing a needle and syringe with a former schoolmate, he quite deliberately drew his own blood into the syringe, mixed it with the cocaine and gave it to her.

The three other women were included in the study, although they were not infected, since their partners were, and they were referred to the INPer in order to prevent possible infection and vertical transmission of HIV. In the three cases, the men were infected via blood, one as a consequence of a transfusion; in the other two cases, the infection was transmitted to them as adolescents as a result of intravenous drug abuse.[8]

Why did most of the patients get involved with men who, from the very first date, showed clear signs of personality disorders, mainly of the antisocial or borderline type, some of them already in trouble with the law? Why did others begin a relationship with partners much older than they, married or divorced men, with age differences of at least fifteen years and a history of multiple sexual partners? Why didn't they develop self-care behaviour? What happened to the self-preservation instincts of Freud's first drive theory? Why did the death drive increase or prevail over Eros? I should like to suggest some hypotheses in this regard in order to explain these findings.

The thesis I wish to propose hinges on the fact that the psychic subject is constituted through intersubjectivity, in the interplay of drives, identifications, and representations with one another. In this particular group, the primary object of love, identification, and attachment—the biological parents or substitute figures—were unable to establish good enough relationships of object love and recognition for their daughters to achieve the internalization of a representational system of care and appreciation of themselves (possibly due to a complex set of socio-economic, cultural, and transgenerational factors). They were also unable to awaken the processes of thought, symbolization, and mentalization that would have allowed their offspring to overcome adversity. On the contrary, these relationships were characterized by violence, sadism bordering sometimes on filicide, or the abrupt loss of the mother and/or father during childhood or adolescence, or again of a particularly significant brother or sister (Lartigue, 2004).

The mechanisms of identification with the aggressor and the sum of accumulated traumata are clearly evident in these patients, with disavowal of the affects associated with these traumatic experiences, so that in adolescence they do to themselves actively what before they suffered passively. Three types of life style can be evidenced here: in the first, some patients took refuge in alcohol and drugs, acting on Thanatic impulses (in seven cases, the father had a severe problem of alcoholism, in two the mother, and in another, mother, grandparents, and uncles). The second type is that of those patients who had relationships with men who were characterized by this type of addictive pathology and/or an antisocial or borderline disorder; this was the first alarm signal of what would come later. The third type is associated with the structuring of a depressive-masochistic personality disorder, with consequent impoverishment of the ego and loss of interest in living. The deadly repetition compulsion can already be seen in some of the new families, with manifestations of violence that are beginning to be inflicted on the next generation.

Traumatic loss

Since the pioneering work of Spitz (1946), we know the consequences that loss of a parent in infancy may entail; the deprivation of parental figures leaves an indelible mark. The anaclitic depression he observed in the 1940s is still the model that best explains infantile depression, as are Bowlby's (1980) hypotheses on the phases children go through when they are separated from their parents, sometimes with severe blockages in different areas of psychological development: psychomotor, cognitive, emotional, and social. Can these losses be worked through and made meaningful? This is a question that I cannot yet answer.[9]

Viviana, one of the patients whose mother died when she was one year old, was adopted by her older sister; this was a source of considerable confusion for her, since she thought that her sister was her mother and her father her grandfather. Regina's father was "beaten to death for going around drunk" (the patient's own words) when she was fifteen months old. She also "lost" her mother, in the sense that she was left in the care of her maternal grandmother until she was fourteen, because her mother remarried.

The father of another patient separated from her mother when she was three months pregnant with the patient. Bertha met him when she was six years old, when her mother started a new relationship, only to lose him again when she was thirteen; he was murdered in a hold-up in his home town. Two more patients lost their fathers in adolescence, one at fifteen and the other at eighteen.

Abandonment by the father in infancy occurred in six cases (in two cases, when the mother was pregnant with the patient, another when the child was one, another at three, another at five and the last at six); the reasons were quite similar: irresponsibility, lack of commitment, extramarital relationships, problems of alcoholism and/or drug abuse. Lorena told us with deep feeling about the pain and suffering she felt: "After my daddy left, when I was five years old, I began to get depressed, I got sick a lot at that time with flu, vomiting, and fever". Elizabeth lost both parents when she was five, when they gave her away to a maternal cousin.

The parents were separated or divorced in three cases (in Federica's case, the parents separated several times but got together again). In the first of these, when the patient was four and her father attempted to abuse her sexually, her mother decided to separate (the father died of substance abuse when his daughter was fifteen).

In the second case, separation occurred when the patient was four. Adriana said: "Now that I'm older, I think about it and wonder why he wasn't with me, I have a bad image of him, he helped us financially, but not constantly, he had a lot to give us and didn't give us anything." In the third case, the parents divorced when Sonia was fourteen. She said that the relationship between her parents was "strange"; her father was usually in his mother's house, "he was not very affectionate, he was very jealous and had a problem with alcohol"; when her parents quarrelled, her father would leave the house for several days, which made her "feel very bad".

The problem of abandonment by, or separation of, the parents involves an additional loss, since the mother needs to work outside the home to support herself and her children. Feelings of discontent, emptiness, and loneliness are narrated by three patients. Regina (the girl whose father was murdered) didn't see her mother because she was working, feels she needed her very much, since she couldn't go to her school or take care of her when she was ill; she saw her only at weekends, when she was washing and ironing with no time for the children. Since her mother's affection was always scarce, Regina feels that she tried to attract attention in order to get her affection; this is why "I was naughty and *wanted to be ill to get more attention*". It is noteworthy that since her HIV-positive diagnosis, Regina and her mother have been able to communicate better about the reasons why she didn't take care of the little ones; she points out that "this attention is arriving late, but finally she's giving it" (it was her own sentence of death that enabled Regina to get her mother's close attention — a very high price to pay).

Gloria's parents worked constantly to support the family, so that she was left to take care of her older brothers; her father even worked at weekends, so she didn't have much of a relationship with him, since he was always absent; she described him as having old-fashioned ideas. Katia's father was described as an affectionate man, dedicated to her when she was small, but during her adolescence he worked all day long, so he didn't live with his children; it seems her mother had an obsessional neurosis ("the only thing she doesn't wash is soap, because you can't").

Added to the losses are problems connected with the new relationships of both parents, in some cases with the birth of half siblings; this generates conflicts in the reconstituted families. In six cases, the patients had other siblings, one of them seventeen by her father, and another, eight siblings from her mother's four relationships. The former case increased the rivalry and jealousy present in all siblings, the so-called fraternal complex, with discrimination, favouritism, aggressions, insults and rejection; in five cases, the mother or paternal grandmothers clearly preferred a sister, further intensifying sibling conflict and resentment.[10]

Visible and invisible violence (psychic traumata)

All patients had experienced some form of domestic violence and child abuse; these traumatic events (or adverse experiences in childhood) were perpetrated by the father and/or mother, or by other family members. These traumata, aside from generating defence mechanisms such as splitting or dissociation, blockage of mentalization processes and of the central nervous system (Fonagy, Gergely, Jurist, & Target, 2002), placate the sadism that is turned against the subject's own ego.

The fact that 35% of the mothers of these patients had been cruelly beaten, pushed around, burned and/or stabbed by their partners is more evidence of the violence that women experienced every day.[11] It is noteworthy that in some cases the beatings occurred even when the mother was pregnant; in others, it moved the neighbours to call for police intervention.[12] Hernán Solís (1999) reminds us of the interplay of power, domination, and terror that characterizes choleric couples: hate predates love, and the escalation of violence is unspeakable. Also, witnessing marital violence is as harmful for the psychic apparatus as direct abuse. The feelings of impotence, desperation, anger, hate, and guilt disorganize the ego, which is unable to defend itself, while the pain caused by the chaos of "maddened drives" (Nasio, 1996) encourages excessive or pathological use of projective identification.

Margarita saw how her father abused her mother, one occasion in particular remaining engraved in her mind—when he threw a pan of boiling water on her mother while she was cooking; her burned foot had such severe gangrene that it had to be amputated. She and her brothers were very frightened when this happened, and when the three eldest grew older, they would either retaliate and hit the father back or try to stop him; however, he would always get the better of them and beat them up. The biggest problem, according to the patient, was that her mother always caved in and went to get her father, who welcomed her with another beating, dragged her around, and even tried to hang her.

In these case histories, it must be emphasized that only one of the mothers of these women hit her husband, in a perverse pact of abuse of the daughters, in which the father violated the law of incest.

The situation is equally sinister for girls abandoned by their fathers in childhood, whose mothers find another partner and "choose a substitute father"[13] who takes the cruelty further. This is not only physical and verbal abuse, but sexual abuse and harassment, with a clear and evident observation of pathological behaviour, which adds yet another component to their disillusionment. In two cases, the mothers would not believe that their daughters had been abused, which is experienced as a way of "driving the other person crazy"; complicity in the perverse pact is overwhelming. A total of seven patients were subjected to sexual abuse, two of them by their fathers (one mentioned above), another two by their stepfather, two more by a stepbrother, and in the last case, anal rape by a neighbour.

As for the physical abuse of the children, it is perpetrated by the father in seven cases; he is described as "the typical macho", a violent and impulsive beater who ill-treats his wife and children, sometimes brutally, which makes them victims of double abuse— the actual abuse they receive personally, as well as witnessing the physical, verbal, and psychological abuse of their mother. In one case, it seems that the father's aggression and anger was directed only against the children.

In six families, it was the mother who cruelly beat her daughters and sons; in another, it was both parents. Other aggressors were a stepmother, a grandmother, the paternal uncles and the maternal uncles. A total of 65.38% (17/26) patients were objects of physical abuse. Other patients (five) were victims of verbal, emotional, or psychological abuse, three of them by their mother, and two by their stepfather. According to Vania, her stepfather was a person who damaged her emotionally very deeply, who took it out on her. Today, she cannot question anything at all, because he always said to her: "Never ask idiotic questions". At thirteen, when she began to rebel, her mother forced her to ask his forgiveness; she felt "very humiliated, very bad, felt like disappearing or killing him".

Another type of abuse is exploitation; seven patients began working when they were about eight years old, most of them as domestic servants either in the homes of relatives (grandparents or aunts), stepfathers or stepmothers, or strangers. They were forced to give up all the money they earned. Paulina, whose father also beat his mother when he drank, began working at age eight because of her family's financial problems. She described herself at that age as "shy, fearful, unsociable, afraid that the rain might destroy the house"; since she was so young, she was "afraid of earthquakes, fires, hold-ups, heights"; terrified of the night, her dreams were full of anxiety.

Discrimination, humiliation, and ill-treatment were suffered by five patients. In two cases this was explicitly the mother's doing, in another two the paternal grandparents were the perpetrators, and in the remaining case, the patient's aunt and cousins. Neglect, lack of care, and indifference were quite evident in five more cases. It is striking that physical abuse was the most prevalent (seventeen cases), followed by witnessing marital violence (nine cases), then by sexual abuse (seven), exploitation (seven), verbal abuse (five), discrimination (five) and neglect (five). In some cases, as is obvious, the patients experienced many types of abuse—accumulative traumata, the effects of which are more disorganizing for the psychic apparatus than a single form would have been.

This is a problem of transgenerational transmission. In some case-histories, we have data on the grandparents: Viviana told us that sometimes her father beat her mother in front of her father's family, "so they could see who wore the trousers", and he also disparaged her: "He treated her like an inferior". The paternal grandparents allowed and tolerated the father's violence. In the case of Bertha, casting doubt on the fact that she was their granddaughter, they ill-treated and humiliated her. Angelina's grandmother severely beat the patient's father because he wanted to go on with his studies; she was a single mother, so the father had to go out to work from a very early age, and he ran away from home in adolescence because he could no longer tolerate this situation. Francisca's maternal grandfather was characterized by his intolerance, rigidity, and perfectionism: "you had to do whatever he said", for which the patient's mother also ran away from home in adolescence. The cruelty of some fathers and mothers toward their children is unimaginable, and it is in these families that we encounter the highest number of deceased children.

To this we must add that this group of women, most of whom live in conditions of poverty or extreme poverty, suffers from the multi-deficiency syndrome: low level of education, therefore low level of occupation, with deficiencies of nutrition and stimulation. They have to struggle daily just in order to survive.

What is our responsibility as psychoanalysts?[14] What measures can we recommend or actions take with respect to such situations of social inequality? Can we, and do we want to, work in the field of primary prevention? It is a fact that men and women cannot take sufficient care of themselves to avoid infection by the human immunodeficiency virus if no other person has ever given them such care, love, and protection, which they might incorporate and internalize, in order to acquire this function through identification. To invent strategies for breaking up this intergenerational transmission of visible and invisible violence is one of our greatest challenges. In the meantime, as Bowlby (1951) and Alizade (2001) have said, we cannot leave the parents on their own!

Notes

1. An extended version may be found in Chapter Three of Alizade, M., & Lartigue, T. (Eds.) (2004). *Psicoanálisis y Relaciones de Género*. Buenos Aires: Editorial Lumen. The initial Investigation Project was carried out with the financial support of the Secretariat of Health, the National Council of Science and Technology, the National Institute of Perinatology, the Mexican Psychoanalytical Association, the Research Committee of the International Psychoanalytical Association and the UNAM Medical School, project No. MO252-9911 Conacyt; 212250-50021 INPoer; 01-10 and 011 APM (Lartigue et al., 2000a,b)

2. Who accepted freely and gave their informed consent to participation in the research, and who attended the National Institute of Perinatology (in Mexico City) for prenatal controls between April 2000 and June 2002.

3. Psychometric tests and structured clinical interviews were also used in the two phases of the investigation.

4. My deep gratitude to the patients for allowing me to enter their private life, and to the Research Fellows who were in charge of the diagnostic clinical study of each patient: Martha Pérez Calderón, Patricia Dávila and Antonio Mendizábal, and researcher Itzel

González. The life histories were done on the basis of transcriptions of in-depth interviews that were audio taped.

5. This problem was investigated at the international level by Loris Heise (1996, 1998).

6. Psychoanalytic articles on the AIDS epidemic are surprisingly few in number.

7. With ages ranging from seventeen to thirty-seven. Ten women from the initial sample refused to be interviewed; they are not included in these results. For more information on their medical care in the INPer, see Ortíz (2000).

8. If we consider all thirty cases, transmission was sexual in 83.33% and blood-related in 16.67%.

9. The analysis of the life histories up to the time of the interviews may enable us to draw a series of inferences in this sense.

10. Four patients had a substitute parental figure with capacity for reparation (a grandmother or an older sister).

11. For this reason, in our country legislation to curb domestic violence was indispensable; such a law was passed in 1998.

12. Fonagy (1999) differentiates two types of violent men: type I attacks impulsively at the slightest provocation, while type II carefully plans the attack.

13. In one case, the stepfather helped to rehabilitate the mother, who became an alcoholic when her husband left her; in another case, the stepmother "left them without food", which led to a sister's death.

14. The patients who accepted our proposal of therapeutic help were given it and in one case, the treatment continued for a year and included her partner. Leñero (2002, p. 80), referring to the psychotherapist's responsibility, asks: "How can we go beyond our professional specialization that intends to be ethical but draws back in the face of collective injustice and its real causal links? What is the role in the therapy of economic, political and bureaucratic conditions, corruption and social violence to correct the concrete, material influences on socio-family life, within the context of a given society? What is its ethical obligation, beyond the somewhat unilateral field of psychotherapeutic specialization (as in that of any professional specialization)?"

CHAPTER FIFTEEN

New methods of conception and the practice of psychoanalysis

Sylvie Faure-Pragier

W hat kind of influence does social change have on the mind-structure of women patients who are sterile and who have recourse to the various new techniques of medically-assisted procreation? With sperm donated by another man, it is now possible to have children even though the father is sterile (artificial insemination by donor). A woman born without ovaries or who is prematurely menopausal can overcome these difficulties by means of an oocyte donated by another woman. If the uterus has been surgically removed, she can ask for an embryo, engendered or not by her own gametes, to be implanted in another woman, the surrogate mother; indeed, in some countries (but not in France) surrogate mothers are remunerated and are listed, complete with photograph, in a catalogue! Confronted, as are my patients, with these new procedures that have a considerable impact on issues such as filiation (linear descent), I have observed certain changes in the way they interpret their infertility, as well as modifications in the representations and affects that lie at the heart of our psychoanalytic work. The influence of the *socius* on how the analytic couple functions cannot be ignored.

To summarize, my thoughts on these issues have developed along the following lines over three successive periods of time:

- consultations with women patients in a hospital setting;
- the realization that these one-off sessions were going nowhere, so that I decided to ask other psychoanalysts to collaborate in a research project that has given rise to some specific hypotheses;
- working with new patients who consulted me spontaneously after a book I wrote on this topic was published.

Modifications to my own approach thus correspond to the changed parameters that led these patients to consult me. There has been a shift from denial of the role the mind plays in infertility towards the acknowledgement of the patient's tendency to project aggressiveness on to her immediate circle and doctors, thus holding them responsible for her own sterility.

The hospital setting

I would like first of all to describe my initial experience in this field. In the 1980s, I was working in the context of a medical consultation in which other doctors requested the help of a psychoanalyst.

In this kind of consultation, I was able to catch a glimpse of what is at stake when sterility is a major issue. But these discoveries were limited by the desire to understand, which can lead the analyst (or the medical practitioner), in cases where what the patient says is not sufficiently meaningful in itself, to project on to her material one's own *a priori* conceptions.

In order to attenuate this unsatisfactory state of affairs, we set up "gynaeco-psycho" meetings in which, as colleagues, we could discuss and exchange our impressions; we learned a great deal from these exchanges, which furthered our understanding not only of the patients seen in consultation but also of the whole procedure that was being offered to them in an attempt to treat their sterility.

We were surprised to discover some striking similarities in what the different protagonists had to say. The medical practitioners recounted situations that were often tragic; we regretted the fact that there was no "narrative" of the session itself and of everything that usually structures the encounter between a psychoanalyst and the patient who comes for analysis.

To the question: "What brings you here?", the answer might be: "It's Dr X". In other words, it was as though something was wrong with Dr X and that it was he who needed help rather than the patient—who did not see how our talk could be of any use to her. In this kind of encounter, if the analyst remains silent, the session externalizes the patient's reservations. If the analyst wants to know a little more, the patient may find something of interest in the meeting—and will usually go on to talk of her quietly satisfactory life, often centred on denial and submissiveness with respect to parental models and, in the past, on tragic events (though any link between these and her current sterility is immediately rejected). The therapist is thus placed in a paradoxical situation. Reflection, action, supportiveness—what is at stake in these encounters?

Let us therefore take a closer look at the three actors on that particular stage.

In most cases, *the patient* (or perhaps the sterile couple) is in a counter-request situation. Referred to a psychoanalyst at the doctor's behest, patients often talk in platitudes in much the same way as prospective adopting couples do. "Everything is fine" as far as they are concerned; their main aim is to convince us that they are perfectly normal and that they will turn out to be "good" parents. Given the absence of any real desire to discuss matters with a psychoanalyst, nothing much will come out of such an encounter.

Occasionally, some pathological condition or other may be revealed in the course of this one-off discussion; here again, however, in spite of any theoretical interest this situation may have, it is only very rarely that the patient will derive any benefit from it. Any proposal as to therapy will hurt the patient's feelings; though she may acknowledge the fact that she is indeed in some difficulty, for her the solution is quite simple: once she has a baby, everything will be just fine. She has no desire to work through the conflict situation that underlies her desire for a child. Indeed, the wish to conceive at all costs expresses quite the opposite: repress any ambivalence by engaging in the irreversible act of procreation. Here the analyst is faced not so much with a refusal as with a counter-request: to maintain the denial that psychological considerations have any role to play, since anything to do with the psyche is experienced as disturbing.

If the encounter comes after a fairly lengthy series of medical interviews, etc., it may be experienced as persecutory. The patient blames the physician for not having cured her condition—and she experiences the referral to a psychoanalyst as an accusation against her mental functioning, aimed at clearing the doctor of all blame, as though he or she had said to the patient: "I'm not the one who is powerless or incompetent, you are the bad patient who, without even realizing the fact, does not want to have a baby!"

This rejection—which, when it does exist, is necessarily unconscious—is understood by the patient as a kind of "wild" interpretation, so that it in fact increases her resistance.

In some situations, it is intolerable to have to "admit" that the baby she has done everything possible to conceive is in fact not wanted. It is tantamount to saying that the patient does not desire what she is putting so much effort into obtaining; *she*, not some physical defect or other, is in fact saying "no" when she appears to be proclaiming a "yes". Or else it is the desire itself that is too powerful and runs counter to the objective: "It's because I want so much to be pregnant that it's not working."

Given that the request does not come from the patient, it must come from *the medical practitioner*, whose motives are often complex.

- The desire to understand the patient's distress better, to spare her from committing herself to a lengthy course of treatment which, if it fails, would only aggravate the feelings of castration that are so much a feature of this pathology.
- The desire to avert iatrogenic mental distress, in other words disorders caused by the treatment itself. Is the couple able to accept artificial insemination by donor (AID)? If the father has not come to terms with his sterility, will he tend to overcompensate by lavishing affection on the child? Will the mother be able to tolerate proving her fecundity by becoming pregnant while her partner feels castrated? The fear of inflicting such a wound may lie behind many AID failures, in cases, for example, where the physician proposes this treatment too hurriedly, in an attempt as it were to repair the sterility that he or she has just announced to the couple.

- The desire to have a better understanding of the messages issuing from the Unconscious: perhaps a phrase or two in what the patient said may explain everything? The gynaecologist may want to develop this understanding on a personal level, and as a result may be more attentive to what patients have to say and more aware of his or her own desire to repair sterility at all costs (or, on the contrary, to reject certain couples).
- Perhaps the wish to be helped in making an ethical decision as to indications for treatment.

And what of *the psychoanalyst* in all this? Especially a psychoanalyst who, like me, has undertaken this kind of work and has learned to identify certain patterns, but who realizes that any action must be restricted to an investigation that is difficult to conduct outside of classical psychoanalytic treatment. Psychoanalysis is, by definition, a theory derived from practical experience. When a patient evidences no wish for therapy, can any theoretical considerations be derived from what may be taking place? Absolutely not.

The second phase of my itinerary. Back to the actual practice of psychoanalysis

The reader will not be surprised to learn that, having reached this stage, I decided to leave hospital work behind me and focus on consultations, in private practice, with those sterile patients who, thanks to physicians who knew something of what was at stake, had evidenced the wish to discuss matters with a psychoanalyst. The *in-conceivable*, which is the psychological side of biological sterility and which I have tried to describe, carries with it a denial of the mind's role; this seems to be the main obstacle to undertaking psychotherapy with an analyst. Generally speaking, patients talk of their quietly satisfactory life, in the midst of which their sterility has brought scandalously unfair distress. In their past, some tragic elements may be revealed, but the link between these and procreation is too often refused. If they have no other problems in their life, patients just do not see what there is to talk about. I therefore had to modify my classically neutral analytic stance and adopt a much more active approach in proposing treatment.

I agreed to enter into the patients' defensive system and advised them to have a trial series of sessions. In my book *Les bébés de l'Inconscient. Le pychanalyste face aux stérilités féminines aujourd'hui* (Faure-Pragier 1997), I describe several therapies that began in this manner. They were all helpful, with some patients in fact giving up their idea of having a baby.

Curing sterility does not necessarily imply facilitating procreation. Some infertile women, once they become aware of their fear of the imaginary child on to whom all of their ambivalence is projected, decide not to become pregnant and succeed in renouncing the motherhood they had "wished-for". In this way, they avoid the organic failures or complications that may well have occurred if, without this personal growth and development, they had continued with the whole series of solutions that some medical units propose.

Other changes occur too. Just as with psychosomatic patients, the analyst has to adapt. A more active approach is often called for, so that patients may "tame" their thoughts and fantasies and allow them to develop. A space for playing opens up, with words and representations, thereby creating a transitional space in which it becomes possible to conceive, to let an unknown child emerge within the patient's self—not only the child that the patient herself is, but also the one that will thereafter be able to grow in the privacy of her body.

During this phase of individual practice, a new research modality began to take shape. I had often discussed my ideas with other psychoanalysts. Some had, on their couch as it were, patients who had initially consulted for other reasons, but who later proved to be sterile or had successive miscarriages. We decided to set up a workgroup. Its founding principle was at that each member should write down his or her observations on a clinical case that we would then study at a later date (so as to avoid being influenced by the work we would be doing on it). In this group, various hypotheses were put forward. I shall discuss simply the often controversial *wish for a child* in infertile women.

When the wished-for child takes a long time coming, is there always—behind the motherhood project and beyond the wish to have a child—the desire to give birth to a child conceived with a loved partner? Does the distress that is masked by this wish really have to do with the fact of not having a child? Is the child not some-times a means of getting rid of some primitive suffering or other (even though having a child is not the solution)? What lies within this "desire for a child" that justifies, in the eyes of the doctors involved in medically-assisted procreation, setting in motion a whole battery of therapeutic procedures? René Frydman (1999[2003]) admits that he is a practitioner of "desire medicine" because, with the exception of a few cases of serious injury, sterility is not an illness leading to physical pain (and therefore justifying treatment), but something that leads above all to the frustration of the wish to be a parent. Does this desire, as Freud thought, corre-spond to the reparation of what he called "female castration", or has it to do with something entirely different? Will the study of sterility help us to make progress in our understanding of "female castration"?

As a preamble, I would simply remind the reader that the prob-lem situation that I am about to describe may exist without bring-ing about sterility; the birth of a child may or may not ease these conflicts.

Becoming involved in sterility treatment procedures would seem to be proof that the desire to have a child really does exist. Given the non-satisfaction of this wish for a child, at a time when medical science has shown itself capable of astonishing technical prowess, it is not suffering that is the key issue but the need for action. In agreement with her gynaecologist (otherwise she would simply consult another one), an infertile woman will nowadays lay down her requirements—the "right to have a child", as I have called it. This has to be granted in order to avoid asking questions about what her true desire may be.

Thus, the child is desired not simply for him- or herself, but also as the bearer of some phallic quality or other. Does this have to do with penis envy, as Freud suggested: the reason behind the desire to have a child, a penis-substitute? This would not appear to be the case with patients who do not cathect the masculine or paternal image as being particularly enviable. In becoming pregnant, these patients try to identify with the image of a fulfilled mother, one who has everything she could possibly wish for, the image they have of their own mother. They are searching for a maternal phallicism more than for a masculine penis.

This representation is that of an all-powerful archaic mother, the counterpart of the father of the primal horde that Freud describes in "Totem and taboo" (Freud 1912–1913). Sterility generates a passionate need that has to be fulfilled at all costs in order to repair their wounded narcissism; it is not so much the desire for a child that has to be satisfied as a determined "will to be a mother". The ideal is that of a mother who lacks nothing, within a mother–child totality of which the patient once was part—she needs both to break free of it and to find it again through herself becoming the same kind of phallic mother.

In such cases, the patient's mental functioning is characterized by *denial*—or more exactly by *refutation*—of any affect, fear, or desire that has not been screened by an ego ideal that is all the more demanding when sterility carries the meaning of castration, incapacity, or anomaly—in other words, when it aggravates an already intolerable narcissistic wound. In such cases, it is not depressive suffering that predominates, but anger, envy, feelings of injustice and iniquity, at least at this phase of the medical treatment.

The demand for a child, in many of these patients, is an expression of their wish for normality and conformity to social expectations, of their desire to be considered as fully-fledged adults and to fulfil their moral obligation to their husband and in-laws. They are completely unaware of this deep distress, which brings in its wake desperate defensive mechanisms in an attempt to keep it hidden; these defences are externalized as character traits and as non-deferred immediate actions. It is that distress that makes their sterility so intolerable; it is seen as a repetition of childhood traumata, some of which may have been deeply disturbing. It gives them the feeling that they will never be able to become adults, it produces unbearable regression towards dependence on the maternal figure (dependence that, in fact, these patients have never managed to overcome). The maternal figure never really cathected her husband; she transferred all her hopes on to her daughter, but without validating the latter's femininity—all the more so since the maternal figure was much more a mother than a woman.

There is a narcissistic deficiency that can no doubt be explained by the weakness of the mother's capacity for reverie, thereby hindering the development of the ability to process issues in fantasy. Their discourse is less associative than factual, and they rarely report dreams. Their superego has been taken over by a highly restricting ideal ego.

The child they desire is not an Oedipal child given by the father. He failed to separate mother and daughter, and he plays only a minor role. The link with the mother predominates and often underpins a mother–daughter "community of denial". The real mother is experienced as being the only possible mother. The daughter tries to become a mother in order to escape from this, but any child that emerges would be engendered by the maternal figure or for her, so that, given the weight of projection, the plan is doomed to failure anyway. The imaginary child must be destroyed by these patients, otherwise they themselves would run the risk of dying. Deficiencies in symbol formation mean that self-preservation is a dominant feature of these women, given the fundamental nature of the violence they experience: "it's either him or me".

Becoming involved in a treatment procedure helps them escape from their depressive collapse and the self-disgust that their failure to conceive brought in its wake. But the price to pay for this relief is a heavy one indeed.

Having a child would lend support to the magical possibility of self-reparation; sterility generates the desperate need to force the body to satisfy that illusion. Infertility—shameful and hidden—is often experienced as a handicap that, with immense courage, they try to overcome. These patients submit to painful treatment procedures that are protracted and exhausting; they are carried away on a spiral of technological sophistication that hardly facilitates insight into the true nature of their desire for a child.

Nowadays, I participate in a growing number of genuine requests for psychotherapeutic help

Since my book was published, I have witnessed some extraordinary developments in the requests for therapeutic help, both on the part of the medical practitioners with whom I work and on that of the patients themselves.

The gynaecologists are now able to give much more precise indications. These, it is true, were already being fine-tuned in the course of our interdisciplinary meetings. They are now much more experienced. In return for their more passive approach, they are now much more attentive to what their patients have to say and they allow more time for spontaneous expression on the patients' part. As a result, the patient's background history is much more detailed than it used to be. Painful secrets of filiation sometimes give the opportunity to point out that the psychological effects of private dramas must be taken into account and not denied or pushed aside by the wish to procreate. This does not imply that the physician interrupts the prescribed medical treatment; for me, this is a crucial point.

Patients no longer feel rejected or dismissed as being "bad", as I described the situation as it then was, some twenty years ago. The complex nature of sterility—and in particular the recursive character of what transpires between mind and body that is a feature of this symptom—is acknowledged nowadays by the gynaecologists who have worked with me on this project.

The fact that infertile women now make their own request for psychotherapy has transformed that treatment too. In such cases, there is no room for denial. The wish to understand is predominant. Articles, books, television programmes—these have laid the groundwork for processing conflicts that have become consciously acknowledged. Among these new cases, I would make a distinction between simple sterility and those which lead to a break in filiation (such as "experimental sterility" brought about by sperm donation).

Patients whose sterility is not attributable to their husbands have the same psychic structure as those I have described *supra*, thus confirming the accuracy of my reconstructions over a much larger sample. However, the denial of the part played by the mind has disappeared. Such patients tend spontaneously to lay the blame on their immediate circle or on the fact that they had experienced severe traumata. Their own drive-related conflicts remain unacknowledged, however, and the analyst's task will be to encourage awareness of the role the patient herself plays in the ambivalent relationship with the maternal figure.

Access to more information at least leads them away from *denial*, the mind-set that they probably shared with most other infertile women, and towards *projection*, which lends itself to psychoanalytic work. The narcissistic trauma can at last find expression and be repaired through the transference. I have wondered about this latter element; when I think about my experience with such patients, I have the feeling that the transference is paternal in nature, or perhaps it is the existence of a theory about sterility that introduces triangulation

Are there cases in which the maternal figure does not act as a focus for all these demands and claims? Sometimes we could well think so. A death or a miscarriage sometimes seems to be the root cause of the patient's incapacity to conceive. One patient, for example, made several unsuccessful attempts to have a second child; she immediately suggested to me a possible explanation for this "secondary sterility" in which psychological factors were uppermost. She was in love with a man who was not her husband, and she wanted to become pregnant so as not to seek a divorce. Was this a conflict between a desire and a superego prohibition? That would have been highly unusual. The analysis highlighted the patient's inability to find any other way out of her dilemma, because she was so dependent on her husband, who played the part of a good mother for her. Divorce would have meant her regressing to the helplessness and despair she had known as a child; her husband was vital to her as a "self-object" (in Kohut's [1971] sense of the term).

Another patient claimed it had all to do with her sisters' ungratefulness; she (the patient) had sacrificed fifteen years of her life for them, yet they all refused to donate the oocyte that she required. Such conflicts lead to sterility because they cannot be dealt with in any other way, given that there is no link with a paternal figure and no capacity for symbol formation.

Thanks to the *treatment*, this kind of alienating link can be loosened fairly quickly. Often, a little freedom is enough to make conception possible. In general, my patients tend to interrupt the therapy as soon as they succeed in becoming mothers, and after showing me their baby. Their Oedipal situation has not yet reached a level where it could facilitate structuring, even though a weak link with the paternal figure may have been unearthed (this is always a sign that pregnancy can henceforth take place). The actual presence of the baby seems to be required before these patients can enter into triangulation. Many of them have abandoned the idea of continuing their therapy. Some have come back later, more mindful of their affects, after some difficulty or other with their infant. Having thought herself freed from a "hateful" but passionate dependence on the maternal figure, who constantly threatened to commit suicide if she was not granted absolute obedience, one patient described to me how her three-year-old son would bully her; she felt the same rage and the same guilt towards him as she had felt towards her mother. That was a deeply distressing discovery for the patient, but it enabled her to make significant changes, now that the demand for pregnancy was no longer the main issue.

Breaks in the continuity of filiation, where AID is the procedure used, involve different psychodynamic conflicts. They bring about real experimental sterility. The feeling of being sterile is immediately striking: patients deny their husband's azoospermia, just as they ignore the influence the donor has on their infertility. Since they have taken the decision to consult a CECOS,[1] why are they not pregnant? In this way, they take on board their partner's infertility and suffer from feelings of personal "incapacity".

In some of these patients, the prevalent maternal link is similar to that in the previous situation: would they have been sterile with a different partner? Perhaps? It is no surprise that failure is the result when these patients are in an "in-conceivable" frame of mind (in this sense in which I have used the term, supra).

There is another, more specific, pathological condition. In cases like these, the father's role seems to be a decisive factor. The Oedipal hypothesis, which up till now has had to be left to one side in our work, now becomes a distinct possibility. Women who cannot allow themselves to be fecundated by the sperm of an anonymous donor are sometimes very much attached to their father and are in rivalry with their mother. That said, their Oedipal complex has not been "resolved" and these feelings have not been repressed because their post-Oedipal superego is not strong enough.

Their incestuous desires are almost conscious; sometimes their dreams attest to this, as when, for example, they show a donor who looks like the patient's father, thereby revealing the state of arousal that the insemination generates. The paternal figure is highly cathected but does not lay down much in the way of prohibitions—in many cases, he will openly have shown that he preferred his daughter to his wife; the latter may well have accepted this abandonment, thereby unconsciously making the daughter feel guilty.

For example, in an initial interview, a patient told me:

"I'd like to know more about the donor. Anonymity is useful, but it would be better if there were some kind of descriptive register."

"With what details?"

"Age, especially. I can't stand the idea that he may be fifty years old."

"What does that make you think of?"

"My father."

Twenty years on, there is a further set of problematic issues, this time raised by the recent arrival of intracytoplasmic spermatozoan injection (ICSI) treatment. This is a revolution as far as male sterility is concerned; men now have a much greater opportunity to procreate, so that donor procedures and all the conflicts that these entail should rapidly be superseded. However, the patients who have consulted me seem to feel anxious about this procedure. They put forward various arguments.

- The fear that they are being used as guinea pigs. This has to do with resistance. There is as yet an insufficient number of cases, so that a proper statistical estimate is not currently possible.
- The understandable development of a fantasy of being fertilized by a defective spermatozoon. Is the doctor some kind of sorcerer's apprentice? This hesitation comes into conflict with the loyalty obligation that incites a woman to have a child who descends genetically from her partner.
- Exacerbation of intrapsychic conflict, which is at its height in women who have already undergone AID. One of these patients said to me: "When all else fails, I'll try ICSI." When I tried to point out to her the deadlock she found herself in because of her guilt-ridden desire to have a child by a donor, she began to express a certain degree of hostility towards her husband. In the past, he had steadfastly maintained that sperm donation was a commonplace event and had tried to convince her of that fact. At the same time, he wanted it to be kept absolutely secret. Now he wanted to use his own spermatozoa, however weakly mobile they might be.

- Finally, those couples who have previously had a child through AID. Intracytoplasmic spermatozoon injection (ICSI) procedure gives them the hope of being able to give birth to a child "of their own kith and kin". This gives rise to a new kind of "question of conscience". The mother feels herself to be dispossessed of that particular child, who is no longer "hers alone". She fears that her husband may behave differently towards each of the children. This is the same kind of sometimes conscious de-cathexis that we may find in women who, after adopting a child, then have one of their own; they may have difficulty in accepting the second child: "I didn't save that baby from all kinds of misfortune."

Technological development and innovation entails a certain number of consequences not only in reality, but also in the mind. It would appear to be the case, however, that reality—in genetics, for example—has less of an impact than the unconscious meaning that these new procedures take on in the history of individuals and in the way that they will later have to be retrospectively processed.

Notes

1. Centre d'Étude et de Conservation des oeufs et du Sperme humains—Centre for the Study and Preservation of Human Eggs and Sperm [Translator's note].

CHAPTER SIXTEEN

The impossible being of the mother*

Alicia Leisse de Lustgarten

I n this chapter I take a critical stance in regard to the affirmation that motherhood is what makes a woman. My argument high-lights the fact that procreation, when viewed as the presence of nature in any human phenomenon, defines a woman in terms of being a mother and a mother in terms of being a woman. On the basis of its condition as giver of birth, the maternal function is mistaken for an absolute creator of life, which thereby locks women into an ideal of being everything; this misconception ignores their adult being, which is part of a network of complex relations.

For some time now, a recurrent thought has accompanied me every time I listen to mothers talking about themselves, heavy with reproach and discontent, ignorance and anger, that ultimately reveals the paradox that the ideal always masks: it is an impossible function. Sitting opposite these women, I think of the other side of this meritorious motherhood, containing attitude or diligent willingness. I think of the fatigue caused by a bulging stomach,

---

* This paper was first published in Spanish in *Tropicos*, volume 2, 2001. Reprinted with permission.

impatience with the endless demands of the children, who are by nature exacting. I think, too, of how, to make the psychic existence of a new being possible, a woman must offer her whole self, only to see, in the course of time, the child go his or her own way in life determined by choices that are nearly always different from the mother's.

I remember some images. A woman, tormented by the utter impossibility of conducting a dialogue with her daughters, shuts herself into her room to avoid the daily confrontation that means satisfying their demands, however excessive, in an attempt to silence the guilt that condemns her for what she considers her inadequacy. Or another, frightened by the "peevish look" her adolescent daughter gives her—the girl is always quick to blame her mother for her lack of partners, of friends, and of everything else her mother should have provided for her. Then I remember the woman, determined to see her daughter other than she really is—how she would like the girl to be—driven by her own discontent. And I could go on. No, this is not a question of good and bad mothers. My interest lies in discussing what always underlies the ideal: mother fades out as a female subject in the diversity of her options when she is locked into this condition.

Let us pause for a moment and think about the theme of this meeting—"Catastrophic change; New developments in Latin-American psychoanalysis". Catastrophic change and the impossibility of being a mother: what do they have in common? I will not focus particularly on any violent event leading to death or tragedy, however close this may be to national and worldwide experiences that require our sustained attention and involvement.

Catastrophic change in psychoanalytic thought is a concept that we owe to W. R. Bion (1897–1978), a British psychoanalyst born in India, whose life was characterized by his untiring investigation of problems; his explorations gave rise to important contributions and considerable controversy. The conceptualization of catastrophic change focuses on a constant conjunction of facts observed whenever a new idea appears in diverse fields: the mind, the group, psychoanalytic work, society. The new idea contains a potentially disruptive force that produces a greater or lesser impact on the organization where it is manifested. Of the facts this author names, I will focus on his reference to subversion of the system—the

Establishment—in the sense of exploring the mother's being from the perspective of arguing in favour of a different kind of motherhood. The questioning of certain affirmations that set themselves up as paradigms leads me to insist that these ideas aim not to ignore the fundamental value of the maternal presence, but rather to posit that the mother as a *person* depends much more on who she really *is* rather than on any definition of motherhood.

A quick glance at history shows us that women, as well as almost everything pertaining to the human sphere, are defined in phallo-centred terms, considered here as the discourse of male domination and power. The long-established division of labour places men, producers of work and economic gain, in the public arena and women, as mothers, in the domestic circle, responsible for the care of the children. This leads inevitably to the fact that motherhood is seen as a natural or biological condition, thereby disregarding the cultural dimension involved in all human phenomena. This imposed definition, by ignoring all reference to a symbolic system that includes choice or the expression of a wish, destroys femininity as such by reducing it simply to motherhood, as the social *mores* of our time would have it. The eminent psychoanalyst and sociologist, Nancy Chodorow, with her fundamentally innovative way of looking at these issues (1978), points out how little girls are brought up to be "the woman who feeds" and taught that they must be mothers. They learn that being a girl is not as good as being a boy, they learn to define themselves as future mothers, they learn that a girl must do girls' things and later women's things. My question is: what are women's things? Have they to do *only* with motherhood? *Always* with motherhood? Is this the *only* function or is it *one* function amongst others?

Let us now consider what refers to the mother as a being. Motherhood, defined as an unforgettable personal and psychological experience, crucial for the child's psychic structuring, ultimately sustains the categorizing of women as mothers and mothers as women. Let us consider for a moment the female Unconscious. The fact of being a mother is inseparable from a narcissistic wish, with no implication that this is pathological. This wish is appropriate to a woman's self-image and the aspirations that are part of her ideals; it opens up a path to the realization of her fantasies and the satisfaction of her desires. But a woman is also aware of something that revives motherhood in her internal world: the way it is represented in her psyche. There is frequently an irreconcilable difference between a woman's insistence on having a child and the obviously limited commitment she will be able to give it, since her wishes clash with her identificatory references. I remember a young professional woman, determined to be pregnant, for whom the idea of breast-feeding or investing her time to take care of another person was anathema because it was something she herself had never experienced: she saw herself as an ugly, strange little girl rejected by her mother, while the favouritism her father showed towards her seemed to have had somewhat incestuous connotations.

Having a child is always a task that goes beyond reason, since it is impossible to respond to all the demands the child will make. All human beings have to deal with absence, with what is missing or lacking, because this is part of all relationships. The mother-to-be, in pregnancy and at delivery, is seen as the unconditional creator of life and as such is inevitably called upon to fulfil this role, considered to be her ultimate goal in life. Being subjected to long-term demands conflicts with the right to one's own existence, so that motherhood involves a change in the woman's private life as such. The new life cannot but be intrusive, since it requires limits to be modified and more complex adjustments to be made. The woman's own projects are postponed or perhaps abandoned entirely, and she tends to forget that any possible error or insufficiency on her part can in fact motivate a child to seek his or her own path. Clinical practice confirms that the mother is indeed significant as the basis of her children's mental organization: she names them, desires them, and provides the conditions that make their life possible. But if this affirmation were to be accepted without question, it would conflict with the assumption that she possesses overwhelming power and a sense of commitment that, though immense, can never be sufficient. Being in the *locus* of omnipotence does not mean that she is omnipotent. This is a kind of virtual *locus* where what she gives is a "totality" for the child but is inevitably marked by the void of her castration, or, what amounts to the same, that part of her experienced as lacking.

With motherhood, the imaginary illusion of completeness she once experienced—it was necessary then, but never again possible—comes back on to the woman's stage. The experience is sometimes described in terms that I would consider to be "sublime experiences", a kind of fleeting ecstasy. Vegetti (1996) calls it "the imaginary child of the night" while Kristeva (1984) describes it beautifully as the reconstruction of the paradise that the imaginary child experienced. Vegetti points out that, ironically, incompetence is characteristic of the human condition, not of animals. And thus we find women of various ages, some of whom are highly-educated and/or have cultural achievements to their credit, in the same position: facing the annihilation anxieties that giving birth to a child may evoke or fears aroused by the proximity of that different other whom she awaited with so many fantasies.

Although the mother's status as a being is defined also from other perspectives given the constantly changing cultural environment, the importance of motherhood still characterizes identity-as-a-woman, ignoring for the most that we are dealing with a function. In this order of ideas, the creative aspect of motherhood is not limited to the skills, the attunement, or the appropriateness that she develops with her child; it also involves knowledge of her own limits and identificatory determinants, who she is as an individual being and what she is as a social subject. This view questions the idealizing dimension that sees in the mother a kind of icon.

I have, of course, my own opinion on this field of psychoanalytic thought, where a chorus of voices has echoed the social affirmation of a female ideal defined by motherhood. Glocer Fiorini (1996) summarizes Freud's highly eloquent words: "The path to femininity will be a series of successive passages from the mother to the father, from the penis to the child, in which the greatest aim of femininity will be motherhood, which is paradoxically an aim in the phallic order".

Although it would not be true to say that Freud knew nothing about women, he did consider investigation into their sexual organization as a dark continent, a view that could to some extent be attributed to the male chauvinist views of his times. If the Freudian definition is that the girl solves the problem of castration—described in wider terms as what she does not have or what she is not—thanks to the fantasy of receiving a child from her father and, later, from her partner, it shows that the response to her wish is limited to having a child; the phallic object cannot apparently be displaced on to something different. Also, the woman's wish for motherhood as something that makes her complete is not inherent to the female condition, since a man's wish for a child can involve a similar fantasy.

For Melanie Klein, who contributed a great deal to what we know of the first months and years of life, the mother shoulders a great responsibility in that her response is considered to be the determining and defining bulwark as regards the vicissitudes the child will face throughout life. Klein was not the only psychoanalyst to hold that point of view, of course; but her ideas are tinged by this exaggerated and excessive maternal dimension. For Lacan, the tendentiously phallo-centric distribution is present when, from another perspective, he emphasizes how the word-of-the-father and the norm it establishes rescues the child from the entrapment involved in being at the mercy of the mother's desire. He argues that the "third party" or *tiers*, the name-of-the-Father, provides order where once chaos reigned. The theoretical backdrop to this would appear to oppose a "body" perspective to a "law" one, thereby reinforcing a dichotomy that is already biased. I have always thought that the phallus-as-signifier, representative of an "everything", though a metaphor of the male sexual organ, ultimately shifts the weight of establishing order on to the masculine dimension.

The idea of a different kind of motherhood leads me to consider some paradoxes and myths that conceal the impossibility of what they maintain.

1. The first refers to "learning" the maternal function. The parental condition is one of those occupations that follow the old model of apprenticeship without formal learning; that is, one is mainly what one has witnessed or with what one is identified. Motherhood is linked to personal history, mixed with unfulfilled longings, the reparation of one's objects, and repetition of experiences. It is a special kind of learning impregnated with what each has experienced in relationships marked by gratification and frustration, conflict and lack; it is an unavoidable fate. The mythic construction of what must be defines a mother-who-is-pure-and-who-represents-"everything", the person in whom all knowledge is deposited, and her shortcomings will be labelled in consequence. When this

happens, she soon begins to search for indicators to explain her bewilderment. Centres for developing parental skills clearly show that anxiety concerning their ignorance hinders integration of theoretical ideas that could function as reference points. The urgent need for answers shows that these programmes must target the kind of experiential knowledge that, for different reasons, these parents have not themselves managed to acquire.

2. Many influences have reshaped the image of mothers, particularly with regard to idealization. Motherhood is an identificatory ideal, a goal to be reached that functions as a criterion upon which they will be judged. What is not apparent is the fact that the feminine dimension—the woman-as-such—is here sacrificed by being defined solely in terms of her child; she renounces that sphere and lets it fade into the background. The sleepless nights, the days without respite, the conflicting aspirations bear witness to the fallacy of attempting to sustain this. Lending herself to fusion, or trying to respond to the limitless demands, can only undermine the mother's narcissism, her self-identity, and her integrity, that other self-identity she possesses. The relationship with her infant is asymmetrical; though she may be everything for the infant in the early period of life, the child is not everything for her in her life. Further, by stimulating her child's desires, she limits her own, and the supposedly unconditional response the child requires at the beginning is simultaneously a warning to the mother that her child is not her property. Thus, motherhood and personal fulfilment may ultimately be incompatible. The pressure of an ideal model is revealed by demands that are impossible to satisfy. Those peaceful, composed, and containing images, with their idealizing halo—they symbolize everything a woman is supposed to be and lock her into the maternal function. Being her child's first love object on the one hand, and the requirement to satisfy the ideal on the other, are hardly ever compatible. The discrepancy between the goal and what actually occurs means that the promise contained in that image of the mother is untenable; the fact that she is also an individual in her own right as a woman, part of a network of relationships and having a project of her own, is to all intents and purposes ignored.

3. Having children implies acknowledging demands and paying a price; having made the choice, the mother is of course willing to accept these. Ties of blood alone, however, cannot guarantee the quality of a relationship. Motherhood may give her the illusion of possessing something that could symbolically resemble a missing part of herself, but every child has her or her own desires, hopes and expectations, experienced in terms of the relationship situation that evokes them. What the mother is looking for does not necessarily correspond to the person her child is or will be; each manifests this fact, since it opens the path—perhaps painful but also, fortunately, feasible—towards self-identity, towards becoming oneself.

Finally, a word about guilt, a kind of constantly present weight associated with any ideal that is impossible to attain. Doing things simply "well" is experienced as not being adequate. Winnicott was one of the few illustrious psychoanalytic theorists of his time to acknowledge feelings of rejection and hostility in a relationship that involves so many demands; it is thanks to him that we have the felicitous term: *the good enough mother*.

My aim in putting forward these ideas is to call into question the assumption that motherhood is the only choice or even the primary choice that a woman can make, and to emphasize that any response defined in terms of an ideal is untenable. Motherhood is a function that a woman may or may not embrace. If we divide the universe into "good" and "bad", we necessarily ignore who each person is and what he or she chooses. Bion used to say that he didn't know the answers to these questions and that, even if he did, he would refuse to give them; for him, it was important that each of us try to find his or her own answers (Bion, 1977).

REFERENCES

Alizade, A.M. (1992). *La sensualidad femenina*. Buenos Aires, Amorrortu editores. English edition: *Feminine Sensuality*. London: Karnac, 1999.

Alizade, A. M. (1995). *Clínica con la Muerte*. Buenos Aires: Amorrortu Editores.

Alizade, A. M. (1998). *La Mujer Sola*. Buenos Aires, Editorial Lumen.

Alizade, A. M. (2000). El final del complejo de Edipo en la mujer: De la duplicación a la individuación. Trabajo leído en la Asociación Psicoanalítica Argentina. Ver también cap. 7 de La Sensualidad Femenina (1992), ant.citado.

Alizade, A. M. (2001). Maternidades. In: *La Mujer Sola. Ensayo sobre la Dama Andante en Occidente* (pp. 163–183). Buenos Aires: Lumen.

Alizade, A. M. (2002). The fluidity of the female universe and its psychic consequences. In: A. M. Alizade (Ed.), *The Embodied Female* (pp. 25–36). London: Karnac.

Amati Mehler, J. (1999). Perversioni: struttura, sintomo o meccanismo? *Psicoanalisi*, 3(1): 59–66.

Argentieri, S. (2005). Incest: yesterday and today. In: G. Ambrosio (Ed.), *Incest* (pp. 17–49). London: Karnac.

Aslan, C. M. (2000). La feminidad primaria. In: A. M. Alizade (Ed.), *Escenarios Femeninos. Diálogos y Controversias*. Buenos Aires: Lumen.

Badinter, E. (1981). *L'Amour en Plus*. Paris: Flammarion.

Badinter, E. (1987). Maternal indifference. In: Toril Moi (Ed.), *French Feminist Thought* (pp. 150–178). Oxford: Blackwell, 1989.

Baldini, U. (1990). Masaccio unveiled. *Review*. The *Guardian*, 29 March.

Baranger, W. (1991). Il narcisismo nell'opera di Freud. In: J. Sandler, E. Spector Person, & P. Fonagy (Eds), *Studi critici su Introduzione al Narcisismo*. Milano: Cortina, 1992.

Bégoin-Guignard, F. (1987). À l'aube du maternel et du féminin. Essai sur deux concepts aussi évidents qu'inconcevables. *Revue française de Psychanalyse, LI*(6): 1491–1503.

Benjamin, J. (1998). *Shadow of the Other. Intersubjectivity and Gender in Psychoanalysis*. New York and London: Routledge.

Benkov, L. (1998). Yes, I am a swan: Reflections on families headed by lesbians and gay men. In: C. G. Coll, J. L. Surrey, & K. Weingarten (Eds.), *Mothering Against the Odds: Diverse Voices of Contemporary Mothers* (pp. 113–133). New York: Guilford Press.

Berezin de Guiter, J. (2000). Violencia hacia la mujer. Una mirada psicoanalítica. In: A. M. Alizade (Ed.), *Escenarios Femeninos. Diálogos y Controversias* (pp. 299–303). Buenos Aires: Lumen/International Psycho-analytical Association COWAP.

Bergman, A. (1987). On the development of female identity: Issues of mother–daughter interaction during the separation–individuation process. *Psychoanalytic Inquiry, 7*: 381–396.

Bergman, N. J., Linley, L. L., & Fawcus, S. R. (2003). Randomized controlled trial of skin-to-skin contact from birth versus conventional incubator for physiological stabilization in 1200g to 2199g newborns. *Acta Pediatrica, 93*: 779–785.

Bernstein, (1983). The female superego: a different perspective. *International Journal of Psycho-Analysis, 64*: 187–201.

Bion, W. R. (1961). *Experiences in Groups and Other Papers*. London: Tavistock.

Bion, W. R. (1962). "A theory of thinking". *International Journal of Psychoanalysis, 43*: 4–5. Also in Bion, W. R. (1967). *Second Thoughts. Selected Papers on Psycho-analysis*. London: Heinemann.

Bion, W.R. (1977). *Two Papers: The Grid and Caesura*. Rio de Janeiro: Imago Editora [reprinted London: Karnac, 1989].

Blanck-Cereijido, F. (1983). A study of feminine sexuality. *International Journal of Psychoanalysis, 64*: 93–104.

Blanck-Cereijido, F. (1996). Panel report: Infertility, surrogacy and the new reproductive techniques. *International Journal of Psychoanalysis, 77*: 129–133.

Blanck-Cereijido, F. (1997). Psicoanalisis y nuevas técnicas reproductivas. En: Heil Mórales Ascencio (Ed.), *El Laberinto de las Estructuras* (pp. 155–163). México: Siglo XXI.

Bleger, J. (1967). *Simbiosi e Ambiguità*. Lauretana, Loreto, 1992.

Bleichmar, H. (1997). *Avances en Psicoterapia Psicoanalítica*. Barcelona: Paidós.

Bowlby, J. (1951). *Maternal Care and Mental Health*. Geneva: WHO Scientific Publication no. 164; London: HMSO.

Bowlby, J. (1980). *Attachment and Loss, Vol. III. Loss, Sadness and Depression*. London: Hogarth.

Braudel, F. (1969). *Scritti sulla storia*. Milan: Mondadori, 1973.

Braunschweig, D., & Fain, M. (1975). *La nuit, le jour. Essai psychanalytique sur le fonctionnement mental*. Paris: Presses Universitaires de France.

Britton, R., Feldman, M., O'Shaughnessy, E., & Steiner, J. (1990). *The Oedipus Complex Today: Clinical Implications*. London: Karnac.

Brown, G. W., Harris, T. O., & Hepworth, C. (1995). Loss, humiliation and entrapment among women developing depression: a patient and non-patient comparison. *Psychological Medicine, 25*: 7–21.

Bukatman, S. (1994). X-Bodies: the torment of the mutant superhero. In: R. Sappington, T. Stallings (Eds.), *Uncontrollable Bodies*. Seattle: Bay Press.

Bunting, M. (2004). Messing with life. The *Guardian*, 2 February.

Cachard, C. (1981). Enveloppes de corps, membranes de rêves. *L'Evolution Psychiatrique, 46*(4): 847–856.

Canestri, J. (2003). Le processus analytique et le travail de transformation. *Bulletin de la Société Psychanalytique de Paris*, 70.

Cereijido, M. (1990). *Single Women Who Choose Motherhood*. Michigan: UMI.

Chasseguet-Smirgel, J. (1964). *La sexualité féminine: recherches psychanalytiques nouvelles*. Paris: Payot. 1970. English edition: *Female Sexuality: New Psychoanalytic Views*. Michigan: University of Michigan Press, 1970.

Chodorow, N. (1994). *Femininities, Masculinities, Sexualities: Freud and Beyond*. Lexington, KY: The University Press of Kentucky.

Chodorow, N. (1999)[1978]. *The Reproduction of Mothering*. Berkeley, CA: University of California Press.

Chodorow, N. J. (2003). "Too late": ambivalence about motherhood, choice and time. In: A. M. Alizade (Ed.), *Studies on Femininity* (pp. 27–40). London: Karnac.

Clarke-Stewart, K. A. (1989). Infant day care—maligned or malignant? *American Psychologist, 44*: 266–273.

Cohen, M. (2003). *Sent Before My Time—A Child Psychotherapist's View of Life on a Neonatal Intensive Care Unit.* London: Karnac.

Coleman, R. W., Kris, E., & Provence, S. (1953). The study of variations of early parental attitude: a preliminary report. *Psychoanalytic Study of the Child, 8*: 20–47.

Cooper, D. (1971). *The Death of the Family.* London: Allen Lane/ Penguin.

Cooper, L., & Glazer, E. (1994). *Beyond Infertility.* New York: Lexington.

Cooper, P. J., Tomlinson, M., Swartz, L., Woolger, M., Murray, L., & Molteno, C. (1999). Postpartum depression and the mother–infant relationship in a South African peri-urban settlement. *British Journal of Psychiatry, 175*: 554–558.

Costello, C.Y. (1997). Conceiving identity: Bisexual, lesbian and gay parents consider their children's sexual orientations. *Journal of Sociology and Social Welfare, 24*: 63–89.

Crespi, L. (2001). And baby makes three: a dynamic look at development and conflict in lesbian families. *Journal of Gay and Lesbian Psychotherapy, 4*: 7–29.

Davies, J. (1998). Thoughts on the nature of desires: the ambiguous, the transitional, and the poetic. Reply to Commentaries [on "Between the disclosure and foreclosure of erotic transference–countertransference"]. *Psychoanalytic Dialogues, 8*: 805–823.

De Mause L. (1974). The History of Childhood. Chapter 1. Alianza Universidad. España, 1982.

De Mause, L. (s/f). La historia del ultraje infantil. *Rev. de Psicoan. Número especial Internacional, 7*, 2000, p.

Devereux, G. (1965). *Ethnopsychanalyse Complémentariste.* Paris: Flammarion. English edition: *Ethnopsychoanalysis: Psychoanalysis and Anthropology as Complementary Frames of Reference.* Berkeley, CA: University of California Press, 1978.

Diamond, D., Kezur, M., Meyers, M., Scharf, C. N., & Wienshel, M. (1999). *Couple Therapy for Infertility.* New York: Guilford.

Dimen, M. (1995). The third step: Freud, the feminists, and post-modernism. *Gender and Psychoanaylsis, 55*: 303–319.

Dio Bleichmar, E. (1991a). *El feminismo espontáneo de la histeria.* Madrid: Siglo XXI.

Dio Bleichmar, E. (1991b). *La Depresión en la Mujer.* Madrid: Temas de Hoy.

Dio Bleichmar, E. (1991c). *Temores y Fobias. Condiciones de génesis en la infancia*. Buenos Aires: Gedisa.

Dio Bleichmar, E. (1995). The secret in the constitution of female sexuality: The effects of the adult's sexual look upon the subjectivity of the girl. *Journal of Clinical Psychoanalysis*, 4: 331–342.

Drucker, J. (1998). *Families of Value: Gay and Lesbian Parents and Their Children Speak Out*. New York: Insight Books/Plenum Press.

Duby, G., & Perrot, M. (Eds.). (1990). *A History of Women in the West*. Harvard University Press, 10 Vols., 1993.

Duvignaud, F. (1981). *Le corps de l'effroi*. Paris: le Sycomore (*El cuerpo del horror*. Fondo de Cultura Económica. México, 1987).

Ehrensaft, D. (2000). Alternatives to the stork: fatherhood fantasies in donor insemination families. *Studies in Gender and Sexuality*, 1: 371–397.

Eliacheff, C., & Heinich, N. (2002). *Mères–filles une relation à trois*. Paris: Albin Michel.

Elise, D. (1997). Primary femininity, bisexuality, and the female Ego Ideal: A re-examination of female developmental theory. *Psychoanalytic Quarterly*, 66: 489–517.

Elliott, A. (1992). *Social Theory and Psychoanalysis in Transition. Self and Society from Freud to Kristeva*. London: Blackwell (2nd edn 1999) (*Teoría Social y Psicoanálisis en Transición. Sujeto y Sociedad de Freud a Kristeva*, Buenos Aires: Editorial Amorrortu, 1995).

Faure-Pragier, S. (1997). *Les bébés de l'inconscient. Le psychanalyste face aux stérilités féminines aujourd'hui*. Paris: Presses Universitaires de France.

Ferenczi, S. (1929). The unwelcome child and his death-instinct. *International Journal of Psycho-Analysis*, 10: 125–129.

Ferenczi, S. (1932). *The Confusion of Tongues Between Adult and Child. Final Contributions to the Problems and Methods of Psycho-Analysis*. New York: Brunner-Mazel, 1980.

Fonagy, P. (1999). Male perpetrators of violence against women: An attachment theory perspective. *Journal of Applied Psychoanalytic Studies*, 1: 7–27.

Fonagy, P. (1999). Persistencias transgeneracionales del apego: una nueva teoría. *Aperturas Psicoanalíticas. Hacia modelos integradores 3* (www.aperturas.org).

Fonagy, P., & Target, M. (1996). Playing with reality: I Theory of mind and the normal development of psychic reality. *International Journal of Psychoanalysis*, 77: 217–233.

Fonagy, P., Gergely, G., Jurist, E., & Target, M. (2002). *Affect Regulation and Mentalization*. New York: Other Press.

Freud, S. (1905d). Three essays on the theory of sexuality. *S.E.*, 7: 130–243. London: Hogarth.

Freud, S. (1910h). A special type of choice of object made by men: contributions to the psychology of love. *S.E.*, 11: 165–175. London: Hogarth.

Freud, S. (1912–1913). Totem and taboo. *S.E.*, 13. London: Hogarth.

Freud, S. (1914c). On narcissism: an introduction. *S.E.*, 14: 67–102. London: Hogarth.

Freud, S. (1919e). A child is being beaten. *S.E.*, 17: 179–204. London: Hogarth.

Freud, S. (1919h). The uncanny. *S.E.*, 17: 217–256. London: Hogarth.

Freud, S. (1921c). Group psychology and the analysis of the ego. *S.E.*, 18: 65–144. London: Hogarth.

Freud, S. (1923b). The ego and the id. *S.E.*, 19: 1–59. London: Hogarth.

Freud, S. (1924). *A General Introduction to Psychoanalysis*. New York: Pocket Books.

Freud, S. (1924d). The dissolution of the Oedipus complex. *S.E.*, 19: 173.

Freud, S. (1924c). The economic problem of masochism. *S.E.*, 19: 159–170. London: Hogarth.

Freud, S. (1925j). Some psychical consequences of the anatomical distinction between the sexes. *S.E.*, 19: 241–259. London: Hogarth.

Freud, S. (1931b). Female sexuality. *S.E.*, 21: 223.

Freud, S. (1933a). Femininity. In: New introductory lectures on psychoanalysis. *S.E.*, 22: 112–135.

Freud, S. (1937c), Analysis terminable and interminable. *S.E.*, 23: 209–253. London: Hogarth.

Freud, S. (1950a [1895]).Project for a scientific psychology. *S.E.*, 1: 295–391. London: Hogarth.

Frydman, R. (1999). *Dieu, la médecine et l'embryon* (2nd edn 2003). Paris: Odile Jacob.

Gaddini, E. (1953–1985). *Scritti*. Milan: Cortina, 1989. A selection from *Scritti* published in English as *A Psychoanalytic Theory of Infantile Experience*, A. Limentani (Ed.). London: The New Library of Psychoanalysis, 1992.

Gaddini, E. (1984). Whether and how our patients have changed up to the present day. In: *Changes in Analysts and in their Training*, IPA Monograph, Series 4.

Gissler, M., Berg, C., Bouvier-Colle, M. H., & Buekens, P. (2005). Injury deaths, suicides and homicides associated with pregnancy, Finland 1987–2000, *European Journal of Public Health*, 15: 49–93.

Glocer Fiorini, L. (1996). En los límites de lo femenino: Lo otro. *Rev. De Psicoanal.*, *LIII*(2): 429–455.

Glocer Fiorini, L. (1998). The feminine in psychoanalysis: a complex construction. *Journal of Clinical Psychoanalysis*, 7: 421–439.

Glocer Fiorini, L. (2001). *Lo femenino y el pensamiento complejo. (The Feminine and the Complex Thought)*. Buenos Aires: Lugar Editorial.

Glocer Fiorini, L. (2001). El deseo de hijo. De la carencia a la producción deseante". *Rev. de Psicoanálisis*, *LVIII*(4): 965–976. (The desire for a child. From the theory of "lack" to a theory of productive desire.) Paper read at the 42nd IPA Congress, Nice, France, 2001.

Glocer Fiorini, L. (2002). Fertilización asistida. Nuevas Problemáticas (Assisted fertilization. New issues). In: E. Wolfberg (Ed.), *Prevención en Salud Mental* (pp. 161–172). Buenos Aires: Lugar Editorial.

Glocer Fiorini, L., & Giménez de Vainer, A. (2003). The sexed body and the real—its meaning in transsexualism. In: A. M. Alizade (Ed.), *Masculine Scenarios* (pp. 101–108). London: Karnac.

Gottman, J. S. (1989). Children of gay and lesbian parents. *Marriage & Family Review*, 14: 177–196.

Green, A. (1972). *On Private Madness*. London: Rebus .

Greenacre, P. (1963). *The Quest for the Father*. New York: International Universities Press.

Greenson, R. (1968). Dis-identifying from mother: its special importance for the boy. *International Journal of Psychoanalysis*, 49: 370–374.

Guignard, F. (1984). Adolescence de la féminité. *Adolescence*, 2(2): 221–236. Also in Guignard, F. (1997). *Épître à l'objet*. Paris: Presses Universitaires de France.

Guignard, F. (1985). Le sourire du chat. In Guignard, F. (1997). *Épître à l'objet*, op.cit.

Guignard, F. (1993). Différence des sexes et théories sexuelles. Désir et danger de connaître. *Revue française de Psychanalyse. LVII*: 1691–1699.

Guignard, F. (1995). Le Maternel et le Féminin, deux espaces de la vie psychique. *Psychologie clinique et projective*, 1: 2–12.

Guignard, F. (1996a). Prégénitalité et scène primitive. In: F. Guignard (Ed.), *Au Vif de l'Infantile*. Lausanne: Delachaux & Niestlé.

Guignard, F. (1996b). Éprouvé d'amour, déni d'amour. *Revue française de Psychanalyse, LX*(3): 805–812.

Guignard, F. (1996c) L'infantile dans la relation analytique. In Guignard, F. *Au Vif de l'Infantile*, op. cit.

Guignard, F. (1997a). Généalogie des pulsions. In Guignard, F. (1997). *Épître à l'objet*, op.cit.

Guignard, F. (1997b). Le Moi et l'objet dans tous leurs états. In: F. Guignard (Ed.), (1997). *Épître à l'objet*, op.cit.

Guignard, F. (1997c). L'envie, terre de désolation. Jalousies, envie et scène primitive. *Revue française de Psychanalyse, LXI*(1): 123–139.

Guignard, F. (1997d). Entre deuil et traumatisme: le masochisme. In: F. Guignard (Ed.), (1997). *Épître à l'objet*, op.cit.

Hardin, H. T., & Hardin, D. H. (2000). On the vicissitudes of early primary surrogate mothering II: Loss of the surrogate mother and arrest of mourning. *Journal of the American Psychoanalytic Association,* 48: 1229–1258.

Harsch, E. H. (1990). Ammen und Kinderfrauen—Zugang zum Trauma einer Patientin durch ein literarisches Werk. *Jahrbuch Psychoanal.* 26: 102–131.

Harsch, H. E. (1994). Freuds Identifizierung mit Männern, die zwei Mütter hatten: Ödipus, Leonardo da Vinci, Michelangelo und Moses. *Psyche, 48*: 124–153.

Harsch, H. E. (2001). Wie Kinder aufwuchsen. Zur Geschichte und Psychodynamik der Doppelbemutterung. *Psyche, 55*: 358–378.

Heise, L. (1996). Violence against women: Global organizing for change. In: J. Edelson & Z. Eisikovits (Eds.), *Future Interventions with Battered Women and their Families* (pp. 7–33). Thousand Oaks, CA: Sage.

Heise, L. (1998). Violence against women: An integrated ecological framework. *Violence Against Women, 4*(3): 262–290.

Howes, C. (1999). Attachment relationships in the context of multiple caregivers. In: J. Cassidy & P. Shaver (Eds.), *Handbook of Attachment* (1932) (pp. 671–687). New York, London: Guilford Press.

Jacobson, J. (1976). Ways of female superego formation and the female castration conflict. *Psicoanal.* 45: 525–538.

Jones, E. (1922). Notes on Dr. Abraham's article on the female castration complex. *International Journal of Psychoanalysis, 3*: 327–328.

Jones, E. (1935). Early female sexuality. *International Journal of Psychoanalysis, 16*: 263–273.

Kestenberg, J. (1956). On the development of maternal feelings in early childhood: observations and reflections. *The Psychoanalytic Study of the Child, 11*: 257–291.

Klein, M. (1928). Early stages of the Oedipus conflict. In *Love, Guilt and Reparation. The Writings of Melanie Klein*, vol. I. London: Karnac and the Institute of Psychoanalysis, 1992.

Klein, M. (1932). *El psicoanálisis de niños*. Buenos Aires: Asociación Psicoanalítica Argentina, 1948.

Klein, M. (1932). The effects of early anxiety-situations on the sexual development of the girl, and The effects of early anxiety-situations on the sexual development of the boy. In *The Psycho-Analysis of Children. The Writings of Melanie Klein*, vol. II. London: Hogarth and the Institute of Psychoanalysis, 1986.

Klein, M. (1932). *The Psycho-analysis of Children*. London: Hogarth.

Klein, M. (1945). The Oedipus complex in the light of early anxieties. In: *Contributions to Psycho-Analysis*. London: Hogarth Press and the Institute of Psycho-Analysis. Also in *Love, Guilt and Reparation. The Writings of Melanie Klein, vol. 1*. London: Karnac and the Institute of Psycho-Analysis (1992).

Klein, M. (1946). Notes on some schizoid mechanisms. In: *Envy and Gratitude* (pp. 1–24). London: Hogarth, 1975.

Klein, M. (1957). Envy and gratitude. In: *Envy and Gratitude* (pp. 176–235). London: Hogarth, 1975.

Klein, M. (1958). On the development of mental functioning. *International Journal of Psycho-Analysis*, *39*: 84–90.

Kohut, H. (1971). *The Analysis of the Self. A Systematic Approach to the Psychoanalytic Treatment of Narcissistic Personality Disorders*. New York: International Universities Press.

Kristeva, J. (1984). *Histoires d'amour*. Paris: Seuil (Coll. "L'Infini"). Reissued in 1985. English edition: *Tales of Love* (Leon S. Roudiez, trans.). Columbia University Press,1989.

Lacan, J. (1949). Le stade du miroir comme formateur de la fonction du Je telle qu'elle nous est révélée dans l'expérience psychanalytique. Paper read at the 26th IPA Congress, Zürich, Switzerland, 17 July 1949. In: *Ecrits*. Paris: Le Seuil (1966). El estadio del espejo como formador de la función del yo tal como se nos revela en la experiencia psicoanalítica. En: *Lectura estructuralista de Freud*. México: Siglo XXI Editores, 1971.

Lacan, J. (1966). *Écrits*. Paris: Seuil.

Lacan, J. (1972–1973). *Le Séminaire Livre XX*. Paris: Seuil.

Laing, R. D. (1959). *The Divided Self*. London: Pelican, 1965.

Laplanche, J. (1987). *Nuevos Fundamentos para el Psicoanálisis*. Buenos Aires: Amorrortu, 1989.

Lartigue, T. (1991) Madres adolescentes. Análisis de la interacción maternoinfantil. *Cuadernos de Psicoanálisis*, *XXIV*(1–2): 51–58.

Lartigue, T. (1996). Determinantes tempranos de la maternidad. En: T. Lartigue & H. Ávila (Comps.), *Sexualidad y reproducción humana en México*. Volumen 1 (pp. 219–244). Plaza y Valdés, México: Universidad Iberoamericana.

Lartigue, T. (2001). La patología borderline durante el embarazo. Evidencias clínicas y de investigación en la ciudad de México. en Tropicos. *Rev. de Psicoanálisis. Fondo Editorial Sociedad Psicoanalítica de Caracas, IX*(2). English version, this volume.

Lartigue, T. (2004). VIH/SIDA y fallas en la parentalidad. Una investigación en el INPer desde las teorías psicoanalíticas y de género. En: M. Alizade & T. Lartigue (Comps.), *Psicoanálisis y relaciones de género* (pp. 57–77). Buenos Aires: COWAP-IPA/Editorial Lumen.

Lartigue, T., Vives, J., De La Cerda, D., Vázquez, M., Córdova, A., López, D., Bukrinsky, R., Ávila, H., & Feinholz, D. (2000a). Risk factors for borderline pathology in pregnant women. Effects on the newborn and affective interaction mother–infant. Investigation project with the economic support of the Research Advisory Board of the IPA.

Lartigue, T., Ávila, H., Casanova, G., Vives, J., Nava, A., Sánchez, B., Aranda, C., Figueroa, L., Ortíz, J., Feinholz, D., & Narcio, L. (2000b). ETS-VIH/SIDA y trastornos de personalidad en mujeres embarazadas y sus parejas. Detección y prevención de prácticas de alto riesgo. Proyecto de investigación.

Le Goff, J. (Ed.) (1979). *La nuova storia*. Milan: Mondadori, 1980.

Lebovici, S. (1983). *Le nourrisson, la mère et le psychanalyste. Les interactions précoces*. Paris: Centurios.

Leisse de Lustgarten, A. (1999). El ser imposible de la madre en Tropicos. Rev. de Psicoanálisis. Fondo Editorial Sociedad Psicoanalítica de Caracas, Año IX, vol. 2, 2001. English version, this volume.

Leñero, L. (2002). El interés por la ética y estética de la terapia familiar en México. *Psicoterapia y Familia, 15*(1): 77–84.

Levinton, N. (2000). *El Superyó Femenino. La Moral de las Mujeres*. Madrid: Biblioteca Nueva.

Lévi-Strauss C. (1949). *Les structures élémentaires de la parenté*. Paris, PUF. 2ème edn, Paris, Mouton & Co, et Maison des Sciences de l'Homme, 1957. English edition: *The Elementary Structures of Kinship*. J. H. Bell (trans.), J. Richard von Sturmer, & R. Needham (Eds.), revised edn. Boston: Beacon Press, 1969.

Magis, C., Bravo, E., & Rivera, P. (2002). El SIDA en México en el año 2000. In: P. Uribe & C. Magis (Eds.), *La Respuesta Mexicana al SIDA: Mejores Prácticas* (pp. 13–22). Mexico: Consejo Nacional para la Prevención y Control del SIDA. English edition: Uribe, P. & Magis, C. (Eds.) *Best Practice: The Mexican Response to AIDS*. Mexico: The National Council for HIV/AIDS Prevention and Control.

Martinez, M. (1996). *Comportamiento Humano. Nuevos Métodos de Investigación* (2nd edn). Mexico: Trillas.

Mayer, E. (1985). Everybody must be just like me: Observations on female castration anxiety. *International Journal of Psycho-Analysis, 66*: 331–348.

Mayer, E. L. (1995). The phallic castration complex and primary femininity: paired developmental lines toward female gender identity. *Journal of the American Psychoanalytic Association, 43*: 17–38.

Mitchell, V. (1996). Two moms: Contribution of the planned lesbian family to the deconstruction of gendered parenting. In: R. J. Green, J. Laird, & V. Mitchell (Eds.), *Lesbians and Gays in Couples and Families: A Handbook for Therapists* (pp. 343–357). San Francisco, CA: Jossey-Bass.

Money, J. (1988). *Gay, Straight and In-Between*. New York: Oxford University Press.

Money, J., & Ehrhardt, A. (1982). *Desarrollo de la sexualidad humana (Diferenciación y dimorfismo de la identidad de género)*. Madrid: Morata.

Motz, A. (2001). *The Psychology of Female Violence: Crimes Against the Body*. Hove: Brunner-Routledge.

Nasio, J. D. (1996). Le livre de la douleur et de l'amour. Paris: Payot. English edition: *Book of Love & Pain: Thinking at the Limit with Freud & Lacan*. D. Pettigrew (Trans.), 2003.

NICHD—Early Child Care Research Network (1997). The effects of infant child care on infant–mother attachment security. *Child Development, 68*: 860–879.

Papaligoura, Z., & Trevarthen, C. (2001). Mother–infant communication can be enhanced after conception by in-vitro fertilization. *Infant Mental Health Journal, 22*: 591.

Paschero, L. M. (2000). Aportes sobre el superyó femenino. In: A. M. Alizade (Ed.), *Escenarios Femeninos. Diálogos y Controversias*. Buenos Aires: Lumen.

Phillips, J. L. (1981). *Piaget's Theory: A Primer*. New York: W. H. Freeman.

Pines, D. (1982). The relevance of early psychic development to pregnancy and abortion. *International Journal of Psycho-Analysis, 63*: 311–319.

Pines, D. (1986). A woman's unconscious use of her body; a psychoanalytic perspective. Carol Dilling Memorial Lecture, New York.

Pines, D. (1993). *A Woman's Unconscious Use of her Body*. London: Virago.

Raphael-Leff, J. (1986). Facilitators and regulators: conscious and unconscious processes in pregnancy and early motherhood. *British Journal of Medical Psychology*, 59: 43–55.

Raphael-Leff, J. (1990). If Oedipus was an Egyptian. *International Review of Psycho-Analysis*, 17: 309–335.

Raphael-Leff, J. (1992). "The baby-makers": an in-depth single-case study of conscious and unconscious psychological reactions to infertility and "baby-making". *British Journal of Psychotherapy*, 8: 266–277.

Raphael-Leff, J. (1997). Procreative process, placental paradigm and perinatal psychotherapy. *Journal of the American Psychoanalyic Association* (Female Psychology suppl.), 44: 373–399.

Raphael-Leff, J. (2000a). "Behind the shut door"—a psychoanalytical approach to premature menopause. In: D. Singer & M. Hunter (Eds.), *Premature Menopause—A Multidisciplinary Approach* (pp. 79–97. London: Whurr.

Raphael-Leff, J. (2000b). "Climbing the walls": therapeutic intervention for post-partum disturbance. In: J. Raphael-Leff (Ed.), *Spilt Milk—Perinatal Depression, Loss and Breakdown* (pp. 60–81). London: Routledge.

Raphael-Leff, J. (2003). Eggs between women—emotional aspects of gamete donation in reproductive technology. In: M. A. Alizade (Ed.), *The Embodied Female* (pp. 53–64). London: Karnac.

Raphael-Leff, J. (2005). *Psychological Processes of Childbearing*, London: Anna Freud Centre [Karnac].

Rascovsky, A. (1985). *El filicidio*. Buenos Aires: Ediciones Orion.

Riquer, F. (1996). La maternidad como fatalidad. In: T. Lartigue & H. Ávila, (Eds.), *Sexualidad y Reproducción Humana en México*, Vol. 1. Mexico: Plaza y Valdés/Iberoamerican University.

Riviere, A. (1991). Acción e interacción en el origen del símbolo. In: A. M. J. Palacios & M. Carretero (Eds.), *Psicología evolutiva. Desarrollo cognitivo y social del niño*. Madrid: Alianza.

Rossi, A. (1998). In vitro. In: J. Bialosky & H. Schulman (Eds.), *Wanting a Child* (pp. 60–68). New York: Farrar, Straus and Giroux.

Saal, F. (1991). *Algunas consecuencias políticas de la diferencia psíquica de los sexos*. In: M. Lamas & F. Saal (Eds.), *La Bella (In)diferencia* (pp. 10–34). México: Siglo XXI.

Sandler, J., Spector Person, E., & Fonagy, P. (Eds.) (1991). *Introduction to Narcissism*. International Psychoanalytical Association, Educational Monograph.

Schaeffer, J. (1997). *Le refus du féminin*. Paris: Presses Universitaires de France.

Schaeffer, J. (2002). Negotiating the antagonism between feminine and maternal spheres. In Alizade, M. (ed.) (2002). *The Embodied Female*. London: Karnac.

Schafer, R. (1995). The evolution of my views on nonnormative sexual practices. In: T. Domenici & R. Lesser (Eds.), *Disorienting Sexuality: Psychoanalytic Reappraisals of Sexual Identities* (pp. 187–202). New York: Routledge.

Scher, A. (2001). Facilitators and regulators: maternal orientation as an antecedent of attachment security. *Journal of Reproductive and Infant Psychology*, *19*: 325–333.

Scher, A., & Blumberg, O. (1992). Facilitators and regulators: cross-cultural and methodological considerations. *British Journal of Medical Psychology*, *65*: 327–331.

Scher, A., & Blumberg, O. (2000). Night-waking among one year-olds: a study of maternal separation anxiety. *Child Care, Health & Development*, *26*: 323–334.

Sharp, H. M. (1995). Women's expectations of childbirth and early motherhood: their relation to preferred mothering orientation, subsequent experience, satisfaction and postpartum depression. Doctoral thesis, University of Leicester.

Sharp, H. M., & Bramwell, R. (2004). An empirical evaluation of a psycho-analytic theory of mothering orientation: implications for the antenatal prediction of postnatal depression. *Journal of Reproductive and Infant Psychology*, *22*: 71–89.

Silverman, D. (1987). What are little girls made of? *Psychoanalytical Psychology*, *4*: 315–334.

Solís, H. (1999). El odio es más viejo que el amor: la pareja colérica. In: J. Vives, (Ed.), *Violencia Social, Sexualidad y Creatividad* (pp. 35–45). Mexico: Mexican Psychoanalytic Association/Plaza y Valdés.

Solís, L. (2002). La construction de la parentalité. In: *La Parentalité. Défi pour le Troisième Millénaire. Un Hommage International à Serge Lebovici*. Paris: Presses Universitaires de France.

Spitz, R. (1946). Anaclitic depression. *The Psychoanalytic Study of the Child*, *2*: 313–342.

Steele, B. (1970). Parental abuse of infants and small children. In: E. Anthony and T. Benedek (Eds.), *Parenthood: Its Psychology and Psychopathology* (pp. 449–471). New York: Little, Brown.

Stoller, R. (1968a). A further contribution to the study of gender identity. *International Journal of Psychoanalysis, 49*: 364–368.

Stoller, R. (1968b). The sense of femaleness. *Psychoanalytic Quarterly, 37*: 42–55.

Stoller, R. (1976). Primary femininity. *Journal of the American Psychoanalytical Assocation (Suppl.), 24*: 59–78.

Stuart-Smith, S. (2003). Egg donation. In: J. Haynes & J. Miller (Eds.), *Inconceivable Conceptions* (pp. 166–178). New York: Brunner-Routledge.

Tasker, F. L., & Golombok, S. (1997). *Growing Up in a Lesbian Family: Effects on Child Development.* New York: Guilford Press.

Tort, M. (1989). L'Inconcevable. *Topique, 44*: 235–256.

Tort, M. (1992). *Le Désir froid.* Paris: La Découverte (*El deseo frío.* Nueva Visión. Buenos Aires, 1994).

Tubert, S. (1991). *Women Without a Shadow. Maternal Desire and Assisted Reproductive Technologies.* London: Free Association.

Tyson, P. (1994). Bedrock and beyond: An examination of the clinical utility of contemporary theories for female psychology. *Journal of the American Psychoanalytic Association, 42*: 447–467.

Urrutia, E. (1994). Presentación del Foro de Discusión sobre la mujer y el SIDA. In: *Mujer y SIDA. Programa Interdisciplinario de Estudios de la Mujer* (pp. 7–10). Mexico: El Colegio de México.

Vegetti Finzi, S. (1996). *Mothering.* New York & London: Guilford.

Vovelle, M. (1979). Storia e lunga durata. In: J. Le Goff (Ed.), *La nuova storia.* Milan: Mondadori, 1980.

Welldon, E. V. (1988). *Mother, Madonna, Whore: The Idealisation and Denigration of Motherhood.* London: Free Association Books [reprinted New York: Guilford Press, 1992].

Welldon, E. V. (1999). La ripetizione dell'abuso e dei maltrattamenti da una generazione all'altra in Molfino and Zanardi (Eds) *Sintomi Corpo Femminilita: Dall'isteria alla bulimia* (pp. 327–346). Bologna: Clueb Cooperativa Libraria Universitaria Editrice.

Welldon, E. V. (2003). Risk-taking in the assessment of maternal abilities. In: R. Doctor (Ed.), *Dangerous Patients: A Psychodynamic Approach to Risk Assessment and Management* (pp. 97–106). London: Karnac.

Winnicott, D. W. (1953). Transitional objects and transitional phenomena: a study of the first not-me possession. *International Journal of Psychoanalysis, 34*: 89–97.

Winnicott, D. W. (1956). Primary maternal preoccupation. In *Through Paediatrics to Psycho-Analysis.* London: Tavistock.

Winnicott, D. W. (1963). From dependence towards independence in the development of the self. In *The Maturational Processes and the Facilitating Environment*. London: Hogarth.

Winnicott, D. W. (1970) Dependence in child care. In *Babies and their Mothers*. Wokingham: Addison-Wesley.

Wolf, D., & Gardner, H. (1981). On the structure of early symbolization. In: D. D. Bricker (Ed.), *Early Language and Intervention*. Baltimore: University Park Press.

INDEX

adoption, 36–37, 40, 42, 149
Alizade, A. M., 52–55, 63, 174, 199
Amati Mehler, J., 19, 43, 199
anger, 2–3, 6, 9–10, 62, 64, 163,
    171–172, 184, 191
Aranda, C., 174, 208
Argentieri, S., 16, 19–20, 199
artificial insemination, 13–14, 38–40,
    68, 114, 120–121
    by donor (AID), 40 177, 180,
    188–190
Aslan, C. M., 73, 200
Ávila, H., 174, 208

bad mother, 60, 192
Badinter, E., 48, 116, 200
Baldini, U., 66, 200
Baranger, W., 12, 200
Bégoin-Guignard, F., 98, 200
Benjamin, J., 165, 200
Benkov, L., 92, 200
Berezin de Guiter, J., 162, 200
Berg, C., 151, 204
Bergman, A., 80, 200

Bergman, N. J., 151, 200
Bion, W. R., 97–98, 128, 192, 198, 200
birth control see: contraception
Blanck-Cereijido, F., 114–115, 117,
    200–201
Bleger, J., 201
Bleichmar, H., 81, 201
Blumberg, O., 154, 211
Bouvier-Colle, M. H., 151, 204
Bowlby, J., 127, 168, 174, 201
Bramwell, R., 154, 211
Braudel, F., 16–17, 201
Braunschweig, D., 107, 201
Bravo, E., 161, 208
Britton, R., 14–15, 201
Brown, G. W., 157, 201
Buekens, P., 151, 204
Bukatman, S., 142, 201
Buntin, M., 70, 201

Cachard, C., 48, 201
Canestri, J., 20, 201
Casanova, G., 174, 208
Cereijido, M., 121, 201

changes [sociological, cultural, etc.],
        ix, 11–21, 66, 116–117, 123, 136,
        145–146, 177
    catastrophic, 192
Chasseguet-Smirgel, J., 114, 201
Chodorow, N. J., 54, 62, 64, 87, 95,
        193, 201
Clarke-Stewart, K. A., 127, 202
Cohen, M., 151, 202
Coleman, R. W., 6, 202
conflict(s)/conflictual, 2, 5, 7, 26, 32,
        46, 48–49, 51, 61–62, 70–71, 74,
        83, 87–88, 90–92, 96, 110,
        119–120, 123, 125–127, 130–132,
        138, 141, 155, 159, 164, 170–171,
        179, 183, 186–189, 194, 196–197
    Oedipal, 54
contraception, 23, 45, 64, 120, 147,
        150–151
Cooper, D., 66, 202
Cooper, L., 25–27, 31, 202
Cooper, P. J., 160, 202
Córdova, A., 174, 208
Costello, C. Y., 95, 202
countertransference, 13, 21,
        108–109, 131, 163
Crespi, L., 92, 202
cybernetics, 139–140, 143

Davies, J., 24, 202
De La Cerda, D., 174, 208
De Mause, L., 47, 202
defences, 6, 10, 13, 20, 24, 28, 33, 55,
        60, 70, 104, 105–106, 108, 114,
        120, 165, 184
    anality, 104
    castration complex, 106
    depression, 105
    displacement, 165
    foreclosure, 165
    hypochondriasis, 105
    splitting, 165, 171
Devereux, G., 163, 202
di Lampedusa, G. T., 21
Diamond, D., 26, 202
Dimen, M., 95, 202

Dio Bleichmar, 78, 81–82, 202–203
disappointment, 7–8, 61, 63, 96, 125
domestic violence, 162, 171, 175
donors (of eggs, sperm), 25–32,
        37–41, 65, 114, 136–139, 142,
        146–147, 153, 188–189
Drucker, J., 95, 203
Duby, G., 162, 203
Dukrinsky, R., 174, 208
Duvignaud, F., 137, 203

ego, 9, 12, 20, 69, 75–76, 78–80, 90,
        98, 104, 141, 164, 168, 171
    ideal, 3, 10, 79, 81, 164, 184–185
    identity, 74
    needs/goals, 2, 8, 10
Ehrensaft, D., 28, 203
Ehrhardt, A., 75, 209
Eliacheff, C., 83, 203
Elise, D., 73–75, 203
Elliott, A., 138, 203
envy, 3, 31–32, 42, 49, 54, 81, 91, 101,
        125, 130, 157, 184
    mother, 30–33
    penis, see: penis/phallic envy
eroticism, 27–28, 30, 33, 109
    auto/self-, 75, 98, 102
    erotic gratification, 5–6

facilitator, 154–155, 157
Fain, M., 107, 201
fantasy/fantasies, 3, 10, 12, 14, 20,
        25–26, 29–31, 33, 37–38, 45–46,
        51, 54, 57, 60, 67, 69, 76, 79, 88,
        102, 106, 119–121, 125, 136, 138,
        141, 143, 146–150, 163, 165, 182,
        184, 189, 193, 195–196
    about gender, 76–79, 81
    about suicide, 10
    child, 3–6, 8–10, 164
    family romance, 96, 141
    narcissistic, 60
    of fatherhood, 141
    of ménage à trois, 25, 28
    of pregnancy, 61–62
    primal, 99–101, 103–104, 106, 147

projective, 66
sexual/erotic, 25, 27–28, 148
Faure-Pragier, S., 182, 203
Fawcus, S. R., 151, 200
Feinholz, D., 174, 208
Feldman, M., 15, 201
femininity, 24, 42, 52, 74, 79, 81,
    105–107, 117, 119, 123–124, 143,
    184, 193, 195
  and motherhood/maternity, x,
    50–51, 63, 73, 80, 97–111, 193,
    195
  –masculinity pair, 75–79
  primary, 73–83, 99–100
  the mother in the core of, 79–81
  vaginal sexuality and, 73
feminism, 23, 66, 156
  feminisma, 30–31
Ferenczi, S., 161, 203
Figueroa, L., 174, 208
Fonagy, P., 78, 90, 171, 175, 203, 210
Freud, S., 12–13, 15, 17, 21, 24, 28,
    50, 73, 75, 81, 83, 89, 96, 98, 101,
    105–106, 117, 137, 141–142, 148,
    163, 165, 167, 183–184, 195, 204
Frydman, R., 183, 204

Gaddini, E., 14, 18, 204
Gardner, H., 77, 213
gay parents/donors, 25, 85, 87, 89,
    92, 94–96, 148
Gergely, G., 171, 204
Giménez de Vainer, A., 141, 205
Gissler, M., 151, 204
Glazer, E., 25–27, 31, 202
Glocer Fiorini, L., 137, 140–142, 195,
    205
Golombok, S., 95, 212
good mother/motherhood, 1–2, 4,
    7, 10, 31, 132, 192
Gottman, J. S., 95, 205
Green, A., 14, 60, 205
Greenacre, P., 14, 18, 205
Greenson, R., 18, 48, 205
Guignard, F., 97–98, 100–102,
    205–206

guilt, 6–7, 10, 42, 56, 82–83, 103–104,
    126, 130, 132, 151, 157, 171,
    188–189, 192, 198

Hardin, D. H., 129–130, 206
Hardin, H. T., 129–130, 206
Harris, T. O., 157, 201
Harsch, H. E., 127, 130, 206
hate, 2–3, 8, 47, 49, 81, 114, 171, 187
Heinich, N., 83, 203
Heise, L., 175, 206
Hepworth, C., 157, 201
HIV/AIDS, 161–163, 166–167, 170,
    175
Howes, C., 127, 206
husbands/fathers, 4, 6, 8, 14, 25–30,
    38–39, 41, 43, 49–52, 54–55, 62,
    69, 75–77, 80–81, 88–89, 91, 97,
    99–100, 106, 108, 110–111,
    114–119, 126, 129–132, 138–139,
    141, 146, 150, 152, 154, 157,
    165–166, 168–173, 175, 177, 180,
    184–185, 186–190, 194–195
  deceased, 120–121, 136, 159–160
  father–daughter, 131
  father–son, 164
  name-of-the-father, 196
  word-of-the-father, 196

idealization/idealized, x, 1–2, 7, 46,
    49, 79, 125, 136, 138, 140, 156,
    195, 197
  donors, 147
  mother-, 2, 132
identification(s), 37, 56, 76–77, 85,
    91, 95–96, 99, 104–105, 117, 132,
    174
  counter-, 125
  countertransference, 109
  gender, 78
  projective, 78, 99–103, 107, 124,
    128, 171
  with aggressor, 168
  with mother, 3, 42, 48, 61, 75, 79,
    81, 107, 117–119, 124–125, 153,
    155, 158, 164–165, 167

conflictual, 126
  with the object, 78, 99–100
in vitro fertilization (IVF), 40, 114,
  119–120, 148, 160
incest/incestuous, 19, 27, 83, 91, 98,
  106, 116, 172, 188, 194
INPer, 161, 167, 175

Jacobson, J., 82, 206
jealousy, 2, 4, 31, 50, 81, 170
Jones, E., 73, 206
Jurist, E., 171, 204

Kestenberg, J., 80, 206
Kezur, M., 26, 202
Klein, M., 12, 14, 28–29, 31, 51, 60,
  66, 73, 78, 81, 99, 101–102, 106,
  124, 196, 206–207
Kohut, H., 78, 187, 207
Kris, E., 6, 202
Kristeva, J., 195, 207

Lacan, J., 53, 75, 78, 141, 196,
  207
Laing, R. D., 66, 207
Laplanche, J., 75, 78, 207
Lartigue, T., 48, 163, 168, 174,
  207–208
Le Goff, J., 208
Lebovici, S., 164, 208
Leisse de Lustgarten, A., 48, 208
Leñero, L., 175, 208
lesbian parents/couples, x, 23,
  28–29, 32–33, 40, 85, 148
  psychosexual development of
  boys of, 85–96
Levinton, N., 82, 208
Lévi-Strauss, C., 115, 208
libido, 13, 50
Linley, L. L., 151, 200
López, D., 174, 208

Magis, C., 161, 208
Martinez, M., 162, 209
masculinity complex, 23
maternal instinct, 2, 41

maternity/paternity, desire/wish
  for, 36, 41–42, 51–52, 117
Mayer, E., 73, 209
Meyers, M., 26, 202
Mitchell, V., 92, 95, 209
Molteno, C., 160, 202
Money, J., 74–76, 209
mother–child bond, relationship, x,
  4–5, 9–10, 37, 41–43, 93–94, 98,
  118, 123–124, 130, 154, 184
  mother–daughter relationship,
  97, 99, 102, 124, 139, 185
motherhood
  and the female superego, 82–83
  and work, x, 123–133
  in mythology/history, 116–117
  in psychoanalysis, 117–118
Motz, A., 61, 209
Murray, L., 160, 202

Narcio, L., 174, 208
narcissism, 3, 11–13, 52, 75, 164, 184,
  197
Nasio, J. D., 171, 209
National Institute for Child Health
  and Human Development
  (NICHD), 127, 201
Nava, A., 174, 208
new reproductive techniques
  (NRT), x, 40, 43, 46, 64,
  113–116, 120–122, 135–136,
  140–141, 177
non-maternal psychic space, 45–57

object(s), 37, 41–42, 53, 61, 75, 77–78,
  81, 87, 98–99, 109, 117, 121, 196
  good, 61, 125
  libido/libidinal, 4
  love, 12, 50, 61, 97, 100, 118, 165,
  167–168, 197
  narcissistic–libidinal, 4, 9
  of cathexis, 104, 109
  part-/whole-, 24, 29–30, 33
  persecutory, 125
  phallic, 195
  primary, 41, 137, 165, 167

relations, 13–14, 29, 54, 62, 74, 85, 99
self-, 37, 42, 125, 187
sexual choice, 86–87, 89–90, 95
third, 14–15
transitional, 64
omnipotent/omnipotence, 11, 13, 29, 60, 68–70, 99–100, 105, 119, 121, 147, 149, 194
Ortíz, J., 174, 208
O'Shaughnessy, E., 15, 201

Papaligoura, Z., 160, 209
parental complex, 89–92, 94
parthenogenesis, 11, 13, 20
Paschero, L. M., 82, 209
penis/phallic envy, 50–51, 53–54, 81, 99, 106–107, 109, 119, 183
penis–child equation, 50–51, 117
penis–phallus complex, 53–54
Perrrot, M., 162, 203
perverse motherhood, x, 60–61, 64, 104
Phillips, J. L., 90, 209
Pines, D., 14, 43, 61, 124–125, 209
postpartum distress/disturbance, 154, 157–158
pregnancy, 3–5, 14, 25, 27, 31–32, 36, 42, 45–46, 48–49, 56, 61–62, 68, 70, 102, 118–119, 125, 128, 139–141, 146, 150–155, 158–159, 166, 187–188, 194
artificial/assisted, 35–44
post-menopausal, 146
multiple, 149
primary maternal sphere, x, 98–100
Provence, S., 6, 202
psychic traumata, 171–174

Raphael-Leff, J., 69, 149–150, 153–154, 158, 159–160, 210
Rascovsky, A., 48, 210
regulator, 155, 157
reproductive technology, xi, 23, 25–26, 30, 33, 36–37, 39, 59–60, 68–70, 76, 115, 135–140, 142–143, 145–150, 152, 158, 190
Riquer, F., 165, 210
Rivera, P., 161, 208
Riviere, A., 77, 210
Rossi, A., 30, 210

Saal, F., 118, 210
Sánchez, B., 174, 208
Sandler, J., 210
Schafer, R., 87, 211
Scharf, C. N., 26, 202
Scher, A., 154, 211
sex tourism, 20
Shaeffer, J., 53, 105, 107, 211
Sharp, H. M., 154, 211
Silverman, D., 80, 211
Solís, H., 171, 211
Solís, L., 163–165, 211
Spector Person, E., 210
Spitz, R., 127, 168, 211
Steele, B., 63, 211
stereotype(s), 1–2, 66, 78, 94, 155
sterility, 35, 40, 119–121, 177–189
psychogenic, 111
Stoller, R., 74–75, 212
Stuart-Smith, S., 31, 212
sublimated motherhood, x, 52
superego, 20, 46, 48–49, 56, 81–83, 164–165, 185, 187–188
female, 82–83
superwoman, 67
surrogate embryo transfer (SET), 114
surrogate, x, 26, 28–32, 36, 43, 70, 114, 123, 127–130, 136–137, 146, 148, 153, 177
Swartz, L., 160, 202

Target, M., 90, 171, 203–204
Tasker, F. L., 95, 212
technological bodies, 136–139
Thanatos, 13, 47–48, 56, 165, 168
third-ness/triangulation, 14–15, 25, 28, 85–89, 92, 94, 99, 101 108, 123, 128–130, 132, 158, 187

Tomlinson, M., 160, 202
Tort, M., 116, 120, 140, 212
transference, 7, 13, 21, 55, 108–109,
    130, 165, 186–187
    mother-in-the-, 109
traumatic loss, 168–171
Trevarthen, C., 160, 209
Tubert, S., 38, 121, 212
Tyson, P., 73, 75, 212

Urrutia, E., 163, 212

Váquez, M., 174, 208
Vegetti Finzi, S., 195, 212

virtual paedophilia, 20
virtual sexuality, 20
Vives, J., 174, 208
Vovelle, M., 21, 212

Welldon, E. V., 49, 60, 63,
    212
Wienshel, M., 26, 202
Winnicott, D. W., x, 14, 64, 128, 198,
    212–213
Wolf, D., 77, 213
woman = mother equation, 114,
    191–198
Woolger, M., 160, 202